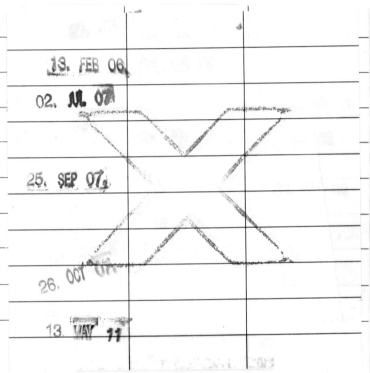

CENTRAL LIBRARY, WESTGATE, OXFORD OX1 1DJ

Renewals: (01865) 241718 - Enquiries: (01865) 815509

To renew this item please quote your reader ticket
number, or the number on the bar code above

Please return/renew this item by the last date shown

XFORDSHIRE
COUNTY COUNCIL
LEISURE & ARTS

THE SOUTH ASIAN PETTY BOURGEOISIE IN BRITAIN

Research in Ethnic Relations Series

The South Asian Petty Bourgeoisie in Britain

An Oxford case study

SHAILA SRINIVASAN

Avebury

Aldershot • Brookfield USA • Hong Kong • Singapore • Sydney

Published by
Avebury
Ashgate Publishing Limited
Gower House
Croft Road
Aldershot
Hants GU11 3HR
England

Ashgate Publishing Company
Old Post Road
Brookfield
Vermont 05036
USA

British Library Cataloguing in Publication Data

Srinivasan, Shaila
    South Asian Petty Bourgeoisie in Britain:
    An Oxford Case Study – (Research in Ethnic
    Relations Series)
    I. Title II. Series
    305.8914041
ISBN 1 85628 972 9

Library of Congress Catalog Card Number: 95-80633

Typeset by Elaine Herman, Nuffield College, Oxford
Maps drawn by Peter Hayward, School of Geography, Oxford University

Printed in Great Britain by Antony Rowe Ltd,
Chippenham, Wiltshire

Contents

Figures and tables

Acknowledgements

I owe my thanks to a great many people whose help has played a crucial part in the completion of this book.

First and foremost, my sincere thanks go to Ceri Peach for the keen interest he has taken in my work - without his encouragement, advice and constant support, this book may never have materialised.

I am grateful to my university supervisor John Goldthorpe for his inspiring supervision. His penetrating analysis and constructive academic advice contributed significantly to the thesis on which this book is based. I owe him much.

My thanks go also to my college supervisor Anthony Heath for his rigorous criticism of my work, as also for his magical help, on many an occasion, in overcoming a 'writer's block'.

I also thank the following people who have read and commented on my work at various stages: Prof. T.O. Ranger, Dr. Duncan Gallie, Dr. Frank Bechhofer, Dr. Tariq Modood, and Dr. A.J. Crowle.

This research would not have been possible without the practical help and moral support of numerous friends. First among these is Dr. Sucheta Martin, who accompanied me on those first apprehensive encounters with the small business owners. She played a key role in the successful completion of the field work in introducing me to Mr. Chopra, an Indian small business owner in Oxford and at the time the president of the Oxford Hindu Mandal. It was Mr. Chopra who drove me around Oxford, personally introducing me to over half the respondents in the survey and making sure that I was granted interviews by all of them. Without his help the survey would not have been possible. I am, indeed, grateful to him.

My thanks are also due to the participants in the survey who were kind enough to permit me to intrude into their lives and their work. Thanks, too, to Harish Sharma of the Oxford City Council for his ready help in obtaining information about the City of Oxford.

I thank Nuffield College for the excellent facilities it has provided for graduate study and also for offering me a funded studentship for all the three years of the D.Phil course. Thanks also go to the University of Oxford for awarding me a scholarship under the Foreign and Commonwealth scheme, and the Charles Wallace India Trust for financial assistance in the final years of study. I am also grateful to the University of Delhi, and Dr. Jaya Gupta, principal of Janki Devi Mahavidyalya, for granting me study leave for four years.

Finally, this book is dedicated to my parents and to my son, Rahul. I express my deep gratitude to my parents for their constant love and encouragement. Their belief in my abilities has been a source of great strength. I dedicate this book to them in partial atonement for the years of absence. The book is dedicated also to Rahul, in apology for the years of having to put up with a mother who was often bad tempered and 'always studying'. I thank him, too, for the practical help he offered in collating the information from the 1991 Census, preparing tables and checking references.

Foreword

This book in an important contribution to the literature on Asian settlement in Britain. It has been developed from a doctoral thesis written while Dr Srinivasan was a student of Nuffield College Oxford. The book examines Asian entrepreneurship in Britain and its implications for assimilation. In particular it examines whether entry into business is forced onto Asians by constraints and racist barriers to employment or whether it is a chosen, preferred course of action.

Work on Asian ethnic enterprises in Britain divides into what one could call the 'ghetto' school and the 'commercial' school. Work by Aldrich, McEvoy, Jones, Cater and others has argued that Asian businesses are a result of white racism, blocking opportunity for progression of Asian workers and forcing them into a kind of stockaded defensive activity, catering to a ghettoised community. Work by Mullins, Ward, Lyons and others has argued that self employment is a preferred way of making money and that the bulk of the entrepreneurial activities cater not to an Asian, but to a broader white clientele. Srinivasan favours the second hypothesis from her Oxford findings but goes further and argues a case based on status aspirations. Essentially, Srinivasan has produced a third school, the 'status school'.

The heart of the book is a survey of all 94 South Asian owned small businesses in Oxford in 1990. Earlier academic studies tended to be in areas of heavy Asian settlement, which were therefore more institutionally complete and where, perhaps, the motivation was different. Srinivasan's study differs from other studies, firstly by examining a city in which the Asian minority is relatively small and secondly by taking the population of Asian businesses and not a sample. The Oxford Asian population was never large enough for an ethnically based business.

Srinivasan argues that there are three status hierarchies to which Asian entrepreneurs relate : (1) in Britain with the British (2) in Britain with the Asian community (3) in the home country with the sending society. Their order of importance is the reverse of the order in which they have been presented. Not only is this the case, but there are considerable differences and ambiguities relating to the same occupational position within the different hierarchies. Thus an Asian shop keeper could appear working class to the British, middle class to the British Asian and upper middle to the Asian community at home. Srinivasan argues that status, not money, is the essential driving force in many of the decisions to change occupations and take up shop keeping: 'If one is an employee one is nothing'

Dr Srinivasan examines the economic consequences of being self employed and argues that it represents important material as well as status benefits over being an employee

Many of the entrepreneurs continue, in any case, to maintain a paid job and use family members, particularly wives, to run the shop. The success of the enterprise tends to be measured in terms of total receipts rather than in income per hour worked. She is perhaps a little uncritical of the willingness of family members to undertake these activities and more accepting of the views of the boss. However, the benefits in terms of job satisfaction, property ownership, flexibility of working hours and the view of the shop as a social as well as an economic enterprise are clearly outlined. In short, self employment is a chosen, not an enforced decision.

Dr Srinivasan investigates whether there is anything specifically ethnic about Asian businesses by comparing the Oxford survey with a national survey of small shop keepers. It shows that Asians work longer hours on average, open on Sundays, have larger families and use family labour. However, it shows that in raising money to start businesses, Oxford Asian business men are less dependent on family and friends and much more dependent on mainstream commercial lenders (high street banks and building societies).

The penultimate chapter, which investigates the extent to which assimilation or acculturation may have taken place, is one of the most interesting in the book. Dr Srinivasan argues that assimilation is often considered on a single scale from non-assimilation to assimilation. However, she argues that there should be two simultaneous scales, depending on appreciation of one's own culture and appreciation of the host culture. Acculturalists could be high on both scales while Assimilationists could be high on the host culture while rejecting their own. Using this quadrilateral scale, Srinivasan concludes that Asian businessmen lead a fairly compartmentalised life.

This is an important book and a significant addition to the literature. It challenges much of the conventional wisdom and will provoke further research.

Erratum

The Foreword on p.xii is by Ceri Peach, Professor of Social
Geography, School of Geography, University of Oxford.

1 Introduction

Aims and objectives

This book attempts to examine South Asian entrepreneurship[1] in Britain and its implications for the 'assimilation' of Asian small business owners into British society. The increase in recent years of the number of South Asians going into shop-keeping and other small enterprises, has excited the attention of social scientists, challenging as it does certain accepted stereotypes regarding the Asian population: for instance, the assumption that Asians are only to be found in lower paid and unwanted jobs, that they are economically dispensable and socially alienated, that the population consists of self-segregating groups who do not enter into competition with the British in any way, etc. (Mullins 1979:403-405). If there is increasing Asian entry into the entrepreneurial middle class, if this is a matter of choice and not so much a matter of discrimination and disadvantage in the labour market, if Asians are successful in their business activity and not merely surviving on the fringes of the economy, if they are performing middleman[2] entrepreneurial functions and are not confined to an ethnic niche, then all the above stereotypes appear to be contradicted.

It becomes interesting, then, to study the role of this recently developed Asian petty bourgeois class in the social and economic structure of British society, and to attempt an answer to the following questions:

1)   what are the reasons for Asian entry into small business?

2)   what is the class position of Asian small business owners, and is business entry a vehicle for upward social mobility?

3)   how 'ethnic' is this Asian business, and is this class of Asian small business owners at all different from the indigenous petty bourgeoisie? and finally,

4)   what are the consequences of Asian entrepreneurship, as far as the nature of Asian ethnicity, as well as assimilation into British society, are concerned?

1

The Asian petty bourgeoisie in Britain *DOES COWLEY PLACE SIMPLY REPRESENT THIS ENTREPRENEURIAL SPIRIT OR MORE?*

Britain, together with the rest of Europe, has seen a steady increase in the petty bourgeoisie (Boissevain 1981), whether due to economic reasons (recession, tax concessions), or political reasons (support of the Thatcher government). What is interesting is that ethnic minorities, and the South Asians in particular, are entering this sector in large numbers. Owen and Green, using Labour Force Survey (LFS) data to examine the changing labour market experience of ethnic groups in Britain during the 1980s, maintain:

> An important feature of employment change in the 1980s has been the massive growth of self-employment (Labour Force Survey data reveals an increase of 993 thousand or 46 per cent between 1981 and 1987-9)...the proportions of persons in work who are self-employed is much higher than the overall British average in many ethnic minorities...In 1981, more than 30 per cent of Bangladeshis and Chinese in work were self-employed, with more than a fifth of Pakistanis and nearly 14 per cent of Indians also self-employed. In contrast, the rate of self-employment was about half the national average for West Indians...By 1987-9 the proportion self-employed had grown substantially in most ethnic groups...(1992:21)

This corroborates the 1984 Policy Studies Institute (PSI) survey, according to which, while only seven per cent of the white working force is self-employed, the corresponding figure for the Asian working force is about 18 per cent (Brown 1984:165). Further, 67 per cent of the Asian self-employed are to be found in the distributive trades, as against only 26 per cent of the whites. According to Brown too, then, the self-employed form a larger proportion among Asians than among whites, and are very much less commonly found among West Indians. By 1990, the LFS shows that as against 13 per cent of whites, 21 per cent of Indians, 26 per cent of Pakistanis, and 19 per cent of Bangladeshis are self-employed. It is, then, well documented that Asians are entering self-employment in relatively large numbers (Owen and Green 1992:7-29; Brown 1984:175; Boissevain 1981:19-20; Ward and Jenkins 1984).

And yet, in the study of migrant groups, emphasis has often been on low paid wage workers, to the extent of clubbing them all together and looking at them as an 'underclass' created by the exigencies of the British economy (Rex and Tomlinson 1979:275-6; Castles and Kossack 1973:477). This ignores the fact that, though a sizeable majority of migrants is to be found in the manual category, a significant minority enters the petty bourgeoisie. As Brown puts it, while it would be wrong to suggest that self-employment is typical for Asians, "...(it)...must be taken seriously into account when discussing Asian employment patterns" (1984:166).

The predeliction for self-employment manifested itself quite early among the postwar migrants from the Asian sub-continent. Holmes, commenting on the diverse pattern of the occupational structure of these migrants, and presenting evidence of entrepreneurship even in the 1950s and 1960s, maintains that "at the side of the working class there were successful entrepreneurs: these individuals were evident, for example, by 1971 in the restaurant business and the textile trade"(1988:231-232).

The signs of a growing involvement in business activity were evident in the development of shops and cafes in Balsall Heath, Birmingham (Holmes 1988:232; Hiro 1971:151), in Bradford (Rose 1969:443), and in Southall, Huddersfield, and Glasgow, as well as Pakistani banks in Bradford, by the late 1950s (Holmes 1988:232). This entrepreneurial zeal is reflected in the 1966 figures for self-employed Asians, especially male Pakistanis in London, who were the only non-European immigrant group to be well represented in this category (Rose 1969:154).

IS THIS PROMINANT IN THEIR SOP? - WHAT DOES THIS MEAN
FOR THEIR SOP?

It was in the distributive trades that the Asians were to find their particular niche. This trend finds a mention in local studies as early as in the 1960s: Pedlars in Birmingham (Desai 1963), Pakistani shopkeepers in Sparkbrook (Rex and Moore 1967), and in the 1970s: Pakistani grocers cum butchers and cafes (Dahya 1974), Shopkeepers and clothing wholesalers in Birmingham (Ballard and Ballard 1977), clothiers in Manchester (Werbner 1979), etc.

The initial impetus was, of course, provided by the needs of the Asians themselves. Thus, according to Banton:

> As Sikh communities built up in Britain, so an ethnic infrastructure developed of grocers, cinemas, goldsmiths, and travel agents to serve an Asian clientele. These establishments were followed by garages, driving schools, taxi services, insurance brokers, and television repair shops (1983:320).

So also, Allen and others, tell us:

> The expansion of a petite bourgeoisie strata in the Asian groups is not restricted to the provision of food stuffs, and although no accurate statistical measures are available, from observation it appears that steady growth has taken place in other sectors as well; insurance, estate agency, the retail of electrical goods, car repairs and so forth (1969:355).

But, as Hiro empasizes:

IS THIS WHAT COWLEY REPRESENTS?

> ...such dynamism and business acumen could not for ever, remain circumscribed within the 'immigrant' market. It had to break out; and it did. Nowadays Asians in Nottingham, for example, buy taxis as soon as they have saved enough from working overtime on the Corporation buses. Others put their money into off-license shops...(1971:152).

Today, Asian enterprise in Britain has established itself and the Asian small shop and the 'Indian' restaurant are no longer confined to particular cities

3

and areas of England, but are an ubiquitous feature of the urban landscape. The magazine *Asian Business* reports that:

> ...there are 104,000 neighbourhood retail outlets in the UK, 80 per cent of which are independently owned, with 70 per cent owned by Asians. In London, Asians own 90 per cent of such outlets...Looking at the UK's 43,700 grocery outlets...more than 30,000...(owned)...by Asians. They generate £7.8bn of annual sales and are used at least once a week by 42 per cent of British adults. Asians also own about 30,000 of the 46,000 confectionery, tobacconist and news (CTN) shops and a significant percentage of chemists and off-licenses. There are 7,000 Indian restaurants...(Ethnic Minority Business Service Newsletter, Oxford, April 1992)

That this Asian business expansion raises certain questions has been noted in the introduction. While detailed reviews of the literature on the four specific questions considered in the book will be dealt with in the relevant chapters, a brief consideration of these issues is now provided.

Reasons for business entry

The first question then is, what are the reasons for this Asian entry into small business? An explanation that is often put forward is the 'cultural' one, which stresses the ethnic advantages of certain groups in business activities, such as an entrepreneurial ethic (Bonacich 1973; Werbner 1984; Boissevain 1981), family support, ethnic networks, protected niches (Hannerz 1974; Aldrich *et al.* 1984), culturally specific economic institutions such as 'rotating credit' associations (Light 1972), and ethnic solidarity (Lawrence 1974; Anwar 1979; Aldrich *et al.* 1984).

    The main difficulty with this approach is that where Asian business activity is concerned, apart from the entrepreneurial ethic and family support, all the other cultural factors appear to vary according to historical period and region. In areas where there is no concentration of Asians, and in a later period of the migration process, it is difficult to find evidence of strong ethnic networks, culturally specific economic institutions, protected niches or a protected market, and yet Asian businesses flourish. And it must be emphasized that family support and the entrepreneurial ethic has been noted among all small business people, not just minority businessmen.

    Yet, certain cultural factors such as values and attitudes towards life, and the cultural rating of occupations, cannot be ignored, so that it is not possible to agree entirely with Aldrich *et al.*, according to whom:

> ...immigrant business activity is shaped more by external forces than by internal characteristics, i.e., the opportunity structure of the receiving society outweighs any cultural predisposition towards entrepreneurship (Aldrich *et al.* 1984:205).

This leads to the 'economic opportunity' explanation, according to which:

...ethnic minority business activity is essentially no different from routine capitalist entrepreneurial activity, depending for its success or failure upon the opportunities presented by the market (Jenkins 1984:231).

Accordingly, the reason for the increase in retailing and other small businesses may well be that: *WHAT TYPE OF BUSINESSES ON THE COWLEY ROAD?*

When an immigrant group establishes itself in a new country, its members look for opportunities that are not being exploited effectively by the native population. These are the niches in the contemporary economic structure in which the competition is least vigorous. Having secured a foothold in such a niche, the group seeks to build upon its success and perhaps to obtain a monopoly upon this kind of work. Its members may then come to regard this as their occupational speciality (Banton 1983:297).

Boissevain also supports this:

It is probably not coincidental that the takeover by immigrants of traditional enterprises such as corner grocers, has been particularly pronounced in Britain. This country has the lowest proportion of small businesses and self-employed in the Common Market...In a certain sense this indicates an empty space in the service sector which ethnic entrepreneurs are filling. The possible relation between such structural and cultural variables needs much more attention (1981:22).

It is worth noting here that despite the variation in the contexts, certain ethnic minorities such as the South Asians, the Chinese and the Jews, have managed to enter the small business sector in the different countries they have migrated to, such as East Africa, Fiji, and the Netherlands, among others. This would seem to suggest that entrepreneurship amongst these minorities is capable of finding the right opportunities and manipulating the context.

Finally, there is also the 'reaction' explanation which looks at ethnic self-employment, "as a reaction against racism and blocked avenues of occupational mobility, a survival strategy for coping on the margins of the white-dominated mainstreams of the economy..." (Jenkins 1984:231).

Nowikowski too, analyses the emergence of businesses among the Asians as a survival strategy and holds that, "For all the Asians, self-employment strategies emerged in the context of structural racial disadvantage in the metropolis" (1984:158).

However, it must be remembered that different ethnic groups experiencing similar levels of discrimination and disadvantage in the white dominated labour market do not exhibit comparable rates of business entry.

It is proposed, therefore, to test these explanations, keeping in mind that they need not be mutually exclusive. A further possibility is also to be considered, namely that the structural position of the migrants in their country of origin would be important in determining the choice of the small business strategy of survival. The significant cultural factor in the case of Asian ethnic minorities may be the prestige accorded to small business in the country of origin. Also, the relative weight of each of these explanations may vary according to the different stages in the growth of Asian retailing. *WHO OWNS WHAT?*

Small enterprise and the class structure

The second question considered is the position of the Asian self-employed in the class structure, and whether small business entry is a means to upward social mobility.

The question of the class position of small entrepreneurs arises because the petty bourgeoisie is of the middle class due to ownership of property and control of the work situation, and yet, not really middle class in attitudes and style of life. But neither is it the working class. Where this 'uneasy stratum' belongs has been much discussed (Bechhofer and Elliott 1968; Gerry and Birkbeck 1981; Scase and Goffee 1982; Boissevain 1981).

The more important question for stratification theory could well be the role of the petty bourgeoisie in social mobility - especially of ethnic minorities, whose large scale entry into this class is well documented (Boissevain 1981; Ward and Jenkins 1984). It has been held that the importance of the petty bourgeoisie lies in its encouragement of intergenerational and career mobility (Bland *et al.* 1978). Studies of minority groups carried out in the United States have consistently shown that small neighbourhood enterprises have served as springboards for upward economic and social mobility, leading to some measure of economic parity with the majority society (Boissevain 1981; Aldrich 1980; Light 1972). According to the 'blocked upward mobility' thesis, barriers to entry into white collar jobs and managerial jobs in white owned businesses may push Asian minorities into starting up on their own. Asian minorities, especially those from middle class backgrounds, forced to take up manual work after migration, may see in self-employment and small employer positions, avenues of mobility out of the working class. As Banton points out, "Running his own business gives a man added status within the ethnic minority"(1983). ~ *hence names on shops!*

But Scase and Goffee, while agreeing that 'marginal' or 'subordinate' groups may see in self-employment avenues of self-advancement and an "alternative to the experience of deprivation in the labour market", feel that proprietorship "does not constitute an 'open' avenue for upward mobility" (1982:188-189). A note of caution is sounded by those studying Asians as well (Ward and Jenkins 1984; Auster and Aldrich 1984; Nowikowski 1984; Aldrich *et al.* 1984). Mars and Ward, thus, ask:

⌄ What is more evident; an entrepreneurial ethic or a religious ethic?

THIS IS PART OF THE QUESTIONNAIRE.

CONSIDERATION TO BARE IN MIND WHEN LOOK'G @ PLACE!

...how far is business an avenue to social mobility and how far a precarious attempt to make a living on the margins of the economy when access to more productive areas is blocked? (1984:5) *but does the place reflect this?*

The questions to be considered then, are, what is the position of the Asian petty bourgeoisie in the class structure, and does movement into the petty bourgeoisie imply social mobility or merely "a sideways shift from lumpenproletariat to lumpenbourgeoisie" (Aldrich *et al.* 1984:191).[3]

Ethnicity of Asian small business

It is one thing to note that a large number of Asians are entering small business, and to attempt an explanation of this phenomenon. But it is quite another thing to maintain, on the basis of large scale entry, that there is something ethnically distinctive about Asian small business which separates it from small business in general. *→ + in what ways*

'Ethnicity', as far as business is concerned, can be said to refer to:

1) an ethnic sub-market based on an ethnic group's own consumption patterns (Mars and Ward 1984:14),

2) a 'protected market' consisting of mainly Asian clientele (Aldrich *et al.* 1984; Boissevain 1981),

3) 'ethnic enclaves', in which Asian businesses function (Auster and Aldrich 1984),

4) reliance on ethnic social networks (Werbner 1984),

5) reliance on family and ethnic labour (Boissevain 1990:132; Aldrich 1980),

6) ethnic business practices, such as working longer hours, not extending credit, etc. (Aldrich 1980),

7) ethnic solidarity (Cater and Jones 1987; Jones 1989).

Is small businesses the way numerica all asian sop is put forward?

In the first place, these 'ethnic' characteristics cannot be presumed to exist from the fact of large scale entry. 'Ethnicity' of business activity, as described above, refers to something more than the mere fact that business owners are of particular ethnic origins. While the General Household Survey (GHS) data has been used (Curran and Burrows 1988) to show that a significant number of small business owners are of ethnic minorities, it cannot in any way demonstrate the 'ethnicity' of these businesses in the sense of whether they serve their own ethnic markets, whether they are dependent on ethnic networks for finance, whether they employ only ethnic labour, whether they are found only in areas of heavy ethnic residential concentration and whether they are significantly different from the native small business owners in such things as attitudes, class

7

origins, education, and mobility patterns. So, large numbers of ethnic minorities may go into 'enterprise activity', but this does not prove that the resulting enterprise activity is 'ethnic'. It may be no different from native enterprise activity.

It has been pointed out with regard to the work ethic of the shopkeepers - the hours worked, business practices, attitudes to family, children and social life, and so on, - that none of this is peculiar to ethnic minorities (Scase and Goffee 1980). Again, Auster and Aldrich (1984:50) have held that relations between ethnic firms would tend toward cooperative mutual adjustment and self-regulation rather than competition, when backed by a strong ethnic economy. However, it may well be that it is Werbner who paints a more accurate picture when she speaks of Pakistani traders in Manchester competing with each other for clientele, and of ethnic identity not being the dominant consideration traders have in matters of credit (1984:186).

On the basis of research conducted in Bradford, Ealing and Leicester, Cater and Jones (1987), and Jones (1989), have emphasized the ethnicity of minority businesses as the cause of both their coming into being and of their lack of success. They speak of the sense of ethnic community, and forms of communal support such as pooling of capital, extended family support, communal insurance against emergencies, all of which is then traced back to the low class-position of migrants. The ethnic community is something created by dire necessity - 'the natural freemasonry of the disinherited', which, they say, is to be found even among the British working class.

This sense of community is then regarded as the principal business resource of the minority group, the chief support in its entrepreneurial activity. The obvious question here would be that if this sense of community is to be found equally among a similarly placed British group, why does it motivate one group and not the other in entrepreneurial activity? Cater and Jones go on to say that this sense of community, while encouraging business activity, is equally the cause of what they see as the lack of success of Asian businesses. It is the sense of community which is supposed to lead to the locational concentration of businesses, the lack of competition among them, and thus to low levels of profitability.

As against all this, it may be that, today, the sense of community which Cater and Jones talk of may not be very evident in the entrepreneurial group. It may well be that with the development of the entrepreneurial group into a 'middle-man minority' group, the competition among these entrepreneurs leads to a philosophy of each for himself.

Asian small shopkeepers may then, be no different from small shopkeepers as such. It is proposed therefore to study how 'ethnic' Asian small business really is, and whether the Asian small business owners are in fact different from their white counterparts.

Self-employment, assimilation and ethnic solidarity

As South Asians, for whatever reasons, have taken to small business on a large scale, the final question would then be, whether the occupation aids their integration into British society. If Asian minorities are taking to self-employment because of the desire to circumvent discrimination in career mobility (Banton 1983:320), and because of lack of fit between socio-economic backgrounds and jobs, large scale entry into proprietorship may be taken as a sign of lack of assimilation. It could be argued that just as the petty bourgeoisie puts up with hardship for the sake of independence and freedom from interference, the Asian small entrepreneur, too, sees in his occupation a measure of freedom from discrimination and prejudice. But, in so far as it does give him a means of circumventing discrimination, the occupation itself may be an aid to integration. Also, as Lord Scarman has argued, a greater involvement in business would produce more community stability and allow ethnic minorities to feel that they possessed a greater stake in society(Scarman 1982:167-8). Again, small business, if successful and lucrative, may actively encourage economic integration. Economic integration, defined by Wright as, "the extent to which the immigrant or minority group is absorbed into, and accepted as part of, the economic system of the host society" (1968:12), has been described by Borrie (1959), as a "way-station to cultural integration". According to Borrie, "it has been taken as axiomatic that reasonable security of employment...(is)...the essential foundation to the long process of cultural integration" (1959:101).

Borrie goes on to say:

> ...to succeed in employment is the first major goal that every immigrant must attain, and to the extent that this can be done by the application of his own skills and initiative the immigrant will be encouraged to make the effort to be integrated in other spheres (1959:111).

EVIDENCE OF THIS
IN COWLEY!

Successful small business activity, especially that of retailing and catering, if not confined to an ethnic niche, may be expected to bring the Asian small business owners into considerable contact with the indigenous population. Thus, on the basis of a survey of Asian retailers in Croydon, it has been maintained that the perception of Asians as forming self-segregating communities and avoiding unnecessary conflicts with white Britons is contradicted by the fact of their undertaking middleman entrepreneurial functions (Mullins 1979:403). Barth (1969), however, would argue that transactional relationships, as between shopkeepers and shoppers, are the single stranded ones which do not carry over into other activities and become the multiplex relationships, which usually remain concentrated within the ethnic group. But, as Granovetter stresses, weak ties often denounced as generators of alienation are to be seen rather as indispensable to individuals' opportunities and to their integration into communities (1978:1378). It is proposed, therefore, to consider the impact of the 'economic integration' of the Asian small business owners on the general integration of this group with the host society, as well as on the nature of their ethnic identification and solidarity.

The extent to which given groups are clustered in particular occupational niches would decide the group's occupational specialization

(Hechter 1978:300), and an occupationally specialized ethnic group is more likely to develop solidarity than one which is unspecialized (Barth 1969; Cohen 1969; Yancey Ericksen and Juliani 1976). But, it is suggested here, that this would depend on the nature of the occupational specialization. If the nature of the employment is such that it does not encourage interaction between those engaging in it, solidarity may not develop. It has been held that the basic perspective of the small business sector remains what Goldthorpe and Lockwood characterized as 'radical individualism' (Bechhofer and Elliott 1968:180-202). If shopkeepers can be shown to have individualist rather than collectivist orientations to action, this may well be taken as implying a weaker ethnic identity and thus, a stronger position *vis-a-vis* assimilation. A situation where individual success or failure cannot easily be attributed to any characteristics of the category as a whole, can be seen as a, "situation encouraging individualistic orientations to action rather than the collectivistic orientations implied by having a strong ethnic identity" (Hechter 1978:299).

The orientation to work of the South Asian small shopkeeper, and its influence on ethnic solidarity, is, therefore, worthy of consideration. Further, as Auster and Aldrich point out:

> ...the extent to which ethnic solidarity persists, once a minority group has achieved prosperity, is important in understanding the link between small business and the persistent salience of ethnicity (1984:51-52).

In a study of Jews, Rosentraub and Taebel (1980), found evidence of declining ethnic collectivism, solidarity and patronage among prosperous Jews. Does this hold true in the case of the South Asian shopkeepers?

Ethnic group solidarity is, in the last resort, the strength of feeling binding the individuals into a collectivity. If this feeling or sentiment is to be measured, there is, according to Hechter:

> ...a general consensus that endogamy is the ultimate measure of the salience of boundaries for intergroup relations...Each group's willingness to cross ethnic or class lines in its marital behaviour should reveal something about the salience of these respective categories as social boundaries (1978:304-309).

Hechter found a strong positive relationship between a group's overall level of ethnic endogamy and its preference for marriage across class as against ethnic lines. It is proposed to examine the level of endogamy among the Asian shopkeepers and its consequences for assimilation and ethnic solidarity.

Reasons for studying the Asians as a whole

A brief mention must be made here of the reasons for studying the South Asians as a whole. As noted earlier, by 'Asian' is meant all those originating from the Indian sub-continent, that is from India, Pakistan and Bangladesh. Researchers in the field of ethnic group relations do not usually approve of such an obvious over-generalisation. It is pointed out that the use of such a blanket term for the many and varied cultures included within it, may be dangerously misleading (Ballard 1990:219). It should first be admitted that there is a great deal of truth in this: in theory there are salient differences not only between the Indian, Pakistani and Bangladeshi groups, but within these groups as well (Robinson 1980 1982 1986). However, there is also a danger of being over-specific: to confine oneself to just the Mirpuris in Oxford or the Gujeratis in Leicester, would be to lose sight of the common processes within the different groups.

It must be pointed out that empirical studies of entrepreneurship among the South Asian groups have not been able to establish significant differences: Rafiq, attempting a comparison of Muslim (Pakistani and Bangladeshi), and non-Muslim (Indian and East African) businesses in Bradford, concludes that overall rates of participation in business and business performance is the same in both groups, and that differences in participation in certain trades and in employment practices are the result of differences in socio-economic status rather than of culture (1992:58).

So also, Aldrich *et al.*, in their study of Asian businesses state:

> ...there is very little evidence of a specific Gujerati, Sikh or Pakistani effect and no sign of any particular impact exerted by the East African business heritage (1984:205).

In a survey of the modes of adaptation by Asian immigrants in Slough, Levine and Nayar, found, "so few differences between these two groups (Indian and Pakistani) on the majority of items...decided to combine them into one sample" (1975:357).

Even more significant is Dahya's emphasis on the traits shared by the immigrants *qua* immigrants:

> ...their ambition for economic success, an emphasis on deferred gratification (willingness to make sacrifices in terms of time and comfort), and on hard work and the goal of self-employment. Taking all these attributes into consideration, one can say that South Asian immigrants in Britain, internally divided though they may be in terms of caste, religious affiliation, language, ethnic and national origins, etc., can be regarded as a single category which I shall refer to as 'Asian' (1988).

Since the purpose of the present work is not to explore the culture content of the various ethnic sub-groups, the argument that 'Asian' is too broad a term would not hold good. The emphasis is more on process, on the dynamics underlying entrepreneurial entry and the use of ethnicity. It is, therefore argued that the risks involved in over-generalisation are relatively few, and that much would be lost by over-specificity.

A note on methodology

With the foregoing as the theoretical background, a survey of South Asian small business owners[4] within the City of Oxford was conducted between November 1989 and June 1990. Detailed information was collected about these self-employed Asians, in terms of their socio-economic background, their previous work history, their educational level, their family and residential patterns, their business practices, their attitudes to racism and assimilation, their ethnic solidarity, their hopes and aspirations, providing an ethnographic account of this particular occupational group of South Asians in Oxford.

Given the difficulties in obtaining a suitable sampling frame, as well as the relatively small number of businesses, it was felt that the representativeness of a *sample* would be vitiated, and that any sort of survey should attempt a complete coverage of the entire population. The total population of one hundred and five South Asian owned small businesses within the City of Oxford, was, therefore, approached, and 94 business owners consented to the interview, providing a response rate of 90 per cent.

As the reasons for undertaking this primary research, and for the choice of Oxford as the research setting, are provided in a methodological appendix[5], it will suffice to say here that a study of cities like Oxford may help to balance the picture presented by the studies of South Asian entrepreneurship in cities like Bradford, Birmingham, Leicester, etc. These places, with a heavy concentration, and residential segregation of Asians, are likely to be 'institutionally complete' in Breton's (1965) sense of the term, and thus, to have different patterns of retailing and business growth, as well as different levels of ethnic solidarity, and assimilation, from smaller cities without a heavy concentration of Asians, but a significant number of Asian shops and restaurants - of which Oxford is a good example.

Finally, it is on the validity of the data that the success of a social survey depends. In this study, the survey data were supplemented by in-depth qualitative research, in as much as a considerable amount of time was spent in observing and interacting with the respondents. This was possible both within the precincts of the shop and restaurant, as well as in their homes in the case of some respondents. There were also social occasions, such as weddings and religious festivals, when observation and interaction were possible. As pointed out by Vidich and Shapiro:

> ...the techniques of participant observation and the sample survey are not competitive, but, in the well conducted community study, will be complementary. The survey provides representative information which is given meaning by the anthropological observer (1970:522).

The structure of the book

The substantive issues to be discussed in the book have been raised and the theoretical and methodological background to the study have been sketched. Chapter 2, titled *'The Research Setting - The City of Oxford'*, provides the empirical background, that is, a description of the City of Oxford, in terms of its location, population, the local economy, and the position of Asians within it. A brief sketch of the migration of Asians into Oxford, the size of the Asian population, its employment patterns, unemployment levels, geographical locations, and socio-economic status, is also provided. The chapter concludes with a description of the Asian business community.

Chapter 3, titled *'Reasons for Large-Scale Business Entry'*, considers the reasons for the large-scale entry of South Asians into small business. It begins with a review of the sociological explanations offered in the literature, which are divided into those that emphasize the constraints which push ethnic minority members into self-employment, and those that emphasize the cultural resources that encourage small business entry. These explanations are then examined in the light of the survey evidence, to see whether Asian businesses in Oxford do, in fact, have the characteristics suggested by these theories.

Chapter 4 offers *'An Explanation for South Asian Business Entry'* in Oxford. Where the previous chapter had identified the specific constraints as well as resources of the Asian entrepreneurs, an attempt is now made to assess the relative weight to be given to constraints, resources and choices, in an explanation of Asian business entry.

Chapter 5, titled *'The Class Position of the South Asian Petty Bourgeoisie'*, goes on to examine whether the increase in the number of Asians going into retailing can be seen as evidence of the rise of an Asian middle-class in Britain, and whether movement into the petty bourgeoisie implies upward social mobility for the Asian small business owner. The 'market', 'work', and 'status' situations of the Asian small business owners in Oxford are analysed in order to assess their class position.

Chapter 6, titled *'Ethnicity at Work'*, looks at how 'ethnic' South Asian business activity is, and the salience of ethnicity for the Asian small business owner in the actual situation of work. A comparison of South Asian entrepreneurs with the native English entrepreneurs is attempted, on the basis of existing research on the British self-employed, with a view to seeing whether the Asian small business class is at all different from the British petty bourgeoisie.

Chapter 7, titled *'Assimilation and Ethnicity'*, first provides a brief elucidation of the two concepts as found in the literature. It then brings together the evidence presented in the foregoing three chapters to assess the nature of the assimilation of the self-employed South Asians in Oxford into British life, as well as on the nature and salience of their 'ethnicity'.

Chapter 9 provides the *'Summary and Conclusions'*. Here the conclusions of the previous chapters are summarized and drawn together to sketch a picture of South Asian entrepreneurship in Oxford and its bearing on the question of the assimilation of Asians into British life.

Despite the enormous amount of literature on South Asian migrants, and some studies of South Asian retailers as well, it can be agreed with Robinson that, "theory which can stand close scrutiny and claim to be unique to ethnic studies is still a rarity" (1986:2). It is hoped that this study, by considering the relative weight of the factors of class and ethnicity and the influence of these on assimilation, will make some contribution towards filling this gap.

Notes

1.   The small business owners studied in this book are those of Indian, Pakistani or Bangladeshi origin, whether referred to as 'Asian' or 'South Asian'. Studies of ethnic entrepreneurship in Britain have largely used the term 'Asian' to refer to entrepreneurs of Indian, Pakistani and Bangladeshi origin (cf. Allen 1969; Hiro 1971; Mullins 1979; Ward and Jenkins 1984; Aldrich et al. 1984; Leach et al. 1990; Patel 1991; Cross 1992; Rafiq 1992; Srinivasan 1992). Tinker explains his use of the term 'Asian' for the overseas communities from India, Pakistan, and Bangladesh, as follows:

The term 'Asian' became current in East Africa in the 1950s instead of the term Indian and has been introduced elsewhere as synonymous with South Asian. It is thus employed in this book (1977:ix)

Recent work on the diaspora from the South Asian countries appears to be changing this usage to 'South Asian'(cf. Clarke Peach and Vertovec 1990; Vertovec 1991)

2.   Middleman Minority is the term applied to ethnic minorities performing middle status commercial and business functions in 'status gap' colonial societies by Blalock (1967) in 'Towards a Theory of Minority Group Relations'. The theory is extensively reworked by Bonacich, (1973) to describe immigrant groups whose business ownership is extensive enough to provide a major source of livelihood for group members. Overseas Indians are cited among a lengthy list of groups who have acquired a reputation for middleman activities

3.   The term 'lumpenbourgeoisie' appears to have been first used by Mills (1951:28), according to whom, "If we may speak of a 'lumpenproletariat' set off from other wage workers, we may also speak of a 'lumpenbourgeoisie' set off from other middle class elements. For the bottom of the entrepreneurial world is so different from the top that it is doubtful whether the two should be classed together.' The term has also been used by Frazier (1957) to

emphasize the small scale and marginality of black business in the USA

4.   As there were no South Asian wholesalers or manufacturers, or Asian owned launderettes, theatres, or pubs, in Oxford, by small business owner is meant in effect, the small shop-keeper and restaurant owner.

5.   The methodology used for the collection of the data, and for its analysis and interpretation are provided in the appendix. Details of the secondary sources of data utilized, as well as the reasons for accepting the validity of the survey research, are also provided.

2 The research setting – The city of Oxford

Introduction

This chapter provides a brief account of the local economy of Oxford, the background of its South Asian population, and the position of these Asians within the local economy. The very limited data available on the demographic and settlement patterns of the South Asian communities in Oxford have been pieced together to provide a backdrop to the growth of Asian self-employment within the city. The chapter concludes with a brief description of the South Asian business community at the time of the survey, in terms of length of residence in Oxford, reasons for migration, type of businesses, location both business and residential, duration of businesses, employment of business owners previous to self-employment, as well as the social class background of the entrepreneurs.

Oxford - its location and character

At the very middle of Middle England, it is said, stands the middle-sized city of Oxford. According to Morris's classic account:

> It is a municipal and parliamentary borough,...a county town, the seat of a university and of an episcopal see, with a population in 1986 of about 114,000 and factories for the production of cars, agricultural implements, printed goods and marmalade (1987:5).

The comparative study of the social and economic differences of British towns (Moser and Scott 1961:17, 84), based on 1951 census data, classifies Oxford with the spas, professional and administrative centres, so that the city could be quite comprehensively described as "an educational centre with an industrial appendage" (Winchester 1975).

The socio-economic structure of pre-war Oxford

Up until the first world war, the city of Oxford was entirely dominated by the University, on which the citizens were heavily dependent for their livelihood. While the Oxford University Press, with a labour force of 300, was the largest single employer, the majority of the 20,000 who worked in the City were in domestic service and the distributive trades, catering mainly for the dons and students (Collison 1963:54). Though the city of Oxford of this pre-war period had been growing, growth was slow and due largely to the general and widespread drift to the towns, and the city remained untouched by the industrialisation that had radically re-shaped and expanded so many other cities (Spooner 1979:8).

A quite sudden and dramatic change in the economic and social structure of Oxford city was brought about by the opening of the Cowley car works in 1912 by William Morris, later Lord Nuffield - an event that was to radically transform the character, size and shape of the city and its surrounding areas. This infant car industry was well established by 1923 and rapidly expanded to include Morris Radiators in North Oxford in 1924, and the Pressed Steel Company at Cowley in 1926. The car industry had arrived in Oxford, which had now come to combine its traditional function as a university centre with that of an industrial city. The years upto 1939, saw the integration of Oxford into the national economy, in that the dominant sector of the labour force became dependent on an industry serving a national market, rather than just the needs of the university (Whiting 1978:1). Throughout the 1920s and 1930s, migration into Oxford from other parts of the country became an important feature, accounting for the veritable population explosion in the city from 62,000 people in 1911 to 96,000 by 1939 (Collison 1963:55). Undoubtedly, the growth of the car industry was the main pulling force that drew the migrants to Oxford, so that nearly half of the city's motor workers were immigrants[1] and nearly half the immigrants were car workers in July 1936 (Spooner 1979:9). However, according to Spooner, it was the local bus company that employed the highest proportion of migrants (1979:9). In any case, unemployment ceased to be a problem and Oxford became one of the most prosperous areas in the country.

The migration had a profound effect on the size and shape of the City. Up until the decade beginning in 1921, most of Oxford's expansion had been in the north wards and either within the City boundaries or just beyond. The post 1921 expansion increasingly pushed beyond the City limits and into areas within easy reach of the Cowley works. In particular, the Headington, Marston, Cowley and Iffley areas expanded at a remarkable rate in the 1921-31 period. The Extension Act of 1928 was the administrative recognition of the new reality - Headington, part of Marston, Cowley, Iffley, Wolvercote and Cutteslowe were incorporated into the City of Oxford. Most importantly, the new growth areas were overwhelmingly occupied by industrial workers (Spooner 1979:11). The housing estates which grew up around the car factories - Morris Motors and Pressed Steel - constitute the 'new' city which differs from the 'old' not only in geography but in political and industrial attitudes and behaviour

(Whiting 1978:2). The ecological pattern of Oxford thus provides, according to Collison and Mogey, a contrast to the usual pattern of American cities, in that people of the highest social class live closest to the centre of the town and are heavily concentrated in the north sector, while the Registrar-General's social class 3 of skilled workers is disproportionately represented near the city boundary (1959:599).

The very first south Asian presence in Oxford

It was during this period of booming growth that the first non-student South Asian presence in Oxford established itself. In 1937, an Indian Law student in London, having successfully established the first Indian owned restaurant in London,[2] moved to Oxford and opened a second one - the Taj Mahal on Turl street, which continues to the present day, though now under a different management. The restaurant was staffed, as became the tradition, by Indian[3] seamen who had jumped ship. The earliest Asians in Oxford, then, belong to the very first category of the Indian immigrant population in Britain - "...the seamen (who) formed a part of the coloured colonies in the 1930s which grew up in ports..."(Desai 1963:3-4). Their number was, of course, negligible, but their presence was quite noticeable as the Taj Mahal achieved considerable popularity among the university students, especially the American ones who continue to return, 'children, gold cards and all'. In addition to the South Asians employed in the restaurant, there were also a few other pioneering settlers who had been door-to-door pedlars in South Wales, Glasgow and Newcastle, and had come to Oxford before 1950 in order to try the same occupation there (Shaw 1988:33). This too, was quite in pattern, in so far as hawking textiles and clothing is one of the earliest occupations taken up by the immigrants in the United Kingdom,[4] starting in the thirties when a few dozen Sikhs began to operate, mainly in Liverpool, Glasgow, and northern Scotland, with some moving to Yorkshire and the Midlands in 1947 (Desai 1963:64-67; Hiro 1971:120).

The post-war new Commonwealth immigration

Oxford's experience of 'black' migration really begins in the post-war period of the 1950s. Though this period was one of balance in terms of net migration for Oxford, there were migrants moving into the city to replace people moving out rather than supplementing the existing population. The new element in this post war migratory flow was that many of these 'replacement' migrants were coloured. According to Spooner, these black migrants differed from those of the inter-war years in other respects too:

> Theirs is an international rather than national migration; their movement to Oxford is part of a larger pattern; for them the drawing power of Oxford is more than just an expanding car works; their background is over-whelmingly rural (1979:22).

The post-war migratory flow of coloured workers into the City of Oxford began in the mid 1950s. This reflected the national situation as the South Asian migration into Britain became numerically significant only after 1952. The economic expansion in the United Kingdom after the Second World War and the resulting shortage of labour attracted immigrant workers from many parts of the Commonwealth.

While it has been demonstrated by Peach (1968) that, as far as the Caribbeans were concerned, it was this 'pull' of the British economy which was the main determining factor of their large scale migration to Great Britain, rather than population pressure and unemployment as emphasized by Glass (1960:6-7), the evidence is more inconclusive where the Asians are concerned. Thus, Robinson maintains that Asian migration takes place regardless of the state of Britain's economy (1986:28).

After entry to the UK, however, settlement patterns were determined purely by the demand for labour. Peach (1966) argues that West Indians avoided areas of low demand and moved instead to regions where labour demand was high and unsatisfied. That this is also true of the Asians is demonstrated by Jones (1976). He suggests that settlement patterns are determined by two features of labour demand. Firstly, settlement took place in areas where white labour was scarce because of the pace of economic expansion e.g. Greater London, Birmingham, and their respective satellites. Secondly, settlement also occurred in those areas where the demand was for 'replacement labour' in those industries where conditions of employment were poor e.g. the textile industry of Manchester, Leeds, and nearby towns. Spooner argues that except for London and the South East, the proportion of coloured migrants is higher in regions of moderate labour demand than in regions of strong demand, so that it would seem that coloured migrants have gone to regions which have had demand but which have failed to attract sufficient white labour (1979:26).

Oxford fits quite neatly into this framework. Though a few Indians and Pakistanis had been employed in the Indian restaurants for some time, it was not until the mid-1950s, when there was an opening for poorly paid, unskilled and semi-skilled labourers in Oxford (Shaw 1988:33), as well as an economic recession in the North (Griffith *et al.* 1960:33) that the South Asians moved into Oxford in any significant numbers. The first major influx of coloured immigrants into Oxford is attributed to the failure of the local bus company, the City of Oxford Motor services, to attract indigenous labour. With bus conductors and cleaners moving to better paid jobs, such as those at the Cowley car works, it is maintained that the bus service in some parts of Oxford was almost at a standstill. To meet this labour shortage, the bus company recruited some West Indians from the Brixton Exchange in 1955 (Griffiths *et al.* 1960:42). It was not only the bus company that required labour: local English unskilled and semi-skilled labour was also being drawn away from British Rail, the hospitals, construction firms, restaurants and other service industries, by the better paid car factory jobs. Times had changed from the inter-war years when the city was a magnet for workers from all over the country, drawn by new jobs in an expanding car industry. For Oxford city it was now a question of filling the less popular jobs of the service industries, and only Asians and Blacks were willing to move to fill this vacuum.

Together with the labour shortages, economic circumstances in other parts of the country also played an important part in the movement of Commonwealth immigrants into Oxford. From about 1956 onwards there was a steady growth in this immigrant population, with an upsurge between 1958 and 1959 as a result of the 1958 recession in the North. According to Griffiths *et al.*, during the recession, as the employment situation became difficult in the North, Indians and Pakistanis moved to the Midlands and the South. In the late autumn of 1958 they migrated from Bradford, Rotherham and Sheffield to Birmingham, Luton, Oxford and Slough (1960:33). That those who moved did so on the basis of personal contacts with the coloured population already in Oxford, is true of the Asians (Shaw 1988:34), as well as the West Indians (Griffiths *et al.* 1960:42).

Employment and settlement patterns - the first phase

An estimate in 1959 gives the number of coloured workers in Oxford as 400-500, of which 60-70 per cent were West Indians (Griffiths *et al.* 1960:42). At this time the bus company was the largest single employer of coloured men (48 conductors, 6 cleaners and 1 driver) (Spooner 1979:30). While the majority were West Indians, that Asians too, were employed by the bus company is borne out by the report of an Indian, with a post graduate degree from India,[5] whose first employment on arrival in Oxford in 1960, was as a bus conductor, because "Bus crews were provided with hostel accommodation in Oxford" (Baquer 1965:105).

The Indians and Pakistanis, because of their language difficulties, found it more difficult to find work than the West Indians, and were mainly employed as kitchen porters in restaurants and hospitals in Oxford (Griffiths *et al.* 1960:42; Baquer 1965:108-109). Many employers, including the bus company, operated a quota system restricting the number of black and Asian employees, and Asians were unable to get work at all in several other firms, such as Morris Motors Ltd., because of an unofficial colour bar. Work by the Oxford Committee for Racial Integration (OCRI), helped to decrease the discrimination amongst employers and Morris Motors, for instance, changed its policy towards Indians and Pakistanis after receiving a deputation from OCRI's executive (Rose 1969:391).

It was in the 'Indian' restaurants, however, that most Indians and Pakistanis were employed (Griffiths *et al.* 1960:27). A Bangladhasi[6] seaman from the Coventry docks, selling his restaurant in Fulham in 1956, moved to Oxford, and within a year had opened two restaurants on Walton Street - 'The Bombay Restaurant' at No.82 Walton Street, and 'The Dil Duniya' at No.108 Walton Street. These restaurants provided living accommodation for not just the Indians and Pakistanis working there, but temporary shelter for all Asian newcomers to Oxford. According to the proprietor's nephew, the present owner of another 'Indian' restaurant on Walton Street:

> Anyone - Punjabis and Bengalis - who came to Oxford had to come to Dil Duniya for temporary living. Accommodation and food were provided free and they were treated as guests till they found jobs and other accommodation. Dil Duniya was also the place for prayers, as the basement was used as a mosque where thirty people could pray, and for the Friday prayers the whole restaurant became a mosque.

As the numbers increased, by around 1959, the Dil Duniya became overcrowded and people began to look for alternative accommodation and jobs. This was in effect the lodging house era in Oxford, with Asian owned houses on Leckford Road and Southmoor Road notorious for excessive overcrowding. According to the respondent quoted earlier:

> In those days the Bengalis and Punjabis had to be friends. We were all Pakistanis. But the Punjabis were more literate and could find jobs more easily -- in the bakeries and the buses, and they knew how to buy houses. In 1960, the very first Bengali started working in the Boffin Bakery in Osney. The management was very impressed by his hard work and began to employ a lot of Asians. Soon, 80 per cent of those working there were Pakistani or Bangladeshi, and this was so till the bakery closed in 1979.

With the bakery becoming a major source of employment there was a corresponding shift in settlement patterns, with houses being bought in the Osney Mead area of West Oxford. Three of the four houses recorded under Muslim names in the electoral register of 1960 were in West Oxford (Shaw 1988:35).[7] So, while the first small clustering of Asians was off Walton Street, in the Jericho area, the second was off the Botley Road, in Osney.

The fourth house on the 1960 electoral register was in the City Centre. The Cobra restaurant, at St Ebbes, had to shut down around 1962, as a result of the Council's slum clearance programme, but the owners were offered alternative accommodation and moved to the High Street. The restaurants continued to be a popular source of employment as lodging and food went with the job. And there was a steady increase in the number of these restaurants, the *Kelly's Oxford Trade Directory* of 1962, listing six 'Indian' restaurants. The first one on Cowley Road, 'The Himalaya', opened in 1962, and prospered for nearly two decades, drawing a number of its regulars mainly from the student population of Magdalen College, who found that for a little more than the price of a pint and a pork pie, they could get a hot, 'three course' lunch of rice and curry, fruit and coffee.

Changes in employment and settlement patterns - the second phase

The early 1960s was a period of consolidation and growth of the South Asian population in Oxford, as employment opportunities expanded and settlement patterns widened to accommodate these changes. A significant employment opportunity was that provided by the Bicester Central Ordnance Depot (COD), during a transfer of the Didcot COD to Bicester. The COD apparently provided two coaches to transport Pakistanis from St Clements, in East Oxford, to Bicester and back daily (Shaw 1988:38). The bus company quota for Black and Asian bus conductors and drivers was gradually loosening up in the early 1960s as a result of local voluntary organisations' pressure against discrimination in employment, and was finally abandoned altogether following the 1965 Race Relations Act. Employment was also available in foundries outside Oxford, as also in the Kidlington cement factory, and the Sandford Paper Mill. After 1965, however, the most significant change was the employment by British Leyland of West Indians, Indians and Pakistanis, as assemblers, painters, cleaners and storemen.

Those working in the car factory and in the buses found it convenient to live in East Oxford, and terraced houses were available at very cheap prices in East and South Oxford. A number of houses in St. Clements, and on various streets between the Cowley and Iffley Roads, such as Circus Street, James Street, Regents Street, Howard Street, Bullingdon Road, Magdalen Road, as well as streets off the Iffley Road, such as Chester Street and Warwick Street, were bought outright by the South Asians, signalling in effect the end of tenancy and lodging house occupation and the shift to owner occupation. This was the start of what continues to be the major clustering of Asians within Oxford. According to Shaw, the shift in the nucleus of the Asian settlement can be seen from Health Centre records - in the mid-1960s, 20 per cent of the Jericho health centre's patients were Asian, but declined from then on, with the majority registered in east Oxford by the late 1970s (1988:41). East Oxford is the one area of the City which has significant numbers of Indians, Pakistanis, Bangladeshis and Caribbeans, and consequently, in terms of its black population it had by the late 1970s, more than 15 per cent in several of its enumeration districts, and generally higher than 10 per cent, in the rest of the area (Spooner 1979:36).

The regional background of Oxford's Asian immigrants follows closely the national pattern described by Desai (1963:13). The majority of the Indians in Oxford are from the Jullunder district of Punjab, with nearly all the rest coming from Gujerat. Amongst the Pakistanis the majority are from the Jhellum district of the Punjabi speaking area of Pakistan, while a sizeable number are from Mirpur. In the Bangladeshi community, more than 90 per cent are from the Sylhet area. There is also a sizeable Indian Punjabi Christian community in the city, again originating from the Jullunder district. The two smallest Asian communities in Oxford, both just under twenty five families, are those of the Sikhs from the Punjab area, and of the Malayalee Christians from South Kerala.

The start of South Asian retailing

Hiro, discussing the economic infra-structure of South Asians in Britain, maintains:

> The distinctive food habits and sartorial customs of the Asians proved economically advantageous to the community. They provided the initial impetus to enterprising Asians to start businesses to supply goods and services which the community needed, and which the British shopkeepers and supermarkets were unable, or unwilling, to meet. As the Asian community grew, so did the number and size of these establishments...Owners...were, almost always, Pakistani immigrants who had begun as labourers...but had, through self-discipline and ambition, saved to invest in businesses of their own...However, Asian enterprise did not for long remain confined to opening food premises. It also went into clothing...(1971:151).

In Oxford, too, it was a Pakistani, Kamal Ashgar, who first opened a grocers shop, 'Asiatic Grocers' in 1962, within the first area of Asian settlement, at 25 Walton Crescent, to supply the growing population of South Asian men with 'halal' meat, rice, wholemeal flour, spices, and other 'ethnic' ingredients essential for basic home cooking, which these men had been long deprived of. The success of this enterprise is evident from the fact that in 1964, a second shop was opened, right opposite the first, across the road from Walton Crescent, again by a Pakistani, and the two shops continued to do good business, side by side, for many years. It was in 1964 that the first shop in the Cowley area - 'Mohammedi Grocers', opened at 45 Bullingdon Road, later to move to 228/230 Cowley Road and to become the famous 'Raja Brothers'. While the second shop off Walton Street continues in the same area till today, the first, though changing hands a number of times, continued in business till the mid 1970s, when it shifted to Cowley Road where it is a thriving business today. In 1964, then, there were three Pakistani owned grocery shops in Oxford.

These grocery shops were essentially a male domain, where the men hung around after work, exchanging news of home, information about available jobs, business openings, etc. Even after the women began arriving around 1964 (Shaw 1988:44), they rarely ventured into the shops. According to the wife of an Indian shop-keeper (No.3):

> When I arrived in 1967, we women were too scared to get out and go to Cowley Road, so we used the English corner shops. For our Indian groceries, the men from the shops would come home, take our lists and deliver the groceries, so we never needed to go to the shops. In fact, my husband warned me never to go to the Pakistani shops alone. There were always men hanging around, joking and laughing, staring at the women and making comments about them...If at all we went, we went with our husbands, or we would send our lists through them.

23

The West Indian women did not suffer from similar constraints and frequented Raja Brothers for their 'Yams, Green Bananas, and sweet potatoes'. This did not go unnoticed, and the West Indians were accepted as a significant part of the clientele of the Asian shops, the one at 45 Bullingdon Road, being renamed 'Afro-Asian Food Stores'.

One shop, however, which the Asian ladies did visit was the textile shop which opened very soon after the grocery shops, on Cowley Road in 1966. Run by a Pakistani woman, of course with the help of her husband an employee of the car factory, it continues to flourish, finding a mention in Snow's *Oxford Observed:Town and Gown* (1991:199): "...S.K. Fashions, unveiling a gorgeous profusion of Indian fabrics...".

So far the pattern in Oxford is no different from that described by Hiro (1971). It begins to diverge, however, with the opening, in 1967 and 1968, of Indian owned, ethnic emporia, one on the High Street and the other on Little Clarendon Street. It is interesting to note that these shops though opened quite early in the settlement process, were in up-market locations rather than in areas of South Asian settlement, and were clearly oriented towards the indigenous population rather than the Asians. The one on Little Clarendon Street, named 'Oriental Crafts', advertised its wares in the *Kelly's Trade Directory*, as including "Exotic caftans, Batik prints, exquisite filigree jewellery, handloomed bedspreads, fascinating curios...". The impression one gets is of 'educated' Indians, aware of entrepreneurial opportunities, desirous of the ensuing social status, but unwilling to 'dirty their hands' with the more tedious though lucrative, grocery business. This attitude was not to last, and by 1969, the Indian owned 'Oxford Grocers' had opened on Cowley Road. At this time there were eight Asian owned shops in Oxford, four of them on Cowley Road, and all eight continue in business today, though three of them have changed location, and two of these the type of business as well. By 1970, Asian retailing had taken off, with a steady increase in business start-up well into the late 1980s.

What is interesting is that, in Oxford, there was little diversification in the types of businesses. This is unlike the pattern of growth noted in other areas (Allen *et al.* 1969:355; Hiro 1971:152; Banton 1983:320; Patel 1991:145-152). South Asians in Oxford did not start up launderettes, public houses, travel agents, theatres, or Asian sweet shops. While there were at the time of the present survey, a couple of chemists, one delicatessen, a couple of fashion clothes shops, and quite a few subpost-offices cum general stores, the vast majority of Asian shops were 'general stores', i.e., a combination of grocers, florists, CTN's,[8] off-licences and even video shops. Also, there was no attempt to give the shops an 'Asian look' as far as shop fronts, and general physical appearance went, so that even the Cowley Road area, which has a preponderance of Asian shops, lacks that particular South Asian flavour noted in other areas such as Southall, Leicester, Bradford or Manchester. Also, despite the association of the Cowley Road with Asian shops and restaurants, Asian shops today, are no longer confined to the Cowley Road or Walton Street areas, but are to be found all over Oxford. This can be seen from Map 1, which provides the distribution of Asian owned shops and restaurants in Oxford.

Oxford, its economy and its ethnic minorities today

The population of Oxford City and its economy

The Oxford City district is the only one within the Oxfordshire County which experienced a negative population change during the 1980s (Emmerich and Lewis 1991:24). The Census figures for the population of Oxford district, from 1961 to 1991, given in Table 2.1, show a gradual decrease in population. Though the number of people resident in Oxfordshire, shows an increase of 5.2 per cent since 1981, the resident population of Oxford shows a decrease of 1.2 per cent.

Table 2.1 Population resident in Oxford on census night

1961	1971	1981	1991
106,291	108,805	107,770	106,471

According to the 1991 Census, the usually resident population of Oxford City (that is, excluding visitors but including residents who were recorded as absent on Census night),[9] is made up of 110,103 people, 53,499 of whom are male and 56,604 are female.

The employment characteristics of the resident population of Oxford, as provided by the 1991 Census, are shown in Table 2.2.

Table 2.2 Economic characteristics of Oxford population

Percentage of males and females

	Employees	Self employed	Economically Inactive	Unemployed
Males* 16-64	61	11	18	10
Females** 16-59	60	4	31	9

*n=35,764
**n=33,236
Source: OPCS, County Monitor, 1991 Census, Oxfordshire.

Map I - Distribution of Asian owned shops and restaurants in Oxford

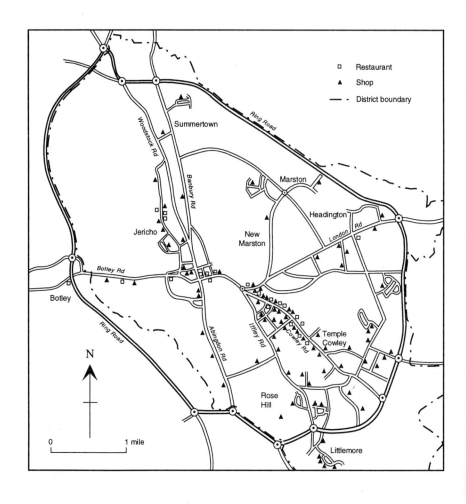

It can be seen from Table 2.2 that 10 per cent of males are unemployed, which is higher than the figure for the county as a whole. Unemployment in the county has always been low. In fact, in the period immediately preceding the present survey, between August 1986 and December 1989, there was a fall in unemployment in Oxfordshire, bottoming out at 2.2 per cent. Since then, the rate has risen to 5.3 per cent. Nevertheless, Oxfordshire still has the second lowest unemployment rate of counties in Britain (Emmerich and Lewis 1991:34). According to the 1991 Census report, unemployment among males has fallen from 6.8 per cent in 1981 to 6.2 per cent in 1991 (1991:10). There is, however, an unequal distribution of unemployment across the County, with higher numbers of people registered as unemployed in Oxford City and Cherwell. And, within Oxford City, unemployment is relatively concentrated in certain wards such as St Clements, Blackbird Leys, East, South, and West wards. According to the 1981 Census, despite the fact that the unemployment rate in the above wards was more than 10 per cent, the unemployment rate in Oxford city as a whole was lower than the national average. The 1991 Census puts the figure for the unemployed in Oxford City at 9.6 per cent.

The prosperity of Oxford is well described by Snow, according to whom:

> Boom was the common experience in Oxford in the late 1980s...The reasons for the boom were clear enough - Oxford's centrality and good communications, its amenities and desirability as a place in which to live...Even in the early years of the Thatcher decade when nationally the economy contracted and jobs fell by two per cent, those in the Oxford region rose by over seven per cent. Small businesses started up at an amazing rate - over one a week, growing by 26 per cent, a rate exceeding the rest of the South East, including London...The Oxford jobless total plummeted to a fifteen year low, 2.5 per cent - a rate which is unofficially regarded as non-existent...Even in Blackbird Leys, traditionally reliant on the car factory next door, the jobless fell from 20 per cent to five per cent...(1991:39-40).

Employment in the whole of Oxfordshire grew rapidly over the 1980s, at an average of 2.3 per cent per annum. There were, however, large changes in the structure of employment between 1965 and 1989, in that there was a heavy decline in employment in manufacturing, and a rise in employment in the service sector. This can be clearly seen from Figure 2.1.

In 1965, the County maintained an industrial structure broadly similar to that of UK as a whole. Over the period 1965 to 1989, the structure diverged from the average, with employment in manufacturing falling more steeply than in the country as a whole. Within this period, 18,000 jobs were lost in the Oxford car industry. The effects of this on the city were particularly severe. Where as in 1965 employment in manufacturing in Oxford, had been 30 per cent above the average, by 1989 it was 15 per cent below. It is this loss of employment in the motor industry in Oxford which accounts for much of the recorded fall in manufacturing across the County. This fall in employment in manufacturing has however, been more than compensated for by rising service sector employment. The largest growth was in the financial services sector, with 11,500 new jobs over the 1980s, two thirds of which were full time. Other growth areas were public administration (6,300), wholesale distribution (6,000), retail (3,500), other services (4,000) and hotels and catering (4,000), the majority of the growth being in full time employment (Emmerich and Lewis 1991:20-22).

Figure 2.2 shows employment change in the City of Oxford during the 1980s. It is apparent that even in 1981, employment in Oxford was dominated by the service industry - the largest sections being public administration and defence, which included the University, Polytechnic and local authorities. Employment in manufacturing, with the exception of the motor vehicle industry, which in 1981 was the second largest category, comprises less than five per cent of total employment in 1989. The City and County Council report concludes that: firstly, the fact that many of the new service jobs have been full time and of reasonable quality being in the public administration and financial sector, and secondly, the fact that Oxford retains a well developed higher education and medical sector which is both a large, high quality employment sector and a generator of future employment through research and development, indicate that the local economy of Oxford City is a healthy one (Emmerich and Lewis 1991:24-26).

The ethnic minorities

The 1971 and 1981 Census figures for the population of Oxfordshire with India, Pakistan, Bangladesh, or East Africa given as the country of birth is provided in Table 2.3.

Table 2.3 Ethnic minority population of Oxfordshire

	1971	1981
India	1,865	3,457
Pakistan	850	1,820
Bangladesh	277	
E.Africa	873	

The 1991 Census included a question on the ethnic group of the population, providing more accurate figures for the ethnic minorities. These, however, are not comparable to the figures in earlier Censuses which did not include the ethnic group question, but depended on 'country of birth' for ethnic classification. According to the 1991 Census, as shown in Table 2.4, the Asian minorities make up 1.4 per cent of the population

Figure 2.1

**Historical employment trends in Oxfordshire and Great Britain
1965-1989**

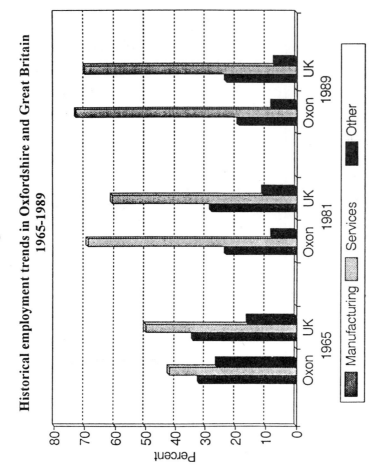

(Source: Department of Employment)

Figure 2.2

Employment in Oxford 1981 and 1989

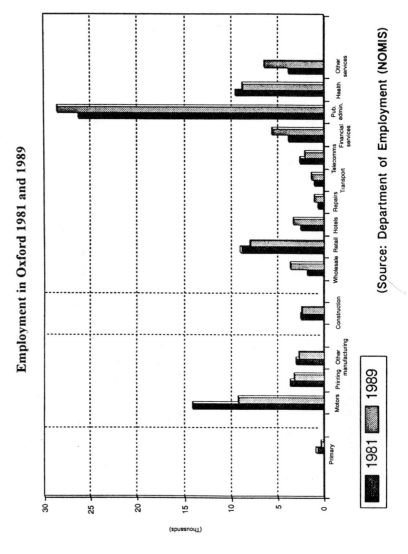

(Source: Department of Employment (NOMIS)

of Oxfordshire, and 4.6 per cent of the population of the City of Oxford. This 4.6 per cent is made up of 1541 Indians, 2092 Pakistanis, 550 Bangladeshis and 881 'other Asians'.[10] The Asian population in Oxford, then, has a greater proportion of Pakistanis, though in Britain as a whole the Indians are the largest Asian group.

Table 2.4 Ethnic group of residents (1991)

% age	White	Black	Indian	Pakis-tani	Bangla-deshi	Chinese	Asian other	Other
Oxford								
County	96.7	1.0	0.5	0.5	0.1	0.3	0.3	0.6
City	90.8	2.8	1.4	1.9	0.5	0.8	0.8	1.2
County	00 per cent= 547,584; City 100 per cent= 110,103							

The settlement patterns of the residents of Oxford City from the New Commonwealth and Pakistan are shown in Map 2. It can be seen from the map that the heaviest concentrations are in the South Eastern parts of the city. According to the 1991 Census, the two wards with significantly high proportions of Asians are St.Clements with a percentage of 13.1 Asians, and East ward with 12.8 per cent Asians. Next in concentration of Asians is South ward with 8.1 per cent, and Temple Cowley with 5.6 per cent.

How does the socio-economic status of the Asian households compare with that of all households in Oxford? House ownership, general housing conditions and car ownership are often used to assess the socio-economic status of groups. Using these as the indicators, surveys conducted in other areas have maintained that Asian households are much more likely to live in overcrowded conditions, to occupy inferior housing and are less likely to own a car than the majority of the population. That this is not entirely true of Oxford is evident from Table 2.5, where the housing conditions and car ownership for Asian households is compared with all households in Oxford, on the basis of the 1991 Census results.

It is quite clear from Table 2.5 that proportion living in owner occupied housing is the same in both groups. Car ownership is slightly higher among the Asians, and the percentage of households lacking or sharing a bath or inside toilet is about the same in both groups. The number of people per room is, however, significantly higher among the ethnic minorities.

31

Map II - Settlement patterns of the Asians in Oxford

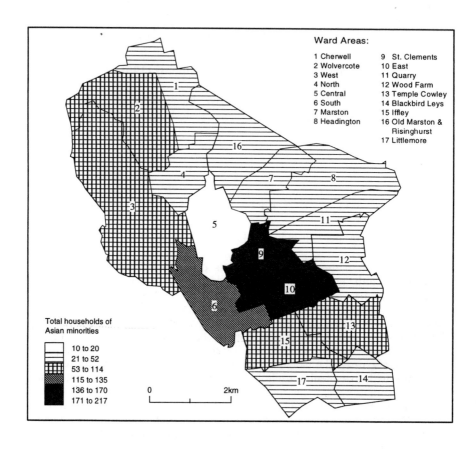

Ward Areas:

1 Cherwell	9 St. Clements
2 Wolvercote	10 East
3 West	11 Quarry
4 North	12 Wood Farm
5 Central	13 Temple Cowley
6 South	14 Blackbird Leys
7 Marston	15 Iffley
8 Headington	16 Old Marston & Risinghurst
	17 Littlemore

Total households of
Asian minorities

10 to 20
21 to 52
53 to 114
115 to 135
136 to 170
171 to 217

0   2km

**Table 2.5 Housing conditions and car ownership for Asian
households compared with all households in Oxford in 1991**

Indicators	Per cent of all households in each category	Per cent of Asian households in each category
Owner occupied Housing	56	56
Households with 1 or more people per room	4.1	27
Households lacking or sharing bath or inside WC	3.4	4
Households with no car	38	36

According to the 1991 Census, 11.8 per cent of the Asian males between 16 and 64, in Oxford City are unemployed, which is higher than the average rate of unemployment of 9.6 per cent in the City. The Asian proportion of the total unwaged within Oxford is 5.7 per cent, though they make up just 4.6 per cent of the total population.

South Asian business in Oxford today

In the City of Oxford, during the period of the survey, 83 small shops, including sub postoffices, and 22 restaurants, were owned by Asians. This constitutes 12 per cent of the shops and restaurants in Oxford.[11] As the Asian population makes up 4.6 per cent of the total population of Oxford, they have a good share of the retail and catering sector.

The type of Asian businesses to be found in Oxford is given in Table 2.6.

Table 2.6 Type and number of businesses

Newsagents	10
Grocers and general stores	43
Sub-postoffice and general stores	12
Textiles	3
Emporia	4
Jewellers	2
Shoes and general stores	1
Motor Parts	1
Delicatessen	1
Fashion Wear	2
Off-License	2
Chemists	1
Tailors	1
Total number of Shops	83
Restaurants	22

It is quite clear from Table 2.6 that these businesses are predominantly grocers and general stores, many of the types of South Asian businesses found in other parts of Britain not being found in Oxford. Nineteen per cent of these businesses had been in existence for more than ten years before the survey, and a further 28 per cent for more than five years, the rest having started their present enterprises after 1984. Some of these, however, signified only a change in location or type of business and not a completely fresh start. Nevertheless, according to the survey, the greater number of existing South Asian owned small shops and restaurants have opened within the five years prior to the survey. This was also the period when unemployment in Oxfordshire was at an all time low. South Asians, then, continue to enter the retailing and catering sector in large numbers, even when there are other employment opportunities.

The ethnic group break up of the Asian small business owners, within the City of Oxford, is as follows: Indians - 31 per cent, Pakistanis - 39 per cent, Bangladeshis -12 per cent, and East African Asians - 18 per cent. The arrival of these businessmen in Oxford, within the thirty year period of 1959-1989, is charted in Table 2.7.

Table 2.7 Ethnic group by year of arrival

	Indians	Pakistanis	Bangladeshis	African Asians	Total
1959-62	5	10	4	1	20
1963-68	10	17	3	1	31
1969-74	5	6	2	3	16
1975-79	2	-	1	3	6
1980-85	4	3	-	3	10
1986-89	3	1	1	6	11
total	29	37	11	17	94

As can be seen from Table 2.7, 54 per cent of the small business owners had arrived in Oxford by 1968, so that they have been resident here for more than twenty years. The earliest residents among this entrepreneurial group are the Pakistanis, three of our Pakistani shopkeepers being residents of Oxford for more than thirty years. As is to be expected, the East African Asians are the most recent arrivals with 53 per cent of them having moved in to Oxford after 1983. While the East African Asians give political reasons - the difficult situation in Kenya and Uganda, and the holding of British Passports - for their migration to Britain, the motivation of the Pakistanis and Indians was quite clearly economic. Thirty eight per cent of the direct migrants from the subcontinent say they came to Britain to earn more money and to further their prospects. They are quite frank about their preconceptions of Britain as a country where 'the streets were paved with gold', and 'money grew on trees', and so on. Thirty nine per cent maintained that they came because they had family members in Britain who had migrated earlier, so that the evidence for chain migration is quite clear.

The regional origin of the entrepreneurs does appear to play a part in the type of businesses they own. The most obvious of these is the almost exclusive Sylhetti, Bangladeshi ownership of 'Indian' restaurants in Oxford. Most Bangladeshi owners are quite emphatic that they would not wish to exchange the 'glamour' of restaurant life, with its 'high class clientele', and much higher profit margins, for the drudgery of shop work. There were, thus, no Bangladeshi owned shops in Oxford at the time of this survey.[12] And, at least a couple of Indian and Pakistani shop owners maintained that they had to close down restaurants which had been doing well because of the difficulty in getting labour, as Bangladeshis preferred to work for the Bangladeshi owners. There is, however, one Punjabi Pakistani, who owns two restaurants, and who has attempted to introduce the North Indian, 'Balti Cuisine' into an area which has known only the 'mixed' Bengali fare, as also one Punjabi Indian restaurant owner. The predominantly Bangladeshi ownership of restaurants is, of course, not true of London, Manchester, and other areas of Britain today (cf. Rafiq 1992).

The more subtle distinctions are to be seen in the greater ownership of grocers cum butchers by the Pakistanis, with the Indians and East African Asians being reluctant to engage in this business which is seen as the lowest in the retail hierarchy in terms of status if not economically. Many African Asians and Indians move to ownership of newsagents shops after a period of grocery ownership, which they see as a step upwards as the work is seen as less strenuous, and the margins of profit are higher. Again, the majority of sub-post offices are owned by the African Asians. The four 'ethnic emporia' are owned by Indians, all of whom have a better than average educational background, and three of whom have never owned or contemplated owning any other type of business. Quite unlike the busy grocery, sub-postoffice or newsagents, the tempo of work in the emporia is slow, the work more 'genteel', and the clientele is of a different order all together, made up predominantly of those with an exposure to, and appreciation of all things Indian. These Indian owners appear to have been more influenced by considerations of 'status' than of significant material prosperity, which to the Pakistani, seems to be one of the dominant considerations in the choice of business type.

This could be indicative of the social class background of the different regional groups, in that, though in all the groups, consideration of the fathers social class reveals a major clustering in Social Class IVa, IVb and IVc, i.e., that of small proprietors and farmers, 24 per cent of Indians and 24 per cent of African Asians, have fathers in Social Class I-III of the Goldthorpe schema, whereas the figures for the Pakistanis is 17 per cent, and there are no Bangladeshis with fathers in these social classes.

The residential location of these entrepreneurs is fairly evenly divided between the areas of heavier Asian residential concentrations and those without Asian concentrations.[13] Thus, 49 per cent resided in areas of heavier Asian concentration and 51 per cent in areas without Asian concentrations. Fifty two per cent of business owners live above their business premises. Where the location of businesses is concerned, the present survey establishes that the one major clustering is on Cowley Road, accounting for 25 per cent of all South Asian owned businesses, and 20 per cent of those actually interviewed in the survey. But, apart from this, the greater share of 58 per cent of businesses are actually located in areas without a residential concentration of Asians (See Map 3). South Asians have then moved away from their own areas of settlement to open businesses in areas where they constitute only a small fraction of the population, quite clearly establishing that ethnic concentration is not a necessary condition for ethnic enterprise as suggested by McEvoy(1987).

What were these small business owners doing prior to self-employment? The employment trajectories are very varied. The mean number of jobs held before business entry is 2.5, with 28 per cent having held at least two jobs and 24 per cent more than four jobs. However, the number who were unemployed or made redundant prior to business entry

Map III - Location of business and residential concentration of South Asian

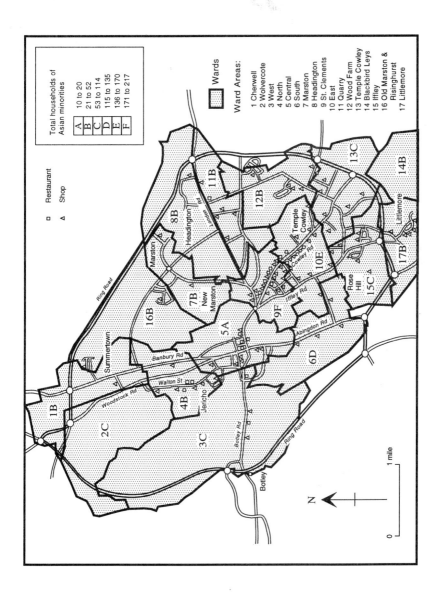

Total households of
Asian minorities

A	10 to 20
B	21 to 52
C	53 to 114
D	115 to 135
E	136 to 170
F	171 to 217

□ Restaurant
△ Shop

☐ Wards

Ward Areas:

1 Cherwell
2 Wolvercote
3 West
4 North
5 Central
6 South
7 Marston
8 Headington
9 St. Clements
10 East
11 Quarry
12 Wood Farm
13 Temple Cowley
14 Blackbird Leys
15 Iffley
16 Old Marston &
   Risinghurst
17 Littlemore

N

0   1 mile

is just five, that is, five per cent of the business owners. The major clustering that stands out is the fact that 27 per cent have at some point in their careers, worked for extended periods at the Cowley Car works, more than half of them as assembly line workers. Forty eight per cent of these British Leyland workers had continued working there even after starting up their businesses, waiting to consolidate their entrepreneurial position before giving up well-paid factory work. A few of them are still continuing with it, leaving the actual running of shops to wives and children. Sixteen per cent of the small business owners had other paid employment, though actively supervising their businesses and doing their stint in the shops after office hours and any other free time.

Summary

While a longitudinal analysis of the growth of Asian retailing over time has not been possible,[14] it is quite clear that there has been a steady growth in the number of shops and restaurants over the period of nearly three decades covered by the survey, beginning with six in 1962 and growing to more than a hundred by 1990. Though the initial impetus for the shops[15] does appear to be the growth of the ethnic community, the shops providing for the needs of the community as well as a business opportunity to their owners, retailing did not remain confined to the ethnic market for long. In fact, apart from a small core of shops which continue to serve this ethnic market, the majority were soon scattered over a wide area of Oxford, catering primarily to the indigenous population. An ethnic infrastructure, with shops satisfying all the needs of the ethnic community, did not develop in Oxford, the type of businesses being limited to the few types which the entrepreneurs felt sure to be economically viable.

Notes

1.   These are immigrants from other areas of Britain and not international migrants.

2.   The very first 'Indian' restaurant, Veeraswamy's in London was owned by an Englishman.

3.   These seamen came from areas which are now in Bangladesh.

4.   Peddling, according to Hiro, was the exploration of areas of self-employment by the large majority of immigrants who, because of their lack of fluency in English, could not find factory jobs before the post-war boom (Hiro 1971:120).

5.   A study in Coventry, reported in *The Morning Star*, (5 January, 1967), showed that half of the Indian bus conductors were

university graduates, and Hiro maintains that jobs on the local Bradford buses remained the exclusive domain of 'educated Pakistanis and Indians (1971:127). The Oxford picture is then, quite typical.

6.   Bengali speaking of Bengali origin, later to become Bangladeshi.

7.   Only a few of the Asian owned houses were actually recorded in the electoral register, as early residents speak of many more than the four recorded in the 1960 register.

8.   'Confectioners, Tobacconists, and Newsagents'.

9.   The 1981 Census excluded households wholly absent on Census night for the resident population base. The 1991 Census includes the households normally resident but absent on Census night. For comparisons with the 1981 figures, however, the 1991 Census uses the 1981 population base.

10.   This does not include the Chinese.

11.   According to the data available with the County Council, there are approximately 843 shops and restaurants within the boundaries referred to above.

12.   About a year after the survey, a Bangladeshi restaurant owner on Cowley Road, did set up shop in premises which fell vacant next to his restaurant.

13.   Areas were distinguished as having heavier Asian concentrations on the basis of City and County Council reports, so that, as mentioned earlier in the text, these areas included East and South Oxford, specifically the areas between the Cowley and Iffley Roads, St Clements, as well as Botley Road and Walton street.

14.   See the concluding section of the Methodological Appendix for reasons.

15.   The restaurants in Oxford have always catered to the majority population, unlike certain areas where restaurants did attempt to attract the single males.

3 Reasons for business entry

Introduction

The previous chapter described the steady growth in small business ownership among the South Asians in Oxford. They constitute 4.6 per cent of the population of the City, but own 12 per cent of the retail and catering outlets. Further, 61 per cent of existing Asian owned small shops and restaurants in Oxford have opened in the last five years. South Asians, then, continue to enter the retailing and catering sector in large numbers.

What is the explanation for this growing entry into small business? Why do the ethnic minorities, and the South Asians in particular, take to petty retailing and catering in such large numbers? While the other ethnic minorities, such as the Chinese, are to be found in the restaurant trade, at the time of the present study there were no Chinese owned shops in Oxford.[1] Though the Afro-Caribbeans make up about three per cent of the population of Oxford, their share of the small business sector is negligible. What then, are the reasons for the proclivity for business start-up amongst South Asians?

Explanations have been many and varied and any attempt at a new explanatory approach must first disentangle the various strands of the different explanations. This chapter, therefore, begins with a review of the explanations offered in the literature for minority business start-up.

Explanation offered in the literature

In view of the extensive literature on entrepreneurship and ethnic business enterprise, with explanations ranging from the psychological and social to the economic, it becomes necessary to exercise a measure of selectivity in the process of reviewing it. The focus, therefore, is on the sociological explanations that consider the social, economic and cultural factors which act as constraints, or as resources, in ethnic business enterprise, rather than on the purely psychological or purely economic explanations. These explanations have been variously subdivided by different sociologists.

40

Thus, Bonacich and Modell (1980:24-30) distinguish between 1) Contextual theories, 2) Cultural theories, and 3) Situational theories to explain entrepreneurship among minorities. The subdivisions provided by Jenkins (1984:231-232), are 1) The Economic Opportunity model, 2) The Cultural model, and 3) The Reaction model. According to Light (1980), explanations may be subdivided into 1) Orthodox (Cultural), and 2) Reactive (Situational and Reactive) models. Waldinger *et al.* (1985:588-594), puts forward the 1) The Cultural approach, 2) The Ecological approach, and 3) The Interactive approach which emphasises the interaction of cultural resources and structural opportunities. To facilitate analysis, the framework that will be followed here is that provided by Bonacich and Modell and the various sociological explanations are discussed under the heads of 1) Cultural, 2) Situational and 3) Contextual theories. While the first type emphasizes the minority cultural 'baggage' that acts as a resource in business activity, the second and third type emphasize the constraints that push some minorities into small business.

Cultural theories

In total contrast to contextual theories which stress the characteristics of the host societies, cultural theories emphasize the culturally specific characteristics of the immigrant minorities themselves, in explanations of their business activity. Large scale entry into business is here attributed to the cultural predisposition or advantages of certain ethnic groups for business.

The 'classic' cultural explanation is, of course, the one which attributes large scale entry to an entrepreneurial ethic. According to this view, ethnic minorities which emphasize values such as 'hard work', 'frugality', 'thrift' and 'profit-making', that is, values similar to those of the Protestant Ethic, would be more likely to enter business (Bonacich 1973; Werbner 1984; Boissevain 1981). Thus, Asians in Africa and the Parsis in India, are believed to be typical examples of minorities whose business success may be attributed to their possession of these values. The under-representation of certain ethnic minorities in business, for instance, the Afro-Caribbeans in the UK, would accordingly be attributed to their lack of the entrepreneurial work ethic. It is to be noted, however, that the entrepreneurial success of Jamaicans relative to American blacks in New York is often commented upon (Foner 1977:132), and has, quite interestingly, engendered, "...an American Negro stereotype of them as 'Black Jews' - aggressive, efficient, acquisitive, calculating and clannish" (Lowenthal 1972:227).

Together with 'hard work', 'frugality', and associated traits, other traits such as 'wanting to be one's own boss', and McClelland's 'need for achievement' (nAch), have been regarded as dominant traits of ethnic minorities, encouraging them to enter small business. McClelland's argument that the single most important causative factor in the rise of entrepreneurship is the prevalence among entrepreneurs of the social psychological drive for achievement (1963:84), has been used to account for differential levels of economic growth among different ethnic groups

(Javilloner and Peters 1973). While it may be agreed, with McClelland and others, that entrepreneurs are likely to have higher levels of nAch, it does not follow that all those with high nAch will become entrepreneurs. NAch may well be satisfied through other routes, so that it cannot be a sufficient condition for business entry. Again, to use nAch theory to account for the higher business entry among South Asians would involve showing that South Asians have higher levels of nAch than other ethnic groups, and there does not appear to be any evidence to support such judgements. While psychological factors *are* important, they cannot be considered in isolation. In fact, an Indian social psychologist, Nandy (1973), has shown that amongst groups where there is community support of business activity, 'n achievement' does not need to be so high for going into business.[2] The importance of this conclusion lies not so much in its denial of the importance of nAch, as in putting stress also on social and cultural factors.

Many social scientists emphasize the need for autonomy - People go into business because it satisfies a social-psychological need to be one's own boss. Empirical evidence for strong psychological inclinations towards independence and autonomy being motivating factors in business start-up has been provided by many (Boissevain and Grotenbreg 1987; Klandt 1987; Mayer 1987). But, if 'wanting to be one's own boss' is a characteristic of all the self-employed (Scase and Goffee 1980), it cannot explain the specificity of South Asian enterprise, that is, why certain ethnic groups such as the Asians have a greater propensity for small business.

Another cultural explanation regards the use of family labour and resources as crucial to the success of ethnic enterprise. The fact that certain ethnic minorities have access to cheap family labour is regarded as a key advantage (Mars and Ward 1984:18; Werbner 1984:168; Aldrich *et al.* 1984:197; Javilloner and Peters 1973:324). Though use of family labour is a feature of all small business (Scase and Goffee 1982; Bechhofer *et al.* 1974), differences in culture do affect the ability to mobilise family labour. This is clearly brought out by the description given by Marris and Somerset (1971:132-50) of the competitive advantage that joint family ideology gave Asians over Kenyan entrepreneurs. Hoselitz (1961) argues that the extended family is possibly the main agent launching an artisan into an entrepreneurial career by providing him the loan to start his own shop. The rise to economic power of certain social groups in India, has been attributed in part to family solidarity which facilitates entry into entrepreneurial occupations by their ability to mobilize capital (Lamb 1965). Werbner, describing Pakistanis in the Manchester garment trade and their reliance on the family, emphasises that, "Pakistanis conceive of their immediate family, usually members of a single household, as constituting a joint enterprise having corporate aims and strategies" (1984:168).

Yet another cultural explanation is one that emphasizes the role of culturally specific economic institutions such as Rotating Credit Associations (RCAs), in financing business start-up among ethnic minorities. A RCA has been defined by Ardener as follows:

...an association formed upon a core of participants who agree to make a regular contribution to a fund which is given in whole or in part, to each contributor in rotation (1964:201).

The role of such economic institutions, which certain groups bring from their country of origin, has been stressed by Light (1972), in his explanation of the over-representation in small business, especially retail trade, of Chinese and Japanese in the U.S. Correspondingly, the lack of such institutions among the Blacks in the United States, and hence their inability to overcome discrimination in lending practices by banks is, according to Light, an important factor in their low involvement in business. Evidence of the use of Rotating Credit Associations to set up businesses in Britain is provided by Werbner (1981) in her study of Pakistanis involved in the rag trade in Manchester. It must, however, be pointed out that though similar institutions are to be found among the West Indians in Britain (Davison describes the 'pardner jackpot' among Jamaicans; 1966:96, 102-103), it does not appear to have encouraged small business activity amongst them here (Foner 1977:132). Light, however, has attributed the business success of West Indians in New York to their Rotating Credit Associations known as 'partners' (1972:32-6).

A fourth variant of the cultural explanation emphasizes the ethnic solidarity amongst certain groups which encourages business entry. Weber, for instance, has argued that the development of 'Pariah Capitalism' among the Jews was encouraged by the Jewish religion with its laws against intermarriage and commensality, which made them into 'pariah people' for whom trade was the only feasible occupation. Similarly, the Asian tendency to form exclusive, self-isolating groups with fraternal networks providing financial help and information, is seen as an ethnic advantage in small business activity (Dahya 1974). Light has shown that the business success of the Japanese in the U.S.A. is due to the high degree of ethnic solidarity amongst them and their reliance on ethnic economic institutions. Though many theorists see ethnic solidarity as supported by host group hostility and antagonism ("the natural freemasonry of the disinherited", cf. Cater and Jones 1987), others see it as primarily self-generated and a positive cultural resource (Anwar 1979; Jeffrey 1976; Watson 1977; Werbner 1984). Auster and Aldrich, refer to a network of communal solidarity as an 'ethnic enclave', and regard ethnic enclaves as important supports for ethnic businesses. According to them:

The most salient feature of early business efforts by immigrant groups is their dependence on an ethnic community for support. Support is provided at two levels: informal support from the friends and relatives of aspiring business owners, and support from the larger networks of ethnic institutions...Strong community support, based on ethnic ties, allows some degree of independence from the core community (1984:49-54).

Another version of the 'enclave hypothesis' emphasizes the culturally based needs of ethnic minorities which can only be met by the development of ethnic businessmen. This creates what has been variously referred to as 'protected niches' (Hannerz 1974:54; Evans 1989:951), 'protected markets' (Light 1972; Aldrich *et al.* 1986:52; McEvoy *et al.* 1979; Cater and Jones 1978), and 'enclaves' (Borjas 1986). That ethnic businessmen benefit from being able to serve the special consumer tastes of their coethnics, has been stressed in the literature on ethnic entrepreneurship. With regard to minority business success in the U.S., it has been maintained that:

> An ethnic group may have not only its own language, but its own habits and customs that are better understood by business establishments operated by members of the group. The demand for foods not particularly popular among others is manifest in the Jewish and Italian areas...restaurants...serve the type of foods generally liked in a particular group (Aldrich *et al.* 1986:52).

Aldrich *et al.* go on to maintain that because Blacks in the U.S. do not have consumer demands different from the majority population, they lack this base for a separate economy (1986:53). The quite distinct hairdressing, music and food needs of the Blacks, amongst others, appear to have been overlooked here.

Where South Asians in Britain are concerned, there appears to be considerable divergence in the literature regarding the dependency of Asian businesses on the ethnic market. According to Dahya (1974:93), ethnic institutions emerge to provide the needs of the immigrants and depend on ethnic patronage. So also, Aldrich *et al.* (1986), Cater and Jones (1978), and McEvoy *et al.* (1979), have maintained that in the three urban areas of Bradford, Leicester, and Ealing, studied by them, the extent of Asian shop-keepers' dependence on co-ethnic trade was certainly high in that Asian shop-keepers served on average 72 per cent of Asian customers, compared with only 14 per cent for white shop owners (1986:52). McEvoy's study showed that only 30 per cent of the customers of Asian owned shops were white, and that dependence on ethnic custom was highest in restaurants and clothing shops (1979:36-43).

However, it must be noted that Aldrich (1980), Mullins (1979), Brooks (1983), Wilson (1983), Rafiq (1988), in their surveys of Wandsworth, Croydon, Lambeth, Brent, and Bradford respectively, have concluded that the dependence on the ethnic market is low. It has been suggested that the studies reporting low dependence have been conducted in and around London, whereas those showing high dependence have been conducted in areas specifically chosen for their large concentrations of Asians (Rafiq 1988). Mullins has further suggested that Muslims tend to depend more on an ethnic market than Hindus, so that there are inter-ethnic as well as inter-regional differences in the nature of the clientele.

It is very likely that the provision of ethnic needs is a platform for the take-off of ethnic businesses. Light has noted that:

> ...among both Chinese and Japanese immigrants, there was also a marked tendency for small business to depend at first on an

exclusively ethnic clientele and only later to branch out to a wider trade (1972:14)

It is, however, highly unlikely that ethnic businesses will continue to be dependent on an ethnic clientele after the take-off stage. Whether they remain dependent or not may well be a measure of their success.

Although different cultural explanations focus on different cultural traits, all of them attribute the economic behaviour of minorities to factors internal to these minorities. They all, in the words of Bonacich and Modell:

> ...share the notion that these minorities are not simply creatures of a particular environment; instead, the groups are seen as bringing to the environment characteristics of their own,... (1980:28).

Situational theories

Among situational theories may be included those explanations which regard entrepreneurial activity as a form of economic adaptation to the particular situations in which immigrant groups find themselves. Entrepreneurial entry is, then, determined neither by the context nor by cultural 'baggage' alone, but by the nature of the immigrant situation.

One variety of such explanations regards the 'sojourner' mentality of migrant groups as the cause of their business activity. It has been argued that the commercial prowess of migrants is essentially the result of their illusory belief in eventual return, or a 'sojourner cast of mind', which creates an interest in the rapid accumulation of money to invest 'back home' (Bonacich 1973; Mars and Ward 1984:12; Aldrich *et al.* 1984:192; Lawrence 1974; Anwar 1979). Bonacich and Modell hold that the feeling of being sojourners or temporary migrants, promotes concentration in trade, both directly, by encouraging thrift and hard work (qualities regarded as necessary for small business), and indirectly, by promoting ethnic solidarity which according to the cultural theorists aids small business (1980:30). Recent studies in Britain do not lend support to this view. A study of South Asian shop-keepers in Glasgow reports that there is no evidence to support the sojourner hypothesis as only 20 per cent of the respondents expressed a desire to return to their country of birth to settle (Krcmar 1984:106)

Another situational approach would be the 'ecological succession' theory advanced by Aldrich and Reiss (1976). The emergence of ethnic entrepreneurs is here attributed to the residential concentration of minorities in certain areas which are subsequently vacated by the local population. Together with the indigenous population, there is an out-migration of indigenous businesses as well, providing opportunities for ethnic business formation (Aldrich 1975; McEvoy *et al.* 1979). It is necessary to point out, however, that the concentration of Blacks in ghettos in the U.S. did not lead to business formation among them. Again, when ethnic business development takes place outside areas of heavy residential concentration of minorities, this theory does not hold.

In so far as situational theories concentrate on the process of immigrant adaptation as the underlying cause of business entry, a different theory for each stage of the essentially dynamic adaptation process would be required. The orientation towards return, as well as the patterns of residential location, are features of the immigrant situation which can be expected to, and do, change during the course of adaptation, but business entry is a more or less constant phenomenon.

Contextual theories

'Contextual theories' regard the entrepreneurial activities of migrant minorities as largely a function of their social, economic or political contexts, and as having little to do with the qualities of the migrants themselves. As Van den Berghe puts it:

> Such similarities as exist (among middleman minorities) must be sought principally in the *social structure of the plural society as a whole*, and only secondarily in the characteristics of the immigrant groups (1975:198)

Thus, minorities concentrate in trading activities not because of any inherent talents or inclinations, but because the surrounding society pushes them into doing so.

Prominent among contextual theories is the one which traces the rise of minority trading groups to status gaps that exist in colonial societies between the colonisers and the colonised, and which require middlemen minorities to bridge the discontinuity between the superior and subordinate groups (Blalock 1967:79-84). The rise of Asian traders in the African countries would then be explained in terms of the contextual requirement for a middleman group to mediate between the British colonisers and the African colonised.

Another variant of the contextual explanation is the 'economic opportunity' model provided by Jenkins, according to which:

> Ethnic minority business activity is essentially no different from routine capitalist entrepreneurial activity, depending for its success or failure upon the opportunities presented by the market (1984:234).

The favourable economic environment has been stressed to account for the rise of ethnic small business activity in Britain. With the 1980s, the era of the entrepreneur is said to have begun (Goffee and Scase 1987; Hertz 1986). According to official sources, the long term decline in small businesses in Britain, together with the rest of Europe, has bottomed out. The Confederation of British Industry pointed out quite recently that since 1976, the number of small enterprises and extent of employment in them has steadily increased (CBI 1980). That this could include small shops is indicated by the 1978 report of the Netherlands Association of Retail Traders that noted how for the first time since the Second World War

46

there was a slight increase in the number of retail outlets (Ward and Jenkins 1984:6). OECD figures also indicate that the increase in the number of independent workers is not limited to Common Market countries (OECD 1980). Despite the increase, the small firm sector in Britain remains smaller than in other European countries, suggesting, an 'empty space' in the British economy for ethnic entrepreneurs to exploit. And hence the takeover of traditional enterprises such as corner grocers by immigrants (Boissevain 1981 1984). Banton, too, supports this. According to him, the reason for the increase in retailing and other small businesses may well be that members of an immigrant group always look for the opportunities in the new country that are not being exploited effectively by the native population, as these are the niches in the contemporary economic structure in which the competition can be expected to be less vigorous (1983:297).

The political climate is also believed to be one conducive to small business activity (Goffee and Scase 1987). All over Western Europe, governments appear to be encouraging small business activity by offering various financial and fiscal inducements (Storey 1983). The primary reason for this is the tendency to look on self-employment as the answer to a number of ills such as rising unemployment, increasing labour disputes, increasing dependence on the welfare state, loosening family ties, alienation from work (Goffee and Scase 1987). There are further advantages for the ethnic minorities in that a greater involvement in business is expected to produce more community stability and allow ethnic minorities to feel that they possess a greater stake in society (Scarman 1982:167-8).

A third version of the contextual theory is what Jenkins has termed 'the reaction model' (1984:231-232). Here ethnic self-employment is looked at as:

> ...a reaction against racism and blocked avenues of occupational mobility, a survival strategy for coping on the margins of the white-dominated mainstreams of the economy... (Jenkins 1984:231).

The same view is held by many others (Cater 1984; Aldrich *et al.* 1984; Ladbury 1984; Reeves and Ward 1984). Nowikowski too, attempts to explain ethnic business activity in Britain as "...part of the wider structure of the British political economy". She analyses the emergence of businesses among the Asians as a survival strategy and holds that: "For all the Asians, self-employment strategies emerged in the context of structural racial disadvantage in the metropolis...." (1984:158).

Discrimination in the labour market, lack of fit between available jobs and qualifications, restricted avenues of promotion, are held to be some of the factors which *push* South Asians and other ethnics into self-employment. Thus, Jones produces evidence in his study of Asian retailing that many Asians enter business, "...not from any positive preference or ambition, but from lack of choice" (1982:469). A similar stand has been taken by others as well (Brooks 1983:44; Ladbury 1984:106).

In concluding this section on contextual theories, it may be pointed out that while the importance of the political and economic context cannot be denied, what is sociologically interesting is that despite the variation in the contexts, certain ethnic minorities such as the South Asians, the Chinese, and the Jews, have managed to enter the small business sector in all the countries they have migrated to.[3] This would seem to suggest that South Asian entrepreneurship is not so much determined by, or dependent upon, the right economic and political context, as capable of finding the right opportunities and manipulating the context.[4] Werbner, in her study of Pakistani entrepreneurship in Manchester, maintains:

> The flourishing of immigrant entrepreneurship in an apparently declining economy raises general theoretical questions. If, for example, we are to argue that immigrant entrepreneurship must be understood as responsive to favourable 'opportunity structures' (cf. Ward:1986), then the Manchester case illustrates that such 'opportunities', if they exist, must nevertheless be perceived, recognized or 'discovered'. In other words, the construction of meaning crucially determines economic strategy. Manchester, a city apparently in inexorable decline, has become for Asian immigrants a base for potential economic prosperity (1990:10).

Finally, though economic opportunities for small business may well exist in many areas of Britain, the availability of opportunities would only point to the fact of 'doors being open'. It does not explain why certain groups rather than others choose to go through those doors. The economic opportunity explanation would not account for the greater propensity for small business among South Asians than among Afro-Caribbeans in Britain.

The Contextual theories appear to treat the ethnic minorities as 'structural puppets', largely the creatures of their contexts, their actions determined by external constraints. As maintained by Gambetta, this structuralist approach:

> ...by focussing on the constraints of behaviour rather than on the behaviour itself - tends, so to speak, to *shortcircuit* the agent and attribute, often implicitly, a zero weight a priori to his preferences, expectations, and decision mechanisms (1987:11).

All this is not to suggest that contextual theories have no value. Host society antagonism towards ethnic minorities does, both directly and indirectly, influence the economic activities of these minority groups. What must be emphasized, however, is that any explanation which regards the activities of minority groups as determined only by the societies in which they live, implying further that any minority group could fulfill the same role, is not adequate. There is ample evidence that only some groups, and not others, take to entrepreneurial activities regardless of context. Under such circumstances, no theory, if it is to be adequate, can afford to ignore 'internal factors'.

Summary

As many writers (Jenkins 1984; Bonacich and Modell 1980) have pointed out, the three types of theories are not mutually exclusive. Light, for instance, argues that the 'best fit of theory and evidence' occurs when the additive power of a variety of factors is recognised, including the reaction of immigrants to blocked alternative opportunities, and their consequent concentration in fields which remain open, the use of cultural resources transmitted intact from the country of origin and the development of 'reactive resources' including skills, values and solidarities developed within the country of settlement (1984:201). This interactive approach is advocated by Waldinger *et al.* as well, according to whom:

> ...ethnic businesses proliferate in industries where there is a congruence between the demands of the economic environment and the informal resources of the ethnic population (1985:591).

A complete theory would necessarily have to include contextual, cultural and situational factors to account adequately for ethnic business activity. Certain factors, however, do tend to be more important than others. While the context cannot be ignored, the fact that certain ethnic groups take to business activity whatever the context, and that, within the same context, only some groups concentrate in business, underlines the importance of cultural and intentional factors.

Evaluation on the basis of survey finding

The survey findings are now presented to evaluate the relevance of the various theories discussed above for Asian business start-up in Oxford. The aim is not, and cannot be, to provide any definitive evaluation of the alternative theories, but to examine some of the fairly central claims made by them with respect to the South Asian entrepreneurs in Oxford. Hence, while no attempt is made to test these theories *in toto*, the survey data is analysed to see whether the South Asian businessmen have the characteristics required by the theories discussed, such as the entrepreneurial work ethic, the need to be one's own boss, and so on. The answers to these questions would clearly illuminate the general theories. The examination starts with the cultural traits of individuals regarded as encouraging entrepreneurial activity, such as the Weberian work ethic and the need 'to be one's own boss', and then progresses to the cultural characteristics of the ethnic community, such as family resources, culturally specific economic institutions, ethnic solidarity and the ethnic market which are looked upon as causes of business entry. The characteristics of the migrant situation are then looked at and, in conclusion, the broad contextual factors expected to aid entry into small business are considered.

Entrepreneurial ethic

That South Asian culture and religious values can quite easily produce the Weberian entrepreneurial character traits has been stressed by many (see e.g., Singer 1973; Zarwan 1977; Rafiq 1988). This was quite clearly borne out by the present survey as well, by the general emphasis placed on hard work, frugality, and deferred gratification:

> If you put in hard work, it is easy to make your business successful. The more work you put in the more you can get out of your business... (No.38)[5]

This was said by a 47 year old Pakistani, successful businessman and community representative on various city council committees.

This sentiment was echoed by respondents young and old alike, Muslim and Hindu, Indian, Pakistani and Bangladeshi. An oft-repeated phrase *'jitna gud daloge, uthna mitta hoga'*, translates literally as 'the more the sugar you put, the sweeter it will be'.

There is pride in the hard work. A well-educated, Indian grocer relates:

> ...drunks sometimes come in and say "You bloody Pakis, you come here with 3p. in your pocket, how do you buy all these houses and drive around in fancy cars?" I tell them, I don't stand with my back against the wall all day, drinking beer and idling away my time. I work hard and every penny I've earned is hard-earned money. (No.21)

It must, however, be noted that 'working hard' is something that all South Asian migrants believe in. In fact, the hours worked in a shop are not always much more than those which a factory employee would attempt to work. This is because every chance of working overtime is taken up by South Asian workers. This is well brought out by the following complaint made by a young Pakistani shop owner, the son of a postal employee in Oxford:

> Most of my generation has grown up without their fathers. All the men were too involved in making money. They worked overtime in the factories and all they did when they came back home was to eat and sleep... (No.80)[6]

Similarly, frugality, thrift, and saving for the future, are essential characteristics of the South Asian population as a whole. This is something that Asians themselves believe, as illustrated by the fact that these very qualities, to which successful business activity is attributed, is one that the shop-keepers and restaurateurs decry most in their Asian customers: "Our people don't spend money. They save it all up for the future", is a comment one hears often.

The small business owners certainly appear to be frugal and hardworking, and this picture is one that is in accord with that found in early sociological literature (Mills 1951; Bunzel 1955), but whether it explains *why* people, and especially South Asians, enter small business activity is quite another question. As one shop-keeper asked,

> Why do you make so much of the hard work we do? Don't the doctors work hard and the lawyers? (No.24)

'Being your own boss'

To go on to the psychological inclinations towards 'being one's own boss', the findings for South Asian small business owners in Oxford appear to support the evidence in the literature. The survey revealed that to a direct question on reasons for entering self-employment,[7] 65 per cent answered that they wanted to be 'one's own boss', and 80 per cent considered the same to be one of the advantages of self-employment.[8] But not a single respondent gave 'wanting to be one's own boss' as the only or sole reason for self-employment. Equal importance was given to 'greater prestige' and 'financial improvement'. Thus, as can be seen from Table 3.1, 56 per cent considered entering self-employment because it was financially advantageous, and 53 per cent because they considered it more prestigious. And, as shown in Table 3.2, to the question concerning advantages of self-employment, 56 per cent considered self-employment to be 'more prestigious', and 80 per cent maintained it was 'financially better'.

Table 3.1 Reasons given for entering self-employment
(respondents could give more than one reason)

	to make money	to raise prestige	to be own boss	misc. other
per cent mentioning	56	53	65	34

(n=94)

Table 3.2 Advantages of self-employment

(respondents could give more than one response)

	being own boss	financially better	more prestige	other
per cent mentioning	80	80	56	37

(n=94)

While a few did stress that they 'hated to take orders', 'couldn't work for anyone else', were 'not used to being told what to do', and so on, the vast majority valued "being one's own boss" not so much for its own sake, that is, not because of the control factor, but because being one's own boss implied greater wealth or greater prestige or both. This was a theme one came across time and time again, as can be seen from the following quotations:

An East African computer programmer, recently turned newsagent, maintained:

> When you're in a job, you slog year in and year out, and at the end of the day, you have nothing to call your own. When you're your own boss, the fruit of your labour is yours. Self-employment is the only way you can accumulate money. (No.42)

A 60 year old Indian, a sub-postmaster for the last 15 years, said:

> I always wanted to have my own business, to be my own boss. There is no doubt that it gives you more standing in society. Both among the whites who respect your money power...and among your own community also...Working for others has no value unless you are a doctor or teacher or engineer...You don't have anyone controlling you and telling you what to do and that is why people respect you. (No.54)

According to a young Pakistani in a tiny general store:

> Better to work for yourself, to be your own boss. The more hours you put in, the more rewarding it can be. In the factory you get a set wage and also you can be made redundant or you can be sacked. No one can sack you here. You don't have to worry where your next money is coming from. (No.80)

The concept of self-employment then, incorporates for these respondents both independent, and thus, enhanced status, as well as increased earnings.[9]

Another interesting point brought out by the survey is that it is not employment *per se* which is distasteful, but 'being only an employee'. Once entry into self-employment has been made, to continue with, or take up some other, paid employment, is not felt as a blow to one's self-esteem. A significant minority - 16 per cent of the respondents and 10 per cent of their spouses - had some other paid employment as well. If being one's own boss is as important as it is made out to be, why do so many continue in paid employment even while self-employed?

One 45 year old, simultaneously accountant, management consultant and shop-keeper, explained:

> I feel I can do my job with greater authority and freedom, as I'm not solely dependent on the job. The knowledge that the shop is

there gives me a feeling of security. And, when I work in the shop, I feel the same way about the other job - that I'm not totally dependent on the income from the shop. I function better this way! (No.56)

Self-employment allows one to tackle the paid job with more self-confidence; the position is one of greater strength as one does not need to fear being sacked, or having to put up with the whims and fancies of the employer - the backing of one's own business is there. And the paid employment is an important standby, allowing the small-business owner to be more relaxed in his business activity. Thus, while 'being one's own boss' is a comfortable state of affairs, and regarded as an essential element of self-employment, it is difficult to see it as being in itself the prime motivating factor in business start-up.

Family labour and resources

Though there appears to be some debate about the culturally specific nature of family resources, the evidence from the present survey quite clearly establishes a cultural twist in the manner in which family labour is utilized. To begin with a few statistics, it can be seen from Table 3.3 that 72 per cent of shop-keepers' spouses work in the shop, 46 per cent of them full time. Forty two per cent of the South Asian shop-keepers had their children actively helping in the business. In view of the fact that 38 per cent of the shop owners had children who were too young to work, the actual number of shop owners using children's help where this was available, is 68 per cent. Forty one per cent of shop-keepers also reported help from other family members, for instance, parents of one or other of the spouses, or siblings of the spouses, or nieces and nephews.

Table 3.3 Family members working in shop

Per cent of owners'	Full Time in shop	Part Time in shop	Not Working in shop	N.A.
spouses	46	26	25	3*
children	8	34	20	38**
other family	12	29	59	

n=76,[10]

* No spouses; ** Children too young or no children

When the entire population of business owners is considered, that is, both shop and restaurant owners, the percentage of spouses and children helping out is seen to fall. However, when these figures are compared to the figures for white shop and restaurant owners provided by the SCELI,[11] as presented in Table 3.4, it is found that as against 64 per cent of Asian spouses, the percentage of white spouses working in the business is only 35 per cent. Similarly, while 38 per cent of the children actively help in the Asian business, the figure for the children of white small business owners is only 19 per cent. A greater proportion of South Asian than white wives and children are, then, involved in the business.

Table 3.4 Ethnicity of owner and family help

	Asian*	White**
spouse help(%)	64	35
child help(%)	38	19

* n=94

**n=78 source: Social Change and Economic Life Initiative (SCELI)

To the question, 'If you were to fall ill or had to go away, who would look after the business?', 64 per cent of respondents answered 'family'. Only 10 per cent held that they would leave the business in the hands of employees. Family involvement in the business, then, appears to be relatively high among South Asian small business owners.

This is some evidence for the view that commitment to the family business is an important variable in explaining South Asian small business activity. The responsibility for the family business is one which is accepted by all members of the family, whether employed elsewhere or not. 'From each according to his abilities', is definitely a principle followed here, as evidenced in the factory-worker husband who comes home during his lunch time, to look after the shop, the bank-officer son who returns home at 5pm to do his stint in the shop, the wife who arranges to finish all her house-work by 10am to take over the shop from her daughter-in-law who then leaves for her office job, the wife who works as a nurse in the mornings, and serves in the shop in the afternoons giving her husband time off for other activities, the insurance man who takes a couple of days off during the working week for his insurance work, leaving his wife to manage the 'Take-away'. The permutations and combinations are endless. But, at some time of the day, for some period of time, most members of the family work in the family enterprise. The needs of all are catered to, there is a great deal of responsible cooperation, and considerable flexibility, allowing each member a certain space for his or her own individual activities.

The role of family labour is further accentuated by the fact that the families of Asian small business owners are generally larger than those of their white counterparts. Where the SCELI shows that the mean number of children for the whites is 2.1, for the Oxford Asians the mean number of children is 3.1. Families are then larger, and where the household includes members other than the nuclear family, the pool of available labour is quite extensive.

It is because of this 'collective commitment' on the part of the family that it becomes possible for South Asian small business activity to counteract some of the avowed evils of shop-keeping. For instance, long and unsocial hours is an often quoted disadvantage, which Asians, in contrast to the whites, are believed to ignore, because of their indifference to the low social evaluation of such hours - hence their greater proclivity for small business (Mars and Ward 1984:18). However, the point is not that South Asians are unconcerned about the hours. The point is rather that the ethnic small business owner is able to mitigate the inconvenience of the hours of shop work by calling on the resource of family labour. The need to work long hours is offset by the fact that there is a certain flexibility in the hours worked and also, by the fact that work is shared by various members of the family. So, no one person need work very long hours at a stretch. And, each member of the family may choose times of work convenient to him or her, and also have the time to take up other work if desired.

Further, as quite correctly pointed out by researchers in Australia (Kitay and Lever-Tracy 1990; Lever-Tracy et al. 1991), the assumption that the use of 'family labour' is 'exploitative' is questionable. It is pointed out that 1) possible employment alternatives for the family members working in the family enterprise may not be better; 2) employment of family labour is not so much for the short term benefits to the owners from underpayment of relatives, as to the long term benefits of the family enterprise; 3) family labour may be viewed in terms of the contribution it makes to the family, which may repay them through higher living standards or through support for education etc.; 4) children are certainly not viewed as cheap labour, work in the family enterprise always taking second place to their school or college work (Kitay and Lever-Tracy 1990:23). The present study quite strongly supports all these points.

Forty eight per cent of the wives of respondents do not have educational qualifications. The only jobs available to them are menial cleaning jobs, which are not a viable option, given the class background in their home country.[12] Again, the advantage in employing family labour is never expressed in terms of its being cheap, but always in terms of its trustworthiness and reliability. Lack of trust in non-family labour was an important reason given for not expanding existing shops, as the following statements reveal:

> You have to keep an eye on them, or they'll rob you silly. I had to throw a girl out the other day - she was handing a bag filled with groceries over the counter to her boyfriend. (No.34)

...you can't trust anyone - you cannot leave them in the shop and go out or do something else. Either my father or I have to be here always. (No.18)

I would like to open another shop to sell the rejects and old stock. I have the resources, but its very difficult to get trustworthy people to work. Its just my wife and me, and now with the baby, my wife too, is very busy. (No.1)

Family members can be depended upon to devote their time to the business, even young school-going children being left to man the tills alone and generally to pull their weight in the shops and restaurants. To speak of this as exploitation would, however, appear strange to children and parents alike. These children are also the ones to be sent to private schools, to be given all the advantages of prosperity, and to be placed first in any conflict of interests.

It is also maintained that as a consequence of long hours, 'family life' may suffer - that 'there is no time for the family' is another expected disadvantage of small-business. This, however, does not appear to be the case for South Asian small business owners. In fact, many Asian shop owners believe that with the shop, the family gets more attention. Table 3.5 shows that only 12 per cent mentioned 'no family life' in answer to the question, 'what do you feel are the disadvantages of small business?', while 20 per cent of small business owners regarded being able to give 'more attention to the family' as one of the advantages of self-employment.

Table 3.5 Business as advantage or disadvantage for 'family life'
percentage of respondents mentioning

'No Family Life'[13]	'More Attention to Family'[14]
12	20

n=94

Table 3.6 Residential location
Percentage of respondents living

Above Business	Near Business	Away from Business	Total
52	28	20	100

n=94

Table 3.6 shows that 52 per cent of business owners live above their shops or restaurants, and the number living a considerable distance away from their business premises is very small. The physical presence of the parents in the home, from a cultural point of view, is definitely seen as an advantage.

Thus, the parents of adolescent children maintained:

> Because we are here when they get home from school, they don't get into bad company or feel tempted to spend all their time at the movies, etc. What is the use of high-power jobs outside the home, when your daughters come back to an empty house - that's when they start smoking, taking drugs, etc. (No.16)

A woman working as a clerical officer in an income tax office, left her job to start a shop when she had her first baby:

> My baby was not settling down with the child-minder, so I thought if I had a shop, I would be able to earn and look after the baby at home. (No.34)

The middle aged owner of an emporium, speaking of the flexibility in working hours allowed by shopkeeping, maintained:

> I could take time off in the afternoon, when my wife would take over, and take my children swimming, or for cricket practice. Because of the shop, I was able to give my boys full attention during their growing years. (No.5)

Pre-school children grow up in the precincts of the shop, and even where the shop and home are not one, children are encouraged to spend time in the shop, thus always under the eye of parents and also, unconsciously and effortlessly, learning the trade and the trader's way of life. This is true of restaurants as well - all restaurant owners maintain that even when they were in school, they would hang around the restaurants owned by their fathers or uncles or brothers, working part-time in the kitchens, or waiting at tables, all the while picking up the trade. The family network is, indeed, very strong - the domain of work and that of play intermeshing to strengthen the fabric of the family, which, in turn, becomes an important cultural asset in small business activity.

Culturally specific economic institutions

The role of the institution of 'rotating credit' in financing business start-up among the Chinese and Japanese in the U.S., has been greatly emphasized by Light (1972). Following Light's seminal work on Rotating Credit Associations (RCAs), any attempt to explain the success of business enterprise among certain ethnic groups such as the South Asian ones, as against the lack of it among other ethnic groups such as the West Indian, has to take into account cultural institutions such as the availability of credit within the ethnic communities.

Such culturally specific economic institutions certainly exist among the Asians in Oxford. This study did not, however, reveal any dependence on these institutions for start up capital. While respondents did not deny the existence of RCAs amongst the South Asian migrant population, it was maintained that it was mainly the women who were members of such associations, and that it was not prevalent among the business owners, who were largely male. According to them, the sums of money that change hands are too small to be of much use in business activity. It was further maintained that today, there is no difficulty in obtaining loans from banks for business start-up, 81 per cent of respondents having started their businesses with loans from banks.[15]

It was, however, admitted that in the early stages of immigrant settlement and in the initial stages of Asian business activity, interest free loans were obtained through rotating credit associations called 'kametis'. This is corroborated by Shaw's study of Pakistanis in Oxford, conducted between 1979 and 1983. She maintains that in the 1960s, Pakistani men who moved to East Oxford bought their houses outright. An important reason for this was that kametis enabled men to pay for their houses in cash rather than by taking out mortgages. She goes on to maintain:

> ...(the rotating) form of credit is still used in East Oxford although kametis are now mainly organised by women. The sums involved are often quite large. If, for instance, twenty women each pay £20 per week, each woman, when it is her turn, will receive £400. This provides a useful sum for the down payment for a house or a shop (1988:51).

The working of the institution, called kameti, is referred to as 'parchi katna' or 'cutting chits'. Any particular chit fund is started with a list of people, all personally known to the organiser, a determinate number who have agreed to pay a fixed amount, say £25, every week. The amount to be paid, the duration, as well as the date of repayment to each individual is decided at the time of drawing up the list. Members decide by consensus, when they would like to get paid, though there is a certain flexibility in this to allow for emergency needs. The element of trust enters the transaction in that each person who collects the lump sum, is expected to continue paying in the monthly contribution till all members have collected.

In Oxford, the basis of trust, interestingly, appears to be neither national origin, nor religious background, but the spoken language. Thus, this study found that Punjabi speaking, Indian Hindus and Pakistani Muslims unite in the formation of RCAs, while the Bengali speakers from Bangladesh and the Malayalam speakers from South India, have their own credit associations.[16] Such associations continue to flourish, but are no longer regarded as an important factor in business start-up. They appear to have been, together with pooling of capital, friendly loans, and so on, an accepted ethnic resource in the initial stages of South Asian business activity. Once businesses are established, however, there is a certain reluctance to draw on this ethnic resource, more formal sources of finance being preferred.

While researchers have stressed ethnic solidarity and the sense of communiity among immigrant groups as the reason for the success of business activity (Cater and Jones 1987; Jones 1989), there appears to be little evidence for this in Oxford. What is more apparent than the solidarity is the lack of it, which supports Werbner's position, that the rivalry and competition between ethnic businessmen has, so far, been ignored by social scientists (1984:186, 188).

The Asian business community in Oxford clearly has a coherent structure, in that generally, each person knows of everyone else within it, his creditworthiness, trustworthiness, how well he is doing, even whether he has a Swiss bank account. But, when it comes to actual business activity, it appears to be a case of each for himself and himself alone. The orientation of the ethnic shop-keeper is clearly what Goldthorpe and Lockwood (1963), characterised as 'radical individualism'. Table 3.7 shows that 64 per cent of respondents believed that contact with other Asian businessmen was not very important in order to run their business well, and this includes 25 per cent who dismissed it as entirely unimportant. The 36 per cent who believed that contact was important, stressed that its importance lay in the business information available through such contact, and not in the sense of any practical help.

Table 3.7 Importance of Asian business contacts[17]

Percentage respondents maintaining contacts

Un-important	Not Very important	Fairly important	Very important
25	39	17	19

n=94

Thus, a 20 year old, Pakistani grocer believed:

> It is good to be on good terms with everybody, but, if I'm in trouble, they are not going to help me, are they? It is only my immediate family, my parents and brothers and their wives who are important to me. (No.24)

A 60 year old Indian sub-postmaster, resident in Oxford for 29 years, said:

> There has always been distrust in the Asian community, and there will always be. But sometimes we can rise above the differences and unite for a cause. (No.54)

A 57 year old, successful Pakistani businessman maintained:

I stopped associating with the Oxford people long ago. The Asians here are jealous of my wealth and success. (No.55)

An East African Asian, recently turned shop-keeper, stated quite bluntly that he did not believe in the solidarity of the Asian community:

I just keep away from them. They will stab you in the back whenever they can. So I keep away. Asians in business just cannot get along. (No.42)

It is worth noting that no claims were made regarding ethnic solidarity as a cause of business start-up.

The ethnic opportunity structure

One facet of the opportunity structure that has received wide attention is that of ethnic needs. An immediate objection to this is that if ethnic business activity were dependent on such culturally specific needs, it would never have 'taken off' in the way it has. As already noted in chapter 2, the number of Asian owned shops in Oxford, has gone up, from three in 1965 (all grocers and butchers), to 83 in 1989.

In Oxford, the Asian population has never in fact been large enough to guarantee a market of a sufficient size to maintain a purely ethnic business niche. It has been noted in chapter 2 that the number of businesses oriented towards the satisfaction of ethnic needs (Textiles, Jewellers and Tailors), remains almost constant at six - i.e., just six per cent of business enterprises.

One way of testing out the ethnic niche hypothesis more directly is to look at the percentage of ethnic clientele. If shops have been started with ethnic needs and tastes in view, they should be catering to a predominantly Asian clientele. Responses to the question on the number of Asian customers were quite clear-cut. As shown in Table 3.8, 18 per cent of the shops said they had no Asian customers at all; forty nine per cent said the number was negligible, maybe about one per cent; and 16 per cent reported less than five per cent of their customers as Asian. That is, 83 per cent of shops had less than five per cent Asian clientele. So also, 95 per cent of restaurants reported less than five per cent of its clientele as Asian.

Table 3.8 Business type and Asian custom

Estimated Percentage of Asian Customers

Type of Business	0	1	5	25	90
Newsagents	4	4	1	1	-
General Stores	6	21	7	4	1
Postoffice	3	6	1	-	-
Textiles, Jewellers, Tailor	-	-	-	1	5
Emporia and others	1	6	3	1	-
Total	14	37	12	7	6
Percentage shops (n=76)	(18)	(49)	(16)	(9)	(8)
Restaurants	1	6	10		1
Percentage restaurants(n=18)	(5)	(34)	(56)		(5)

Today, there are only two jewellers and two textile shops in Oxford which report a 99 per cent ethnic clientele. They cater exclusively to Asians as they deal in traditional Asian gold and silver jewellery, and textiles for ethnic clothes. There appears to be no scope for a third jeweller or textile dealer, as even now, one of the jewellers does much better than the other, and there is considerable rivalry between the two textile shops which cater to the same clientele. Any business which catered exclusively to an ethnic clientele could not hope to remain viable if large numbers deal in the same product. The percentage of minority entrepreneurs benefitting from a specialized ethnic market is, then, bound to be small. It is clear from the survey that, in Oxford, only six per cent of Asian shops, and none of the restaurants, cater exclusively to the ethnic community.

Further, while the first three shops in Oxford were grocers cum butchers, catering excusively to the Asians, today there are thirty nine grocers amongst the respondents, only one reporting a 90 per cent ethnic clientele, and thirty four, i.e. 87 per cent of the grocers, reporting less than five per cent of their clientele as Asian (Table 3.8).

A point which is often overlooked is that even where the product is 'ethnic', this may not be an indicator of ethnic clientele or dependence on an ethnic market, but rather a conscious effort to attract the indigeneous population. For instance, Indian emporia selling art objects, curios, rugs, ready-made clothes etc., do not expect to get ethnic customers. So also, no one today, could possibly say that 'Indian' restaurants cater to the Indians.[18]

This goes against the findings of McEvoy *et al.*(1979), and Cater and Jones (1978), which established a high dependence of South Asian businesses on the ethnic market.[19] This is definitely not supported by the present survey. The general transition to wider, non-ethnic markets is clearly evident in Oxford.

In terms of dependence on the ethnic market, it is likely that the type of business is a significant factor, insofar as in areas like Oxford, without a heavy residential concentration of South Asians, the type of businesses is very limited. Shops in Oxford are mainly grocers, newsagents, general stores, post offices, and emporia. There are no ethnic estate-agents, travel agents, pubs, laundrettes, banks, dry-cleaners, or businesses of the kind reported in studies of Bradford, Birmingham, etc.

The lack of dependence on a separate ethnic market is further established by the consideration of the location of the businesses studied. Table 3.9 provides a break down of the different businesses according to their location in areas with or without Asian residential concentrations. While there is some concentration of businesses in the Cowley Road area of East Oxford - 20 per cent of businesses being located in this area, which also contains a larger concentration of Asian residents than any other area of Oxford - what is more important is that 56 per cent of businesses are located in areas where there are very few Asian residents.

Table 3.9 Location of businesses

	Areas with Asian concentration	Areas without Asian concentration
Newsagents	3	7
Grocers, General Stores	16	23
Postoffices	4	6
Textiles, Jewellers, Tailor	6	-
Emporia, chemists, others	4	7
Restaurants	8	10

Total	41	53
percentage	44	56

n=94

Even in areas with more South Asian residents, the Asian shops do not cater to a higher percentage of Asian customers. In fact, as shown in Table 3.10, 73 per cent of the businesses in these areas maintain that their Asian clientele is less than five per cent.

Table 3.10 Asian custom in areas of Asian concentration

Estimated Percentage of Asian Customers

	0	1	5	25	90
Percentage of Businesses	12	34	27	12	15

n=41

When shop-keepers are asked why the percentage of Asian custom is so low, most, of course, have the perfectly valid reason that 'there are very few Asians around here'. But, shop-keepers in areas of heavier Asian residential concentration had other reasons:

> Oh! there are many Asians living on Abingdon Road, but Asians prefer to go to English shops. The whites will go to an Asian shop, but not Asians. They don't like to see their own people doing well. The Asians who come here, come here only when they are stuck, when they want credit or some other help. (No.34)

A grocer who kept Asian spices, pickles, savouries, etc., maintained that he kept them for his English customers:

> The Asians here, on Walton Street, will not buy them unless urgently needed, because they feel the prices are too high. Asians count their pennies. The English are willing to pay more for convenience. They would rather buy the Asian items from this store, at a slightly higher rate, than go all the way to Cowley. (No.7)

In fact, Asian shop-keepers today are not too keen on Asian custom. A young Asian, selling designer clothes, was quite blunt:

My prices are too high for the Asians. They'll never spend so much on a pair of jeans. I don't encourage them at all - They only waste my time. (No.1)

The same sentiments were echoed by an ethnic emporium owner:

I act indifferent when Asian customers come in - They are only interested in comparing prices and bargaining. They never buy anything. (No.3)

One Pakistani claimed he had had to close his Asian Video shop in the Cowley area, as they had run into difficulties because of the clientele being mainly Asian:

Very difficult to cater to the Asians - Too many arguments and you can't really argue with them because you know most of them. (No.80)

The ethnic opportunity structure, then, can no longer be seen as a reason for large scale entry into small business. Except where retailers deal in ethnically distinctive goods which are not required by the native population, (and these are neccessarily few in number), ethnic entrepreneurs do not rely on custom from the ethnic community, and are not dependent on a protected market.

Sojourner mentality

The present research suggests that, while the sojourner mentality could have been operative during the early years of migration and business start-up, once the migrant has evolved into an immigrant, whose economic activity is oriented towards a future, especially for the children, in the country of destination, the interest in business start-up is intensified. There are two points to be made here - First, that migrants have settled down, and are not thinking in terms of eventual return; second, that the business start-up rate continues to increase. Hence, the sojourner mentality can no longer be regarded as important in encouraging small business activity. Forty four per cent of the respondents said they 'wish to return home, but know we cannot'. A further 34 per cent said they did not want to return. So, for 78 per cent there is not even a 'myth of return'.[20]

Today, with more people reconciled to the idea of staying on - "Our children are settled here, what will we do back home?", "I would love to go back, but I know I cannot", "It isn't possible to go back now, we can't adjust to life there" - the importance of stabilising their financial and social position over here is being increasingly recognized.

A Sikh restaurant owner described the evolution thus:

All Indians came here with the intention of saving money and going back. But they had no clear idea of how much money they needed. They worked hard and sent money back home because they were scared that they would be kicked out of the country eventually. When things started settling down, and wives and children started coming over, it became more difficult to leave. And, once families were here, self-employment became an important option, as it gave you more respect in society and also meant more financial security. (No.65)

A 39 year old, Pakistani grocer, with a 21 year old daughter and 19 year old son, maintained that the increase in self-employment was the direct consequence of the decision to settle down in England. He joined his father in Oxford in the 1960s, and according to him:

...people then were interested in getting some money and going back. They would work for three to five years, accumulate money, return to Pakistan, spend the money there, sometimes on building houses, buying land, otherwise just on living well, and then, when the money was finished, they would return to England. This cycle would continue, of accumulation, return to Pakistan, expenditure and return to England. But, in the 1970s, people realised that they would have to think in terms of settling down in England, that it was foolish to waste money going back to Pakistan and building assets there. Instead, if they invested their money here, it would be far more profitable. When people started realising this, businesses were started, to make money and provide for the children who wished to stay on in England. (No.37)

It is, then, the realisation of no longer being sojourners which impels immigrants into small business today.

Ecologial succession

The situational hypothesis of ecological succession, too, does not seem to be applicable in Oxford. It has been shown in Table 3.9 that 56 per cent of businesses are located in areas where there are very few Asians. If South Asian business development takes place outside areas of Asian residential concentration, the ecological succession theory does not hold. Though, as noted in chapter 2, South Asian retail activity in Oxford started off in areas of Asian residential concentrations, that businesses were to be found in areas without Asian residential concentration as well, is evident from Table 3.11.

Table 3.11 Duration of business and location

Business Duration	Businesses in Areas of Asian concentration	Businesses in Areas of no Asian concentration
1-5 years	23	33
6-10 years	8	11
12-15 years	6	5
16-25 years	4	4
Total	41	53
Percentage	44	56

n=94

Lack of job opportunities and blocked mobility

The findings also do not appear to support the claim that South Asians are pushed into the small business sector because there are no other job opportunities. One must distinguish clearly between taking up a *job* in the small business sector, for instance, working in an ethnic restaurant or factory, and starting one's own small business such as a shop or restaurant. Even if it can be argued that, in certain circumstances, the element of choice is very small in the former case, it is clearly there in the latter. Very few immigrants can or do begin their work history in the country of destination with small business. They have to find paid employment - not necessarily in the ethnic small business sector - and only those who take up paid employment for some years and accumulate money, can hope to start their own business. Table 3.12 shows that 46 per cent of respondents began work in semi- or unskilled manual occupations. While Brooks (1983), has shown that for a small proportion of the respondents in his survey (14 per cent), their own business had been their first job, in the present population, though 12 per cent started work in self-employment, this includes the five per cent who started work in their father's shop, so that it is only for seven per cent that their own business is the first job.

Table 3.12 Class of first occupation[21]

	Percentage of respondents
Professional (I, II)	7
Routine Non-Manual (III)	12
Small Proprietors (IV)	12
Skilled Manual (V, VI)	23
Unskilled Manual (VII)	46

n=94

The next question to be considered is whether the paid employment taken up by respondents before self-employment is commensurate with their qualifications. If not, there is some case for the blocked mobility hypothesis. What are their qualifications? Thirty one per cent of the respondents had no formal qualifications. Though 16 per cent of respondents, did have degrees,[22] the general educational background of the present respondents is quite low. It appears clear from Table 3.13 that the class of the first occupations obtained by the respondents matches quite well with their educational qualifications. The evidence, then, does not support Aldrich's stand:

> ...barriers to entry into managerial jobs in white owned businesses push some Asians into going into business for themselves (1980:401).

Table 3.13 Class of first occupation and educational qualifications

Educational Qualifications	Class of First Occupation				
	I,II	III	IV	V,VI	VII
Degree	5	1	-	3	6
Some Qualifications	2	7	10	14	17
No Qualifications	-	3	1	5	20

n=94

Table 3.14 shows that while 11 per cent did give 'no other job opportunity' as a reason for self-employment, an indication that they probably meant that the sort of jobs they would get were not ones they would like, is provided by the fact that only three per cent held that they could find no alternative job. Sixty six per cent said they could find alternative jobs, but, 87 per cent felt that the alternative jobs were worse or not anywhere as good as their present ones.

Table 3.14 Attitudes towards job opportunities[23]

percentage of respondents maintaining

No other Job Opportunity	Alternative Job		
	Available	Not Available	Worse
11	66	3	87

(n=94)

Of course, there are cases of genuine blocked mobility leading to self-employment - the computer programmer who found younger Englishmen being promoted over his head, despite his seniority and greater experience; the school teacher who felt his authority undermined by the English headmaster; the M.Sc. research assistant in India who had to settle for a manual worker's job in Britain - all of these subsequently took to small shop-keeping. But even this minority felt that in shop-keeping they had a 'better' job - it had its compensations in terms of independence and financial prosperity, quite commonly regarded as the basis of respect and prestige in the community.

In general, what respondents regret is not that they do not get the kind of jobs they should get but rather, that they do not have the qualifications to get the jobs they would like to have. There is the acceptance that with their qualifications, they cannot hope for a 'better' job:

According to a successful Sikh newsagent:

> If I had better qualifications, maybe I would prefer something else. But I am very satisfied - this work has helped me build up something I had never dreamed off, which I wouldn't have had otherwise ...Professional jobs are good, but if you can't get the qualifications, then business is a good alternative. (No.30)

A young Pakistani grocer regretted that he had not paid more attention to his studies:

> I would have been able to get a better job then. With my qualifications, the other jobs available are all tedious and dirty - I have worked in a laundry, as a cleaner in a hospital, in a dairy, in a factory doing piece-work - all uncivilized work. (No.18)

A 43 year old East African Asian was quite amused:

> What blocked mobility?! With `O' levels you cannot really hope for a better job. I love it, otherwise I wouldn't have continued doing it all these years. (No.60)

The disadvantages that the Asians in this survey face, or have faced, in the labour market, are then, due not just to their ethnic identity, but also their lack of proper qualifications. However, disadvantage in the labour market due to lack of qualifications, cannot, in itself, be taken as a cause of entry into self-employment - other groups with poor qualifications, the English for instance, do not appear to go into self-employment to the same extent.

It is true that for most, the choice of job types is limited. The alternative jobs which 55 per cent of the sample felt would be available to them, fell into class VII. Thus, for 55 per cent of shop-keepers and restaurant owners, the only alternative to small-business is semi- and unskilled manual work. But, as many as 20 per cent believe they could get jobs of class I and II, that is, professional, administrative and managerial jobs. Another 14 per cent believe their alternative job class to be III, that is routine non-manual jobs. If even those who can obtain jobs of a higher occupational class, do look on small business as a viable alternative, and do choose to go into shop-keeping, entry into small business is certainly not the result of blocked mobility or lack of alternative jobs. The choice, then, is definitely not a stark choice between deprivation and earning a living through self-employment and small business proprietorship, but a genuine choice.

The context

In Oxford, the City Council set up an Ethnic Minority Business Service in 1989, (very much later than in some other areas of Britain), in order:

> To improve the economic situation of ethnic minority communities in Oxfordshire by the start-up, development and diversification of businesses owned by people from ethnic minority communities (Ethnic Minority Business Service Strategic Plan 1990:4).

Help in obtaining loans for business start-up, advice on feasibility of business schemes as well as development and promotion of existing businesses, are some of the aims of the service.

What is interesting is that the ethnic communities are not very interested in the service. Attempts to woo the business community have met with a conspicuous lack of response, indicating that the ethnic minorities feel quite confident of being able to help themselves, to stand on their own feet. That the business community looks upon any sort of political intervention with suspicion is evident in their reactions to any efforts at reaching them. A Hindu school master turned shop-owner, who had sold his successful grocery store a few years ago to start an ethnic emporium, maintained:

> ...all research is available to the government. They just want to find out the secret of our success so that they can put obstacles in our way. When they found out that grocers were making money by staying open longer, they allowed the big stores like Tesco to stay open longer too, thus depriving the small shop of its profit. They want to see how they can control our success. (No.3)

The ethnic shop-keeper is certainly not aware then, of the favourable economic and political climate; he definitely feels he has succeeded on his own merits, despite efforts to curb his success.

It must also be remembered that South Asian business activity in Oxford began in the 1960s, that is, nearly two decades before the decline in small business activity was arrested. In 1964-65, Oxford could boast of three Asian Grocers cum Butchers, to cater to the tiny South Asian population. The entry into business, then, began during the decline and continues to accelerate after the decline has bottomed out. The context, then, does not appear to be a determining factor in Asian entry into small business.

Summary

To sum up the survey findings, there appears to be no evidence of ethnic solidarity, culturally specific economic institutions, an ecological niche or a protected market, among the South Asians in Oxford today. The sojourner mentality, too, appears to be absent now. The analysis is essentially based on the pattern of Asian retailing in Oxford today. The picture may be quite different in other areas of Britain, and even in Oxford at a different period in the growth of business activity.

In the initial stages of immigrant business, retail activity is certainly directed towards the ethnic community. Thus, though retail activity began later in Oxford than in other areas of Britain, (The first Asian shop in Oxford is said to have been started in 1965, whereas literature mentions Asian shops in Britain as early as 1957) it began with the supply of ethnic groceries to the ethnic community. There is evidence of numerous 'ethnic' features - the goods and the clientele were ethnic, start-up capital was obtained informally through ethnic networks, and the 'sojourner mentality' influenced business activity.

It certainly appears that this 'ethnic niche' stage is used as "a platform from which to expand into the wider market" (Mars and Ward 1984:15). Within three years of the start of business activity, in 1968, the first ethnic emporium was opened in Oxford, and a second in 1969, both of which continue their successful business activity to the present day. This type of business - the export of Asian culture - was, however, clearly aimed at an English clientele. The diversification of businesses and the transition to non-ethnic markets had already begun. As Hiro (1971:152) predicted, the ethnic business certainly did not remain circumscribed within the 'immigrant' market .

Today, even grocers cater mainly to a non-ethnic clientele. With the increase in the number of small business owners, in areas without a residential concentration of South Asians, and at a later stage of migrant settlement, it is difficult to find evidence of strong ethnic networks, a protected market, or culturally specific economic institutions. And yet, the number of new entrants into small business continues to increase. Ethnic networks, markets, or institutions, cannot, then, be seen as determinants of large-scale South Asian entry into small business.

Among the contextual factors, there is no lack of fit between educational qualifications and occupations within the South Asian population in Oxford, and the economic and political climate, even if favourable, would not explain the greater tendency among Asians, than among Afro-Caribbeans for instance, to exploit the opportunities the climate offers.

That certain cultural factors such as the strength of the family and the entrepreneurial ethic are important cultural assets in ethnic small business cannot be denied. But these factors should be looked at more as an aid to successful business activity than as dominant reasons for entry into small business. What then, are the reasons for large scale Asian entry into small business? An explanatory approach is provided in the next chapter.

Notes

1. Subsequent to the present survey, two Chinese owned shops started up, both around the same time and in quite close proximity, in the vicinity of the railway station.

2. In his explanation of greater entrepreneurial activity among the Mahisyas than among the upper castes, Nandy holds that among the upper castes, the community self-image gives no support to the entrepreneurial role, hence the threshold of 'an achievement' needs to be higher for entry into business than among the Mahisyas who have a community norm of entrepreneurship, and hence do not require high nAch to enter business (Singer 1973).

3. Some evidence for this is provided by

    1) Indian businessmen in Kenya during the 20th Century, A Case Study (Zarwan 1977)

    2) The Gujeratis of Fiji, 1900-1945, A Study of an Indian Immigrant Trader Community (Prasad 1978)

3) Ethnic enterprise in the Netherlands:the Surinamese of Amsterdam (Boissevain and Grotenbreg 1987).

4.   The success of petty Indian shopkeepers could be attributed to their ability to manipulate conditions in the country area to their advantage to a greater degree than their European counterparts" (Prasad 1978:37).

> "The economic opportunities of a developing area like Kenya were numerous, and Indians were in a position to take advantage of them. The growth of firms was in large part conditioned by the successful exploitation of different commerical and industrial opportunities as they presented themselves" (Zarwan 1977:255).

5.   Numbers in brackets after quotes refer to the number given to the nterviewee on the schedule.

6.   That the hours worked by wage workers are very long, has been noted by Hiro, according to whom:"...many Asians seek jobs offering overtime. An 84-hour week is not uncommon with Pakistani workers in the West Riding" (1971:127).

7.   The question here was, 'What, according to you are the advantages of self-employment?'.

8.   The question here was, 'What, according to you are the advantages of self-employment?'.

9.   A study of Jews in Britain reports that 23 per cent of employees desired self-employment for the increased social status it might give them (Kosmin 1979:51).

10.   Where n=76, the figures refer to just the shop-keepers and not the restaurant owners

11.   Figures for white shop-keepers are obtained from National data sets, in this case the 'Social Change and Economic Life Initiative', as explained in the methodological appendix.

12.   This point is discussed in detail in chapter 4.

13.   his was one of the responses to the question 'What are the disadvantages of self-employment?'.

14.   The question here was, 'What, according to you are the advantages of self-employment?'.

15.   It is interesting to note that a significant number of owners count their bank managers among their personal friends.

16.   There are variations in the actual functioning of these associations. For instance, in one form of the RCA, the members bid for the collective amount every month, the amount going to the 'lowest' bidder, that is, the one willing to accept the highest discount, generally because he needs the money most urgently (Srinivasan 1995:199-208).

17.   The question was, 'In order to run your business competently, how important is having good relations with other businessmen in the community?'.

18.   Trade research has shown that 26 per cent of all housewives now cook Indian food with some regularity. In 1985, an estimated 90 per cent of UK sales of Indian meal ingredients were accounted for by Asians and only two per cent by non-Asians. By 1990 the proportions had changed to 40 per cent of sales to Asians and 60 per cent to non-Asians. This rise in demand amongst non-Asians is attributed to the multi-cultural composition of the UK, increased overseas travel, and changing attitudes to the adoption of foreign food (Thakrar 1992:29).

19.   A possible reason for this finding could be the oversampling of areas of very high ethnic concentration -- cf methodological appendix.

20.   What may be attributed in part to the sojourner mentality, is what has been regarded as a sign of lack of success of South Asian business activity - the apparently high rates of business failure. In the early years of business activity, what appeared to be failure of businesses may have actually been a quick turnover in business activity due to the desire to make a fast buck and return to the home country. Expansion of businesses was just not on the agenda. Once a certain amount was accumulated, the business was wound up or sold off, though, quite often, people returned to start new businesses.

21.   The Erikson and Goldthorpe, class schema has been collapsed in this table to (1+2) - Professional; (3+4) - Non-manual; (5+6+7) - Small proprietors; (8+9)- Skilled manual; (10+11) - Unskilled workers.

22.   Except for one respondent, a young African asian, who had a degree in Pharmacology, and had opened a Chemists shop, the degrees were all obtained from the area of origin.

23.   The answers to three questions have been put together in this table.
       'No other job opportunity' was one of the responses to the question
       'How did you first come to be self-employed?'. The next two
       responses are to the question 'Do you feel there are alternative jobs
       you could get without much difficulty?' The last response refers to
       the question 'Would you say the alternative jobs available to you
       are better or worse than your present one?.

4 An explanation for Asian business entry

Introduction

The previous chapter identified the specific constraints as well as the cultural resources possessed by the Oxford South Asians. In an explanation of their large scale business entry, the crucial issue now appears to be the relative weight to be given to constraints, resources and strategic choices. While the influence of the constraints of poor educational qualifications and racial disadvantage, as well as, the cultural resources of the entrepreneurial work ethic and family solidarity, on occupational trajectories is accepted, what may be added to this are the intentions and aspirations of the Asian population in Oxford. The present study emphasizes that entry into small business is to be interpreted as a strategic choice on the part of the South Asian migrant, for the achievement of mobility aspirations. And it is the contention of this book that these mobility aspirations must be seen in the context of the stratification systems of both the host country and the country of origin.

Position of the Asian immigrant in three systems of stratification[1]

Contact with South Asian businessmen seems to reveal the operation of three systems of stratification in the migrant psyche. There is the status position in British society, which does not appear to be given much importance. There is the status position within the ethnic group, which small business definitely seems to have improved, and there is also the status position in the structure of the home country which is, even after years of migration, given great importance, and which 'business' improves and keeps secure. There is no sense of alienation or isolation from the home country. As shall be shown, the migrants consider themselves as much a part of their communities in the Asian sub-continent as of the South Asian community in Britain.

As an instance of the operation of this phenomenon, there is the case of an Indian, the owner of an ethnic emporium, moderately successful, but well content. Prior to his migration to Britain, he had held the post of a stenographer in a government office in India - a respectable white-collar job. On coming to Britain, he found that the sort of jobs he was qualified for, were among the lower paying jobs, and that they were 'women's jobs' - in Britain, secretaries, assistants, stenographers, were women. The sort of jobs which men went in for, such as construction labour, transport or factory work, were much better paid than the white-collar work. But, these jobs did not have much status in the South Asian community, especially back home. According to this man:

> If I were looking for a bride for my son in India, and I told them I was a bus driver, or a factory worker, it would be disastrous. I would never get a bride from a good family for my son.

Self-employment, whatever the scale of the business, has a certain prestige attached to it. It means more status both within the South Asian community here, as well as back home. He maintained that he belonged to the working class in Britain, as he worked hard and did not employ any labour. He went on to say:

> If I had been English, I would, quite happily, have been a bus driver or factory worker. But being Indian I had to take up an occupation which Indians would respect and consider a status job. (No.5)

While he accepts that he is working class in Britain, he feels that as far as the South Asian group is concerned, he is middle class, and in his home country, he would be upper middle class. The operation of the different systems of stratification thus becomes clear.

Position within British society

Subjective perceptions of class position in Britain do vary. This is quite clear from Table 4.1, which shows that while 43 per cent believe they are working class people, 48 per cent believe they are now in the middle class.

Table 4.1 'To which class do you feel you belong?'

	Percentage mentioning		
Working Class	Middle Class	Upper Class	Don't Know
43 (n=94)	48	4	5

Perceptions appear to vary according to the size and success of businesses, in that claims of upward mobility within British society are generally based on improvement in their financial positions. Thus, a highly successful, tiny minority of four respondents, believe they have moved into the upper class. According to one of these, a young, Bangladeshi owner of three restaurants in Oxford:

So many important people - politicians, bureaucrats, T.V. people, come to my restaurant. They move with me on equal terms, they know what I'm worth. (No.77),

According to a thirty year old, second generation shop-keeper:

They (the British) respect me for my money power, I can move in the highest circles..(No.9)

While perceptions of the class position in Britain may vary, there appears to be general agreement that it is lower than the position they would have in their countries of origin. That there was a discrepancy between their class positions here and back in the country of origin was confirmed by sixty five per cent of the population,[2] and further illustrated by statements such as the following:

I belong to the working class here, but I'm upper middle class in Pakistan. (No.91)

I may be middle class here, but I'm treated like royalty back home. (No.9)

We may be working like slaves here, but back home we have servants, houses, chauffeurs... (No.38)

Here I'm working class, but back home ...automatically place oneself in the top echelons of society, purely because of financial situation and education. (No.68)

...working class here, but middle class in Bangladesh. I get treated more respectfully there. (No.85)

...working class here in England, but in Pakistan we are upper class. We were always landowners there - of the Jat biradiri...but we were poor. Now we have made it there. But here we will always remain working class. The whites will always consider the Asians as working class...But who cares what the whites think... (No.24)

Position within the ethnic community in Britain

It must here be noted here that 57 per cent of the respondents come from a background of small proprietors and small holders, in that their fathers belong to class IV, and only 17 per cent have fathers falling into class VII, the class of semi- and unskilled manual workers. But, as can be seen from Table 4.2, it is this class VII that 46 per cent of the migrants enter, by virtue of their first occupations in Britain.

Table 4.2   Father's social class and first occupation class

Father's Social Class	I,II	III	IV	V,VI	VII	Total%
Professional I,II	3	1	-	6	4	5
Non Manual III	-	1	-	1	1	3
Farmers, Small Proprietors IV	2	7	9	6	27	54
Skld Manual VI	1	-	-	4	5	11
Unskld Manual VII	1	2	2	5	6	17
Total percent (n=94)	7	12	12	23	46	100

It may be expected that those who have experienced downward mobility after migration, will seek avenues of mobility out of the working class, and may look on self-employment as the most accessible route.

What is interesting is the underlying reason for mobility aspirations, because what is often overlooked is the fact that most South Asian migrants were not dissatisfied with the monetary rewards of their labour in Britain. This is well illustrated by the following:

A Pakistani grocer maintained that in the early days:

> ...our people took up any jobs they could get. Even the educated ones had to take up dirty and degrading work. But the pay was good. Given the way of life of our people, they were easily able to save and send home substantial sums of money - substantial because of the rate of exchange. Even people claiming unemployment benefit could save enough out of it to maintain a family back in Pakistan. (No.8)

The reason for self-employment, then, was not so much financial as social. According to a sixty year old, Indian sub-postmaster, who worked for ten years 'on the buses' before buying a shop:

> I always wanted to have a business of my own. There is no doubt it gives you more standing in society. Both among the whites who respect you because of your money power ...bank managers come to you and keep on good terms with you...your credit facilities are excellent. And within your own community also, your prestige is greater when you are in self-employment. Working for others has no value, unless you are a doctor or teacher or engineer. If three or four Asians get together and one is not self-employed, he will be

78

completely left out...he is not given enough respect. Of course, you are better off financially also, but that is not the main thing... (No.54)

Similarly, a thirty eight year old Bangladeshi restaurant owner maintained:

I worked in the car factory for twelve years as an assembly line worker. The money was good and the free time was more. Now I work much harder. Of course the pay is twice as much, but the main thing is the future is much brighter...you feel that you are more respectable. When you go to work in overalls, you do feel a little small. Now you're suited, booted and the owner of a restaurant. The people you work with in a factory are the working class and those are the people you mix with. Here you meet the rich and better off on their own terms. The people you associate with are very different. (No.85)

Running his own business, then, is certainly regarded as giving a man added status within the ethnic community.

Community representatives

One concrete indication of the relatively higher status position of the ethnic small business owner within his ethnic group, is that the representatives of the community, in a variety of instances, are small business owners. Thus, among the eight members co-opted from the Indian, Pakistani, and Bangladeshi communities, to sit on the City Council's Race Relations Committee (1989), five are shop-keepers or restaurant owners. So also, many of the community organisations were headed, at the time of the survey, by the small business owners - The Co-ordinator of the Indian Union, the Presidents of the Hindu Mandal and the Pakistan Welfare association were all shopkeepers, the head of the Nirankari Mission was the owner of a 'Take Away', and those of the Bangladeshi Association and the Bangladeshi Welfare Association were restaurant owners. Executives of various other councils such as the Oxford Mosque council, the Ethnic Minority Business Service, etc., are also chosen from among the small business owners. It could then be maintained that within the ethnic community, the positions carrying a certain measure of authority or control are occupied by small business owners.

Use of women's labour power

The importance of status considerations within the South Asian community is reflected also in decisions regarding the utilisation of the labour power of women. The existence of cultural taboos regarding the entry of South Asian women into the labour force of the host society has been generally noted (Jeffery 1976:78; Mars and Ward 1984:18; Wilson and Stanworth 1985:3; Khan 1979:123-127). Statistics have consistently shown that South Asian women are less likely to be found in the labour market than white women. According to the 1984 PSI survey, there are major differences within the Asian group, in that only 18 per cent of Muslim women were employed as compared to 57 per cent of other Asian women. But the activity rates of these non-Muslim Asian women are lower than those of white and West Indian women (Brown 1984:150). That cultural restrictions on women going out to work are very stringent among the Muslims is well known (Jeffery 1976; Khan 1979). Though restrictions are less stringent among the non-muslims, allowing one's wife to go out to work, especially when the work is menial, detracts from an Asian man's status or prestige. Khan, looking at South Asian women in London, maintains, that for traditional Muslim families and for women with traditional status conscious husbands, the social costs of outside-work in terms of family prestige and child-care responsibilities would be too high, so that home-working is the only acceptable form of economic activity (1979:123).

Running a shop, therefore, provides the opportunity to maintain these restrictions, to uphold one's prestige, and yet utilise the labour power of the women. A significant number (22 per cent) of the shop-keepers maintained that the shop had been started to provide jobs for the wives.[3] According to a 35 year old grocery shop owner of East African Asian origin:

> ...my wife was sitting idle and could not find jobs other than cleaning jobs. I did not want her to go and clean other people's houses, so we opened the shop. (No.7)

The wife of a very prosperous general store owner, of Pakistani origin, who had only primary school education, but was actively managing the shop with four, white, part time employees, maintained:

> ...I worked as a store assistant in a super market...then worked as a liaison health officer for the council. But this involved a lot of going out, sometimes at night, and my husband did not approve of it. So we started the shop... (No.38)

Even where this was not directly stated, it must be remembered that 46 per cent of small business owner's wives worked full time in the business, and a further 25 per cent worked part time, so that the labour power of 71 per cent of these women was being utilised.

The cultural restrictions on work, even among the Muslims, may be overcome if the work is of a higher order. However, as 48 per cent of the wives in the sample do not have any educational qualifications, the only jobs available to them are menial 'cleaning jobs'. Many of the women were quite emphatic that they would never take up such jobs.[4] A thirty nine year old Pakistani woman with a 'matric' and the daughter of a furniture factory owner in Lahore, maintained:

> I did not work for ten years after coming to Britain as the children were very young and the only sort of jobs I could have got easily

were cleaning jobs which I would ***never take***.[5]...I started the shop as my husband could not get leave from the bus company...the work in the shop got too much for one person so he resigned and joined me. (No.28)

It should be noted here, as shown in Table 4.3, that 530 per cent of the wives, have fathers who belong to class IV, and a further 22 per cent had fathers in classes I, II, and III. Seventy five per cent, then, come from a class in the sub-continent, for which menial work is unthinkable.[6]

Table 4.3 Wives' fathers' occupational class

| | Class of Wives' Fathers Occupation | | | | |
	I,II	III	IV	V,VI	VII
Percentage of wives (n=87)[7]	15	7	53	5	20

For a few respondents, even working in their own shop is not regarded as desirable for women. Thus, a 32 year old general store owner of Mirpuri origin, resident in Oxford since the age of twelve, maintained:

> I don't like the idea of my wife serving behind the counter. I wouldn't be able to tolerate it if customers behaved badly or acted funny with my wife... (No.70)

But for many of the respondents, to own your small business is the answer to the problem[8] of women's entry into the labour market. In small business, the labour power of women is being utilised, within the home and without detriment to the family, safe-guarding all traditions regarding menial work or working outside with other men, and the status of the family.

Position in the country of origin

Business entry gives a man more status within the ethnic community here. What is equally important to the migrant is that, self-employment adds to his status back home.

The wife of a car factory worker, the active partner in a very successful shop, maintained:

> Our position in Pakistan was not low. My father was a police inspector and my husband's father was a zamindar.[9] Our status was quite high. After coming here, when my husband was doing factory work, it appeared demeaning to our people. People considered him just a factory worker at home. You cannot keep up standard at home by doing factory work. But 'business' is regarded as prestigious (No.44)

81

The aspirations for self-employment then, must quite clearly be seen in the context of the stratification system of the country of origin which remains an important reference group for the South Asian migrants.

A migrant is not usually asked by people back home what he does, and equally seldom does he volunteer any information regarding his occupation.[10] Entry into 'business' makes it possible for these migrants to break this well established conspiracy of silence surrounding migrant labour. A Sikh science graduate from India, who worked as a bus driver for eleven years in Britain before acquiring a sub-postoffice and general store, said that though the change meant hard work, it allowed him to hold his head high among his friends in India, all of whom, though not as financially well off as him, were gazetted officers in the government. According to him:

> Once, somehow, my friend's children got to know that I was a bus driver. They were very amused and asked if I had gone all the way to Britain to drive buses! I felt very small. Now that I have my own business, I can hold my head high. (No.64)

And to look at the same thing from the point of view of the people back home, Mihir Bose, in the *Independent* magazine of 11th November 1989, speaks of "the growth of something like a new caste called N.R.I." in India. N.R.I's are 'non-resident Indians', normally resident outside India, who are now wealthy enough to think of investing in India. The native Indian elite feel that their identity is now threatened by the N.R.I's who have become so successful in the West, that they now have the financial muscle to change things in India and are consequently being wooed by Indian politicians. N.R.I's are not really socially acceptable as they are emigrants who left India because they could not make it there, but now they flood the five-star hotels in winter, making the most of the cheap rupee, and the elite finds its own economic and social standing threatened by a class it considers inferior.

While the respondents in this study may only in a few instances, fall into Bose's category of N.R.I's, they have still done very well for themselves by Asian standards, and have a material standard of life they could not have dreamt off back home. As the wife of an Indian shop-keeper put it:

> ...the difference is that between the earth and the sky. Compared to India we have improved greatly ...there we used to dream about gold ornaments, now I can have a gold ring a week... (No.33)

And now, when they go back, the cheapness of the rupee *vis-à-vis* the pound allows them a very high standard of living. So, for the migrant, upward mobility *has* occurred, and it is this mobility and how he is regarded in his country of origin which is more important than his status within British society.

Marriage partners

One important reason for the continuing importance to the South Asian migrants of their status position in the stratification system of the country of origin is the desire to obtain marriage partners from there. As seen from the case of respondent No.5, quoted at the start of this chapter, being 'in business' makes it easier to obtain partners for the children. This is seen to be the case in obtaining partners for the respondents themselves as well. If those respondents who got married after migration to Britain are considered, it can be seen from Table 3 that 71 per cent of them have got partners for themselves from their country of origin. A further 25 per cent obtained partners from their ethnic group in Britain, and only 4 per cent married from within the English group.

Table 4.4 From where partner obtained (respondents)

Percentage obtaining marriage partner from

Country of origin	Ethnic Group in Britain	English Group
71	25	4

(n=56)

Seventy five per cent of the respondents in the present study did not have married children. The remaining 25 per cent had between them, 38 children who had contracted marriages. As shown in Table 4.5, 42 per cent of them obtained partners from the country of origin, 40 per cent from the ethnic group in Britain, and 18 per cent married English partners.

Table 4.5 From where partners obtained (children)

Percentage obtaining marriage partner from

Country of origin	Ethnic Group in Britain	English Group
42	40	18

(n=38)

The country of origin, then, remains an important source for obtaining marriage partners. And that 'being in business' is an asset in arranging marriages, is well illustrated by the complaint about her husband, made by an Indian shop-keeper's wife, the daughter of a medical practitioner in India:

...his family had told us that he was in business. Otherwise my father would never have agreed to the marriage. It was only after coming here that I found out that he was actually working on the buses...soon after we moved to Oxford, he started his own business (No.2)

Summary and conclusion

For both men and women, self-employment in small business is preferable in status terms to paid employment, even if in monetary terms both may be equal. It must also be remembered that South Asians do not calculate the family income in terms of number of people working, and the number of hours they put in. It is the total amount coming in that is important[11], and even if this is not, in some cases, significantly more than a salary, small business is more prestigious.

In Oxford then, the answer to the question framed by Gambetta - 'Did they jump or were they pushed?' - they appear to have jumped. There is little evidence of these South Asian shop-keepers and restaurant owners being pushed into self-employment. Entry into small business appears to be a deliberate strategy adopted to raise both economic and social standing. That this is quite in accord with traditions in the Indian sub-continent can be seen from the work of Mines, and of Papanek. Mines, writing about Tamil Muslim Merchants in India, maintains:

> One achieves status and a degree of prestige within the bazaar area neighbourhood by being a successful merchant...being a successful merchant establishes one's position in the network of social ties which links the businessmen of the bazaar area in the contexts of leadership, economic reciprocity, social ties and state and local politics. Thus, the successful merchant has a considerable social, as well as economic, stake in his position as a businessman (1973:51).

Papanek, writing about the Gujerati Memons of Pakistan, states:

> Business activity, especially when compared to middle class occupations, has been much more rewarding financially in Pakistan, particularly in the last decade...the sons of civil servants and others in respected middle class occupations have begun to enter business professional occupations ...Recruitment for business occupations, therefore, takes place in an expanding group of young men...a sign of the rapidly achieved high status of businessmen and industrialists in Pakistan (1973:81).

Self-employment is conceived to be the only route to substantial financial prosperity, and even if this were to prove elusive, the mere jump into self-employment provides status improvement.

The shop-keeper's self perception of success is clearly evident:

If we weren't successful, why should we have stuck on for fifteen years and more? I don't know anyone who has gone bust. Everyone is improving their living standards, expanding their businesses, moving to better locations. If anyone in Oxford says he is not doing well, he is lying. (No.54)

maintained a 60 year old, Indian sub-postmaster, resident in Oxford since 1961.

Another Indian, aged 54, and resident in Oxford since 1962, stated: Though in earlier times, in India, businessmen had a much lower status than doctors lawyers, etc., today it is quite different. With money it becomes possible to improve one's position. I feel I have achieved something. All my children have gone to public schools. They don't lack for anything. We live well and interact with the British on equal terms. (No.53)

That this attitude is not restricted to the older generation, is evident in the following statement made by a 23 year old Ugandan Asian, for whom self-employment was "the only serious option" :

I went into it to prove something to my community. People treat you differently when they know you have your own business. (No.71)

A 20 year old, of Pakistani origin, maintained:

If I want to go out and buy a Mercedes right now, I can. Which of my English friends of my age can do that? (No.24)

A 28 year old of Indian origin, a certified accountant who had recently switched to shop-keeping believed:

People treat you with more respect. They say, "Oh! He is a businessman". If you are in paid employment, they think you are nothing. They have nothing to talk to you about. (No.79)

On the basis of these findings, the important explanatory variable for entry into small-scale entrepreneurship by Asians, is the strength of their status aspirations, which in turn leads to the development of an occupational specialisation, or, what Werbner has referred to as the 'culture of entrepreneurship' (1984:187).[12]

The orientation towards business entry cuts across class lines. Though the proportion of 'professional' turned small business owner is quite small in the present sample, it does include the solicitor cum restaurateur, the management consultant cum grocer, the teacher turned emporia owner, the computer programmer, the accountant, the marine engineer, all newsagents today, and the insurance agent cum 'take away' owner.

It appears then, that small business entry is a strategy which a growing number of immigrants adopt at some point in their career.

There are a few who take to it after years of factory work, as a symbol of having finally arrived. There are others who use shop-ownership as a short term strategy, to work hard and accumulate enough to go on to better things - maybe just a change in business which does not require as much labour. Amongst the present respondents, there is the East African Asian, who after eleven years of successful post-office and grocery ownership, has bought himself a small newsagents, which does not involve as much work. There is also the successful, 'five year old' newsagent, who now hopes to sell the shop, start an old-peoples home, and 'relax a little'.

There are yet others, a small number, for whom the shop provides a living and that is all, but an independent living of some social standing.

There are also some who see shop-keeping as a way of utilising the labour of the women, and providing jobs for the children, within the home, without jeopardising their prestige.

Finally, there are some with good jobs, who yet see in the shop or restaurant a means of further improving their social and economic standing, a definite route to upward social mobility.

The variations on the theme of the desirability of small business are many. Incidentally, these variations only serve to underline the irrelevancy of expansion. The small shop or restaurant is sufficient unto itself. Seventy five per cent of respondents had no plans for expansion. A few may take the big jump into big business, but for the vast majority, small business is quite adequate, socially and economically.[13]

Thus, it is a central contention of this book that even if the actual pattern of retailing and catering varies at different stages of its evolution, the underlying reasons for entry remain the same - that is, entry is a strategic choice, made in order to achieve ethnically oriented status aspirations.

Notes

1.   Any system of stratification can be looked upon as having various components. As will be seen in the next chapter, where the position of the Asian petty bourgeoisie in the class structure is considered, the framework followed is that used by Lockwood (1958) and later by Bechhofer *et al.* (1968), where 'status' is regarded as one component of class position. Nowadays it is more usual to make a sharper distinction between 'class' and 'status'. The two are analytically distinct aspects of stratification: 'class' is more objective and looks at the position of people within the division of labour, while 'status' has to do more with the responses of others. Empirically, however, the two are closely intertwined. That people in general are not conscious of the sociological distinction is seen by responses of the present respondents such as: "...working class here, but middle class in Bangladesh. I get treated more respectfully there" (No.85). For purposes of the present argument,

the focus is on the status perceptions of the South Asian businessmen.

2. This was a spontaneous response to the earlier question, 'To which class do you feel you belong?' That is, respondents tended to qualify what they felt to be their class position in Britain by the belief that 'it was different at home'.

3. This was one of the responses to the question, 'What were your reasons for going into self-employment?', which allowed for multiple responses.

4. That cleaning and domestic work outside the home has very low status has been noted by Khan in her study of South Asian women in London(1979:121).

5. This was further emphasized in Hindi --"kabhi na leti".

6. Dahya has quite correctly pointed out that the immigrants as a whole, cannot be identified with the industrial proletariat in this country or with the landless category in their society of origin. "One has only to witness the plight and the depressed status of the landless category in Pakistan (and, indeed, in the subcontinent as a whole) in order to appreciate the socio-economic significance of ownership of even small landholdings such as the immigrants and their families possess" (1974:81).

7. Unmarried respondents and women respondents have been omitted.

8. Not to utilise the labour power of women would be at odds with the accepted aspirations for maximisation of economic gain among these migrants.

9. Zamindars are the landowners as distinct from the kamin or the artisans and labourers.

10. This attitude was found to be quite common in a previous survey of families of gulf-migrants from Kerala. "I don't ask him what he does there. He may well be cleaning toilets and I don't want to know about it", said one mother (Srinivasan 1984:67). See also Dahya (1988), for instances of migrants who wish to keep their occupations in Britain a secret from their relatives in Asia.

11. The economic value of the work is perceived in terms of 'the total amount earned each week rather than the number of hours worked to earn it'(Hope *et al.*, 1976:28).

12. Prasad maintains that the establishment of this tradition among the gujerati's of Fiji, is the result of the development of a type of `imitative entrepreneurship' which, according to him, is "the manifestation of the sheep mentality" (1978:276).

13. The lack of the desire to expand existing small businesses is discussed in detail in Chapter 5.

5 The Asian petty bourgeoisie in the class structure

Introduction

The large scale entry of South Asians into self-employment coincides with the general rise in small businesses in Britain and other industrialised countries. According to the *Employment Gazette* of June 1989:

> Self-employment grew rapidly in the 1980s in Britain. Labour Force Survey estimates indicate that between 1981 and 1988, the number of people who were self-employed in their main job grew from just above 2 million to more than 3 million. In the 1980s, the number of self-employed have grown by 136,000 each year on average - and most of the growth has consisted of one-person businesses without employees[1] (Hakim 1989:287).

The petty bourgeoisie,[2] then, has belied all Marxian and liberal expectations.

Marx had claimed in the *Communist Manifesto* that:

> The lower strata of the middle-class - the small trades-people, shopkeepers and retired tradesmen generally, the handicraftsmen and peasants...sink gradually into the proletariat, partly because their diminutive capital does not suffice for the scale on which Modern Industry is carried on, and is swamped in the competition with the large capitalist, partly because their specialised skill is rendered worthless by new methods of production (Marx and Engels 1968:42),

Today, however, it is the persistence and continued reproduction of the petty bourgeoisie which demand attention. The petty bourgeoisie is increasingly being regarded as an essential element of modern capitalism, both in terms of its dynamics as well as its utility in new forms of capitalist production.

The increasing importance of the petty bourgeoisie, in social, political and economic terms, is reflected in the heightening of sociological interest in this class. Where Bechhofer *et al.*(1968), in their seminal paper on small shopkeepers, could complain of the neglect of this numerically preponderant section of the petty bourgeoisie, which, according to them, provided a crucial test of the importance of the property ownership criterion in the determination of class position, a little more than a decade later definite themes in the class analysis of small business owners were becoming apparent (Scase 1982:148-161).[3] While neo-Marxists like Poulantzas (1975), Carchedi (1975), and Wright (1978), attempted theoretical reformulations of the class position of the petty bourgeoisie based on the assumption of it's being a survival of the pre-capitalist form of production, Bechhofer *et al.* (1968, 1974, 1976, 1978), at a more empirical level, speak of the importance of the persistence of this 'uneasy stratum', marginal to the middle class. A third position, forcefully put forward by many, regards the petty bourgeoisie as essential to the dynamics of post-industrial society, not only not marginal in its role in monopoly capitalism, but integral to its reproduction (Berger and Piore 1980; Boissevain 1981; Bechhofer and Elliott 1985).

What is then, the position of the petty bourgeoisie in the contemporary class structure of industrialised countries? This question is considered by focusing on actual social relationships, the meaning and experience of the 'actors' in petty bourgeois positions, rather than attempting any sort of theoretical definition. And further, the question is considered in terms of the Asian petty bourgeoisie in Britain.

Aims and objectives

That the Asians have been in the forefront of the movement into the petty bourgeoisie has been attested to by many. It has been noted earlier that the 1984 PSI survey testifies to a substantial growth in the proportion of Asians who are self-employed. Self-employment is more common among Asians than among whites, with a larger proportion being found in the retail and catering small business sector.[4]

What are the implications of this change in occupational patterns for the class analysis of Asians in Britain? Can we speak of the emergence of an Asian middle-class? And is this occupational change indicative of upward social mobility? As stated in chapter 1, while it is generally agreed that minority groups may look upon self-employment as a route to upward mobility, there is considerable doubt regarding the actual improvement of class position (Scase and Goffee 1982; Ward and Jenkins 1984; Auster and Aldrich 1984; Nowikowski 1984; Aldrich *et al.* 1984; Mars and Ward 1984).

The questions then are: What exactly is the class position of the Asian small business owner, and does movement into the petty bourgeoisie imply social mobility or merely a sideways shift from the lumpenproletariat into the lumpenbourgeoisie.

These issues will be explored in relation to the Asian small business owners in Oxford.

Analysis of class position

Along the lines of Lockwood (1958) as well as Bechhofer *et al.*(1968, 1976), the class position of the Asian small business owners is here analysed in terms of their 'market situation', 'work situation' and 'status situation'. According to Lockwood, class position includes:

> First, 'market situation', that is to say the economic position narrowly conceived, consisting of source and size of income, degree of job-security, and opportunity for upward occupational mobility. Secondly, 'work situation', the set of social relationships in which the individual is involved at work by virtue of his position in the division of labour. And finally, 'status situation', or the position of the individual in the hierarchy of prestige in the society at large (1958:15).

Even while agreeing with the Weberian distinction between 'class' ('market' and 'work-situation') and 'status' ('status situation'), it is argued that any analysis of the class position of an ethnic group will have to recognise the primacy of the market and work situations in the determination of its class position within the society at large. The status dimension will inevitably contain contradictions in so far as the status considerations of the ethnic group and the host society do not and cannot be expected to coincide.[5] Any analysis of the status position of an ethnic group would, therefore, have to take into consideration both systems of stratification - that of the group as well as that of the society as a whole.

The market situation of the small business owner

The position of the small business owner in the market, that is, his economic position, is quite evidently crucial to any discussion of his class position. The economic position is here discussed in terms of:

1) income levels,

2) consumption patterns and ownership of property,

3) security of employment, and

4) prospects for advancement.

1) Income levels

Central to the determination of the economic position is, it must be admitted, the levels of income, turnover, profit. The present survey did not collect this information.[6] However, the notorious unreliability of data on income and profit, has been recognised even by those who produce such data to indicate the small slice of the pie that accrues to small business owners (Bechhofer *et al.* 1978:106, 1968:183). It must be pointed out, on the basis of the survey experience, that, firstly, small business owners are highly unlikely to provide accurate figures for income, profit and turnover; secondly, where figures are provided they will probably tally with those provided for tax purposes, and small business owners are the first to admit that small business thrives on 'tax fiddles' - many of the respondents did. Boissevain has pointed out that that the CERC study of the incomes of independent workers concluded, after an extensive study of the consumer durables they owned, that they earned 50 per cent more than their declared incomes (1981:13). Others, too, have indicated that small entrepreneurs not only earn more than do their salaried counterparts, but also pay less tax on what they earn (*Economist*, 25 February 1978 :46).

That the financial position of respondents is generally sound comes through in various ways. For instance, 80 per cent of the respondents maintained that self-employment in small business was 'financially better' than previous employment,[7] 50 per cent maintaining that their current financial position was much better than it had been two years ago. That these small business owners do not experience any budgeting constraints can be seen from Table 5.1, according to which only 15 per cent determine the amount of money for family use on the basis of how well the business is doing. The majority hold that they take as much as they need to meet all family needs.

Table 5.1 Determination of amount of money for family use

Percentage of respondents taking money

On a Fixed amount basis	According to need	According to how business is doing
32	53	15

(n=94)

This indication of financial well-being is further reinforced by responses to an open question on the 'advantages of the present occupation'. Eighty per cent maintained that it was 'financially very good'.[8] More specific responses were : "Never short of cash", "Don't have to watch your wallet, financially better", "No money problems", "Always money in the pocket", "Worth more money, within reason can get anything", "Earn good money", "Short for nothing, no worry about money", "I can afford what I want, good living", "Earning better than other people". The stereotype of the economically marginal small business owner (Bechhofer *et al.* 1974; Scase and Goffee 1982; Cater *et al.* 1977; Mills 1951), struggling to make ends meet, appears to be belied in this case.

2) *Consumption levels and ownership of property*

Further significant indicators of market situation are house-ownership together with the ownership of other consumer durables. It is clearly evident from Tables 5.2 - 5.5 that levels of consumption are very high among the small business owners. Eighty two per cent of them live in their own houses, and 61 per cent own at least one other house than the one occupied, 31 per cent owning more than three houses. Ninety six per cent own cars with 47 per cent owning two or more cars. Also, a wide range of consumer durables is owned by a large proportion. And, 42 per cent own other businesses (Taxi running, lodging houses, catering, parcel delivering etc.).

Table 5.2 House-ownership

Percentage of respondents living

In Own House (including mortgaged)	Rented House (private) (council)		Rented House with parents
82	9	6	3

(n=94)

Table 5.3 Property owned

Percentage of respondents owning

Other business	Two houses	Three+ houses
42	30	31

(n=94)

Table 5.4 Consumer durables owned

Percentage of respondents owning

TV	Fridge	Phone	Video	Washing Machine	Micro Wave	Stereo	PC
100	100	100	93	89	79	75	45

(n=94)

Table 5.5 Car ownership

Percentage of respondents owning

0 cars	1 car	2+ cars
4	49	47

(n=94)

That levels of house ownership are generally high among South Asians is well established. According to the third PSI survey, 72 per cent of Asians as against 60 per cent of whites, own their houses (Brown 1984:68). In Oxford, however, according to the 1991 Census, 56 per cent of both the South Asian population as a whole, as well as the general population of Oxford City, own their houses, as against 82 per cent of Asian business owners. That levels of house and car ownership among the Asian petty bourgeoisie in Oxford is considerably higher than among both Asians as a whole, as well as the general population of Oxford City, is shown in Table 5.6.

Table 5.6 Comparison of house and car ownership

	House Ownership	Car Ownership
Oxford Residents* Percentage households	56	63
Asians in Oxford** Percentage households	56	64
Asian Business Owners*** Percentage respondents	82	96

*   Source: 1991 Census County Monitor, OPCS June 1992.
** Source: 1991 Census, statistics from Manchester computing service.
*** Source: Present survey

Housing among South Asians is generally believed to be of poor quality in terms of space and amenities, and in poorer areas (Brown 1984; Rafiq 1988). At least as far as the Asian small business owners in Oxford are concerned this is not borne out by the survey - 51 per cent of their houses are located in the 'better'[9] areas of Oxford, and as Table 5.7 shows, 49 per cent live in four-roomed houses and a further 43 per cent in houses with five or more rooms.

Table 5.7 House space

Percentage of respondents living in houses with

3 rooms	4 rooms	5+ rooms
8	49	43

(n=94)

As Bechhofer *et al.* have pointed out, the kind of attitude that underlies these crude ownership figures is very important. The respondents in the present survey, like theirs, not only lived in their own houses, but 75 per cent of them bought the considerable number of consumer durables they owned for cash, only 12 per cent maintaining that some of the durables had been bought on terms of hire purchase. The attitude underlying the pattern of outright ownership certainly appears to be the same as that recognised by Tawney (1921) in his discussion of the symbolic meaning of private property when he talked of 'a limited form of sovereignty'. As Bechhofer *et al.* have maintained:

> Owning your own house (and if possible your business premises), 'paying on the nail' for consumer goods ensures that you are beholden to no one and gives you a measure of control over your own fate (1978:109).

Though 75 per cent of respondents did not have any plans to expand their shops or restaurants, this need not be perceived as an obstacle to business growth as Scase and others have maintained (Scase and Goffee 1982; Scase 1982:159). As noted in chapter 4, the decision not to expand existing businesses is a deliberate one.[10] Though profits may not be ploughed back into the shop or restaurant, it is utilized in various other business ventures such as buying houses to let, cars to run as taxis, part-ownership of other restaurants, and so on.

It can be argued, then, that these small business owners are pursuing a policy of rational capitalism, expansion being seen as diversification rather than as the development of departmental or chain stores and restaurants.

This versatility of those who occupy petty bourgeois positions is something that has received little attention. For many of the respondents, the small shop or restaurant appears almost as just a front for the various activities being carried out behind the scenes - a large percentage can easily be described as having a finger in many a pie.[11]

In diversifying rather than expanding existing businesses, the priority is clearly the acquisition of property. Respondents maintain that the shop or restaurant is very useful in this aim as it provides excellent collateral for obtaining loans from banks, bank loans being utilised by 81 per cent of the population, both for starting their shops as well as further acquisition of property.

3) Security of employment

It has been stressed that income and consumption patterns do not constitute the whole of the economic aspect of class stratification, and that security of employment as well as prospects for advancement, must be considered (Goldthorpe and Lockwood 1963:137; Lockwood 1958:15). A point constantly emphasized in the literature is that the persistence of the petty bourgeoisie goes along with rapid turnover in personnel, that the failure rates of small businesses are extremely high and hence for the individual small business owner, his occupation offers little security (Bechhofer *et al.* 1978). While there is not yet conclusive evidence for this, it is beginning to be recognised that ethnic businesses may have much lower failure rates than those of the native born. Lower failure rates and more sustained growth of 'overseas born' small businesses have been clearly established for Australia (Kitay and Lever-Tracy 1990:3; Strahan and Williams 1988:38). For the U.K. as well:

> In preliminary analysis of data from Bradford, Leicester, and London, Aldrich and McEvoy (1983) found a strikingly low failure rate for Asian owned businesses between 1978 and 1980; only about two in ten failed or moved away, compared to one in three white-owned shops (Auster and Aldrich 1984:50).

Wilson and Stanworth, in their study of ethnic businesses in Brent, found that failure rates of Asian businesses (12 per cent) were roughly equivalent to national failure rates (11 per cent) for retailing and services activities (1985:20). It must however, be noted that 'failure' has been treated:

> ...widely...and is taken to mean firstly, clearly observed closure of a premises where trading has ceased (at least overtly); secondly, transfer of a business as a going concern to another owner; and thirdly, significant change in the type of activity operating on the site (Wilson and Stanworth 1985:16).

It may well be this definition of failure which results in reported higher rates. Rafiq has pointed out, quite correctly, that if the failure rate is taken as including movement of the business from one part of a city to another, or the setting up of the business outside the city, it reflects the failure of the business site rather than the business itself, hence leading to an over estimation of failures (1988). That the determination of 'failure' requires greater care, is brought out by the present survey which revealed the following:

> 1) There were a few shopkeepers (five per cent), who appeared to be on the verge of closing down, but all of them contemplated setting up another business, either of a different kind or in a different place;

2) In the three cases of business closure (as distinct from people changing premises, shutting down one business and starting another immediately, etc.), encountered in the course of this survey, one was of a Pakistani, who after more than twenty five years of shop ownership, (during which period he had accumulated a number of properties in Oxford, which had been given out on rent), rented out his shop premises to an Asian restaurateur, and returned home together with his wife and school going children. This could in no way be regarded as a business failure. It also appears to substantiate anecdotal evidence provided by the respondents, according to which there were few business failures in Oxford as most shops which had closed down in the earlier years had done so because owners had made their fortunes and returned to India or Pakistan.

The other two businesses which closed during the survey were owned by transport workers. They tried their hand at shop-keeping for a few months, did not succeed, but were not greatly discommoded as they had retained their jobs and were able to sell or rent their shop premises at a profit.

3) The general impression obtained is certainly one of stability and security. During the survey, a few respondents did specifically mention job security as one of the advantages of small business:

No one can sack you, you don't have to worry about where your next money is coming from. (No.80)

Permanence, security, no worry of losing job. (No.88)

Job security, your job is in your own hands. (No.66)

A job (paid employment) is never secure, but that is not the case with self-employment. Now my Bank Manager comes to me. (No.30)

4) Prospects for advancement

As far as prospects for advancement are concerned, the respondents were clearly of the view that in entering business they had taken the first important step towards success and that self-employment offered the only route to substantial financial prosperity. While entry into self-employment *per se* did result in status enhancement, once entry had been achieved, status rose concomitantly with financial success. That paid employment could never provide the same financial benefits as self-employment was quite emphatically stated by a number of respondents, as can be seen from the following quotes:

Working for someone else is worth nothing. It is of no use. You work and you have nothing to show for it. But in self-employment, if you work hard enough you get results - you can make something of your life. After fifteen to twenty years of hard work in self-employment, you are made for life - you can actually retire earlier than in paid employment. (No.50)

Even if the shop is not doing too well and you are struggling, you are not really a loser because you are getting enough to get by, as much as you would get when working in a factory, for instance. But, in the shop, what you make is all yours. If you work hard, you earn more, and **you** get that, not anybody else. (No.20)

Thirteen years of working as a computer analyst and at the end of the day you have no money in the bank. You work and the money goes into someone else's pocket. In business, you make money, you make a big jump financially. (No.42)

When you are working for someone else you cannot accumulate much. And to buy a house you have to pay a larger mortgage. But if you have a business, you accumulate money, and it is quite easy to make a large down payment which reduces the mortgage. (No.49)

Better to work for yourself - the more hours you put in the more rewarding it can be. In the factory you get a set wage and also you can be made redundant or sacked. (No.80)

Because of my business background I knew where the money was. My shop has helped me build up something I had never dreamed off, which I wouldn't have had otherwise. (No.30)

Working in the factory you don't know what you are doing, where you are going. At least when you are self-employed you are getting the true worth of your labour. (No.19)

There are certainly other jobs I could have, but again, certainly, there's never as much money in anything else. (No.68)

Of course we are all better off financially - all of us who have gone into self-employment. Don't let anyone tell you otherwise. If I hadn't been successful I wouldn't have stayed on in the same business for fifteen years, would I? And, I don't know anyone in Oxford who has gone bust. They have all expanded, got bigger shops, improved themselves. Of course, initially it may be a bit of a struggle, but once the business gets going it is fine. (No.54)

A point that should be emphasized here is that these are the responses of people who are already successfully self-employed, and not merely the pipe dreams of those who would follow in the celebrated Horatio Alger tradition of American society, such as Chinoy's automobile workers or the affluent workers studied by Goldthorpe *et al.* (Chinoy 1955; Goldthorpe *et al.* 1968:131-6). The present respondents are clearly people who see their economic future as being in their own hands - the more work you put in, the greater your rewards - and, all future advancement is visualised in terms of acquisition of more property, to become men of solid worth. The market situation of the South Asian small business owner in Oxford, then, appears to be quite healthy.

According to Bechhofer *et al.*(1971:175-79), some of the strategies which may help the small shop-keepers to improve their market position are: membership of voluntary chains, utilization of Cash and Carry wholesalers, adoption of self-service trading, and formation of traders associations. However, only three of the respondents in the Oxford survey had joined a voluntary chain for grocery supplies. On the other hand, all the general stores, grocers, and newsagents, patronised Cash and Carry wholesalers, (occasionally quite distant ones if discounts or sales were being offered), and all of them had also adopted self-service trading practices. While 22 per cent of shops were members of Commercial or traders associations, 59 per cent of these were the general stores which included sub post-offices where the owners were members of the association of sub post-masters. The general feeling was that membership was not in any way essential for successful business activity. Accepted strategies of improvement are, then, not necessarily the ones adopted by these South Asian small business owners.

What can be regarded as an important strategy adopted by the small shop today is that of extensive diversification of sale products. Any clear cut categorisation of small shops into grocers, newsagents, tobacconists and confectioners, butchers, video parlours, florists, and so on, is no longer possible, as any one shop will carry most items, thus maximising its 'convenience' potential. These shops are able to charge higher prices safe in the knowledge that customers are willing to pay more for the convenience of getting practically anything they need just around the corner, and at practically all hours as well.[12] As one shopkeeper put it:

> When the English think of taking the car out, driving to the supermarket, finding parking space, etc., they prefer to pay a few pence more at the local corner shop. Only the Asian customer grumbles about higher prices and takes the trouble of always going to Tesco's or Sainsbury's (No.7)

Thus, where Bechhofer *et al.*, could speak of the declining importance of the small shop and the erosion of its asset of ready accessibility in the face of multiples and the large retail stores, and of the economies of scale available to the latter, which could be increasingly utilised because of increasing car ownership (1968:184), the picture appears to be very different in Oxford, today.

The work situation of the small business owner

The work situation of the small business owner is discussed in terms of:

    1) his independence,

    2) the social arena of the shop, and

    3) the satisfaction of the small business owner in his work.

1) Independence

Central to the small business owner's experience of his work situation is the fact of independence or 'being one's own boss'. 'Autonomy', 'freedom to do what one wants', 'being one's own boss', 'independence', were the standard responses made by 80 per cent of respondents, to the question, 'What would you say are the advantages of self-employment?'[13] There is nothing unusual in this - all previous literature on the self-employed, irrespective of ethnicity of owner, stresses this factor which is crucial to the perception of the occupation as inherently rewarding, despite the apparent disadvantages of long hours and hard work.

    In the case of the ethnic shop-keeper or restaurateur, however, this factor of 'independence' gains greater importance, as it turns the important arena of work into the one arena where the member of an ethnic minority perceives himself in a position of power or control or authority *vis-à-vis* the host society. Owning your own small business means that "you are creating your own employment", and one in which you "do not have to lick the white man's shoes" (No.18). More importantly, self-employment signifies not just escape from white domination or discrimination, but some measure of control in relations with the white population. This operates at two levels - i.e., that of the small business-owner and his employees, as well as that of the small business owner and his clientele.

The small business owner and his employees

Admittedly, the number of shop-keepers who employ full-time labour is quite small, but over 50 per cent have at least one part time employee. What is interesting is that from amongst those shop-keepers who do employ labour, 42 per cent employ at least one white person, with a small minority of 6 per cent employing 3+ white persons. The employment of white labour is increasingly becoming an important business practice for Asian small business owners:

> Had thought of employing white lady to boost sales... (No.18)
> Would like to have an English girl in the front. Our restaurants don't employ women generally, but I'm thinking of doing it. (No.77)

Good for business to have a white person serving in the shop.
(No.26) (No.1)

If a shop is thinking of taking on an employee, the first preference is often for a white person, a white employee being seen as giving a certain cachet to an Asian shop or restaurant.

The small business owner and his clientele

In the sphere of owner-customer relations, two strands - those of conflict and of cooperation, are quite clearly evident, the ethnic owner perceiving himself as having the upper hand in both. On the one hand, conflict is manifest in the occurrence of racism, but, when the Asian faces racism within the shop or restaurant precincts, he feels better able to handle it:

> It is my shop and I don't stand for any nonsense. If they can't behave I just tell them to get out. (No.17)

> I'm very firm with people who are openly racist. I tell them off properly. You get someone who comes into your shop and says, "where do you get the money to start business? You people always manage it, but it is our money you are taking, etc.," but, I give as good as I get. I tell them I'm paying taxes just as anyone else and even paying for the shirt on his back as he's on social security. (No.34)

> You get these white people coming into the restaurant, after the pubs close, drunk and noisy. I just refuse them admittance, and get them off the premises fast. They can be abusive, but I know how to handle them. (No.82)

However, it is also generally agreed that the sort of whites who would come into the shop or restaurant and cause trouble, ask for credit, or behave in an obnoxious manner, are 'the good for nothing, the tramps and drunks', and these are 'the people you can afford to ignore'.

Generally, harmonious relations prevail between the ethnic small business owner and his clientele, which it must be remembered, is largely white. The adage of 'the customer is always right' is assiduously adhered to, 89 per cent of our respondents answering 'very important' to the question on how important 'good relations with customers' was to the efficient running of their business. As Table 5.8 shows, this is the factor which is given the most importance.

Table 5.8 Factors important to business efficiency[14]

percentage of respondents regarding

	Unimp. imp.	Not Very imp.	Fairly imp.	Very
Business Experience	0	26	17	57
Contacts with Asian Businessmen	25	39	17	19
Talent	0	24	47	29
Customer Relations	0	2	9	89

(n=94)

Successful retailing in a small shop is absolutely dependent on good relations with the customer and the personalised service provided by the Asian corner shop is one of its most important assets. That the Asian shop-keeper is aware of this, is revealed by the following:

> I believe in chatting up my customers. There has to be a good joking relationship with customers. Many local people come into the shop just for a chat. On the way out they may buy a couple of things as well. But if they know they can come just for a chat they are more likely to come in again. The Asian shop-keeper doesn't keep shop-keeping at a purely business level like the British one. (No.9)

> The knack needed in shop-keeping is patience and friendliness. You have to know your customers and be on good terms with them. Often, they just come in for a natter, and my husband and children complain that I spend too much time nattering with them. (No.20)

> People come in wanting to talk, to tell you their problems or share a joke, and if you listen to them and share their problems, they keep coming back. Its not just a question of telling customers the price of goods and taking their money. You have to be friendly and smile even at people you may not particularly like. With many of the regular customers, you know what they come in for, you remember their likes and dislikes - this is the sort of service a chain store cannot provide. (No.13)

> Most of our customers are regulars, some of them 10 years old, as old as the shop. They even tell me their family secrets. That woman over there, she turned her mother out of her house this

morning, and both have been in to tell me their stories. You have to be understanding, and listen to their troubles. (No.28)

Being friendly and polite is really the most important thing. If you are good with your customers, they are good with you. There are many elderly customers who rely on you to help them choose their Christmas presents, birthday cards, etc., and they trust you so much that they hand over their purse to you and ask you to take out the change. (No.34)

Its less than a year since we opened this shop, but we know our regular customers by name. They love it when we greet them by their names, and remember their likes and dislikes. (No.33)

The post-office is very important - because of it, I know the regular clientele by name. I know what most of them are doing, I know when they are unemployed, when they have problems. The post office brings them in, and once they are on friendly terms, they buy things from the shop as well. (No.52)

However, even while making every effort to maintain cordial and friendly relations, the Asian shop-keeper or restaurateur defers to his white clientele, safe in the awareness that the white person is coming to him to be served, and hence, he, the owner, is in a superior position. Thus, according to a fairly upmarket Indian shop-owner:

When you have the shop, people come to you to be served, you are not going out to them, so they have to be polite - the position is different. (No.53)

Similarly, according to the highly successful Pakistani owner of a general store in an area which would be classed as a good residential area of Oxford:

Racism is always there. They don't show it to my face in the shop - they can't. They want to use the shop - its convenient for them, isn't it? So they don't say anything to me...sometimes it gets me angry, but the knack of shop-keeping is to be friendly and pleasant - how else can you keep your customers? You cannot afford to be moody or grumpy. You have to be pleasant, or they will not come again. (No.24)

In his work situation, whether he is resisting racism or being friendly, the owner is at all times aware of the shop or restaurant as his castle. The independence that small business bestows is, then, particularly significant to the ethnic small business owner.

2) *The shop as a social arena*

Some attention has been given to the role of the shop as a social centre. Klingender, writing in 1951, had drawn attention to the small shop as "the working class housewives' neighbourhood club". According to him:

> ...the chat in the queue or over the counter their (the housewives') only chance of social intercourse...This also explains why many shopkeepers (especially women) do not consider their excessively long working hours a hardship: they too enjoy the social life in their shop, thus combining business with pleasure (1951:18).

That, this holds true even today for the Asian shop, is clear from the previous section. And this has two important implications:

First, today, with 80 per cent of the shops reporting 95 per cent of their clientele as non-ethnic,[15] the social interaction in the shop is interaction with the host society. The shop is an important arena of Asian British contact - the exchange of jokes, the banter and camaraderie, the shop-keeper's considerable knowledge of his regular customers family and home life, problems and joys, his role as agony aunt *vis-à-vis* his customers are all indicative of social relations of a high degree of amicability.

It has been maintained (Patterson 1968; Wright 1968:11-13), that 'social integration within the works environment' need not necessarily result in general 'social integration', which according to Wright:

> ...(is) measured by the extent to which race or ethnic group membership per se is a factor determining social distance between members of an immigrant or minority group and members of the host society (Wright 1968:13).

It could be argued that the shop environment presents a work-environment where the level of interaction between the Asians and the English extends beyond that of mere work or business into the social arena, and that differences in cultural background do not impinge on this interaction, so that some measure of integration in social interaction is achieved.

Secondly, if there is no separation between work and social life, between business and pleasure, between shop, home and family, the whole question of long hours, exploitation of family and the drudgery of shop-keeping will have to be reconsidered. Where Mills (1951), Bechhofer *et al.*(1968, 1974), and others highlight these negative aspects of the shop-keepers' work situation, it must be pointed out that on the other side of the coin are the positive aspects of flexible working hours without the necessity of 'clocking in and out', the possibility of dual occupations, a variegated social life within the work environment, and for the ethnic shop-keeper, the utilization of female labour within cultural constraints, and a position of power *vis-à-vis* the white customers. For the Asian shop-keepers, life in the shop is a whole way of life, where neither the hours worked nor the number of people working is consciously calculated. That co-operation of all family members and the consequent flexibility in hours worked by individual members mitigates the 'disadvantage of long hours' has been mentioned earlier.[16] What shop-keepers emphasize is that activities which salaried counterparts may have to postpone for the weekend or other holidays, can be indulged in at any time that suits their fancy. The researcher was told many a time:

> If I were working in a factory or for someone else, I wouldn't have been able to give you so much time. Now my time is my own.

Thus, one shopkeeper takes his sons swimming after they return from school. Another one's wife takes time off from the shop in the morning to be among the first at a Marks and Spencer's sale. The work situation is, then, not looked upon as exploitative by the small business owners or their family.

3) Job satisfaction

Finally, a part of the work situation would be the satisfaction that the shop-keeper finds in his work. Is self-employment a satisfactory job option or is it a case of Hobson's choice? It has been suggested that shop-keepers find their work irksome, that many take to it only because finding a significantly better paid job with the sort of qualifications they have would be difficult, and that more than 50 per cent would like to get out of retailing (Bechhofer *et al.* 1974:112). It is here argued that, to the contrary, with the South Asian small business owners studied, satisfaction with self-employment is very high.

That self assessment of job satisfaction is highly suspect, has been quite well established by now (Goldthorpe *et al.* 1968; Blauner 1960). It may, however, be given some consideration in view of the fact that the very positive responses obtained to the question, 'How satisfied are you with your present job? Please mark yourself out of ten', are highly consistent with the responses to three related questions asked at different places in the interview schedule.[17] These questions were:

> 1) Would you consider the alternative jobs available to you to be better or worse than the present one?

> 2) If you had a choice between your present job and being a paid employee with a higher income, which would you prefer?

> 3) Over the next three years how likely are you to look for a job working for someone else as a paid employee?

The responses to these questions are presented in Tables 5.9 - 5.12.

Table 5.9 Self-assessment of job-satisfaction

Percentage of respondents giving themselves

4-6/10	7/10	8/10	9/10	10/10
7	15	32	19	27

(n=94)

Table 5.10 Job alternatives better or worse?

Percentage of respondents maintaining job alternatives

Better	Worse	Not Sure
6	85	9

(n=94)

Table 5.11 Choice between self-employment and paid employment

Percentage of respondents preferring

Self-Employment	Paid Employment	Paid Employment under certain conditions
75	15	10

n=94

Table 5.12 Likelihood of job change

percentage of respondents maintaining job change

Likely	May be/May be not	Very Unlikely	Don't Know
8	4	85	3

n=94

It must also be stressed that in addition to asking the above questions, the study involved considerable interaction with, and observation of small business owners. Thus, while there were complaints of 'long hours', 'can never take a holiday', 'its a dog's life really', 'Never been sick, can't afford to', it was also evident that even while voicing these sentiments, there was nothing else most respondents would rather do. Business was a way of life on which they thrived, hard work and long hours notwithstanding, as is very clear from the following quotes:

> Oh, I enjoy the work. Otherwise I wouldn't have continued doing it all these years, would I? (No.60)

> I *did* have what you could call a better job - a qualified job - 'A' rate and top wages as shop steward (British Leyland). But I decided to give it up for the shop. 'Interest' is what made me stay in the shop. Its an active life - a challenge to make it go, and I thrive on a challenge... (No.20)

> Once you get self-employed, you will never like to work for someone else. This job is a challenge. This is mine. If I'm working under someone else, my rights are limited... (No.65)

> What better job? This is a cushy job, and no jobs with higher pay (No.1)

> I'm very satisfied. I have worked hard, but now, if I want I can pull out of shop keeping and just sit back - live by simply skimming the cream off my investments... (No.9)

The dismal picture painted by earlier writers (Klingender 1951; Mills 1951; Bechhofer *et al.* 1968), does not appear to be quite accurate - at least not for the South Asians in Oxford today; The respondents appeared well satisfied with their work situation and disinclined to exchange it for any other.

The status situation of the small business owner

In discussing the status aspect of small business, it is necessary to distinguish between:

> 1) the prestige of the occupation as such, of which an important criterion is its being clean and non-manual, and therefore 'respectable'. Other criteria include the rewards and responsibilities the occupation offers, as also the education required for the job (Lockwood 1958:99), and,

> 2) the social standing of those who are involved in the occupation as revealed by the 'relational' and the 'normative aspect of class', i.e. their styles of life, attitudes and values (Goldthorpe and Lockwood 1963).

1) *Status of the occupation*

As far as the first aspect is concerned, there need be little debate; The variety of occupations 'that most people would agree were middle class', includes shopkeeping and business (Lewis and Maude 1949).[18]

In so far as the small business owner is engaged in clean, non-manual work, is independent, an employer rather than an employee, and is in control over his work situation, he would seem to be the incumbent of a 'respectable' middle class position, albeit a lower middle class one. But, in recent years writers have been challenging this middle class status position of small business. Attention has been drawn to the widespread 'ideological' disdain, which grew during the 1960s and early 1970s, for small business:

> 'small' connotated 'archaic', 'inefficient', 'improfitable'...Graduates looking for jobs rarely expressed any desire to enter small business. The real excitement, the chance of a career and the prospects of a fat salary were to be found with the big concerns. Small business then found few champions; it enjoyed little ideological support (Elliott and McCrone 1982:123).

Does this really hold of the South Asians in Oxford today?
According to Lockwood:

> The social status of an occupation depends in part on the social origins of the individuals who enter it. The fact that an occupation recruits its members from higher social strata of the population is at once an index and a cause of its social standing (1958:106).

One way of testing the general standing of small business is, then, to look at the patterns of recruitment into it. That small business has a wide base as far as recruitment goes is well recognized:

> Skilled manual workers can and do move into it from below, while from within its bulging ranks it raises its own spiralists to higher rungs on the income and status ladder. This lower middle class also serves as a net that cushions the fall of the skidders and the superannuated of both the higher middle class and the *grande bourgeoisie* (Mayer 1975:432).

What is interesting, however, is that today, there appears to be a tendency, at least within the South Asian community, for not just 'the superannuated and the skidders' of the higher middle class, but the actively employed, salaried professionals, to take to small business. If amongst the petty bourgeoisie, there are members who are simultaneously members of the salaried professional class, and those who have opted out of   professional jobs to pursue self-employment trajectories, it produces the interesting phenomenon of voluntary movement into the petty bourgeoisie out of the professional occupations, normally regarded as constituting a clear instance of downward mobility (Goldthorpe 1987:43), being regarded as desirable.

Table 5.13 Class of job previous to present one

Previous Job of Small Business Owners (Percentage)

Profession	Non-Manual	Small Proprietor	Manual	Unemployed	Present Job First one
20	9	13	50	3	5

(n=94)

It is clear from Table 5.13 that a significant minority of 20 per cent of the small business owners held professional jobs before starting small business; Most continue with them even after business start up.

If middle class recruitment to small business is increasing (of course the numbers are very small and must be interpreted with caution), then, it is possible that the it indicates an improvement in the general social status of small business. Of course, 50 per cent of the present self-employed come from a background of manual work, and for them self-employment is clearly a step upward. However, if 20 per cent come from a professional background, it appears to indicate some improvement in the status of small business. A possible rationale for this could be:

1) the greater significance given to the criterion of sheer ownership of property as an indicator of class position,

2) the realization that capital accumulation is a viable alternative to educational attainment for upward social mobility,

3) that the only route to substantial capital accumulation is self-employment.

2) The relational and normative aspects

But, to determine whether the incumbent is himself 'middle class', his style of life, his attitudes and values, have to be considered. And, to look at the 'actor' rather than the 'position' is also to keep in mind the differences between ethnic small business owners and their local counterparts, that is, differences in styles of life, as well as in attitudes and values, which are the result of ethnicity rather than class.

Styles of life and behaviour - the relational aspect of class

Among the patterns of social behaviour regarded as characteristically middle class are mutual entertainment between couples and visiting between neighbours, relatively high rates of participation in voluntary associations (Goldthorpe and Lockwood 1963:142; Young and Wilmott 1957:91-95;), as also political affiliation with the Conservative party (Bechhofer and Elliott 1974:115, 1978; Butler and Stokes 1971; Heath 1983).

Some of the patterns of behaviour prevalent among respondents are set out in Tables 5.14 - 5.16.

Table 5.14 Relations with neighbours

Percentage of respondents

Visiting Terms	Casual Chatting	No Contact
21	70	9

n=94

Table 5.15 Leisure time activities[19]

percentage respondents maintaining

No Leisure	Visit Relations	Visit Relations + Friends	TV + Home	Other
41	15	17	14	13

n=94

Table 5.16 Participation in community organisations

percentage of respondents maintaining

Regular Participation	Occasional	No Participation
22	35	43

n=94

That only 21 per cent of respondents are on visiting terms with their neighbours, and only 17 per cent mention visiting friends in their leisure time, is clear from Tables 5.14 and 5.15. That they lead completely home and family centred lives is quite apparent from answers to a question on 'close friends',[20] in that 28 per cent maintained that they had no close friends at all, and associated mainly with family and relations. Some of the oft-repeated responses were as follows:

No close friends. I'm friendly with a lot of people but like to be independent...Prefer to keep to myself (No.32)

No one other than wife and relations (No.40)

Cousins, brothers, - no other close friends (No.19)

The following responses to the question on 'leisure time', revealed a similar pattern:

What leisure time?! If I get any I watch TV and spend time with my family. (No.36)

Read books, watch TV, chat with my wife and visit relations. (No.65)

We have no friends really, we visit relations, sometimes outside Oxford, in Birmingham... (No.67)

On Sundays we drive to London, to see my parents and to go to the temple. (No.1)

Restaurant hours are very unsocial. My social life is in the restaurant. The rest of the time I'm with my family. (No.77)

Life-styles, then, are very different from accepted middle-class ones. There are, however, two points to be noted here:

1) While there may be flexibility in the hours worked by any individual, the business remains open for an average of 78 hours a week, with a minimum of 48 hours for some, and a maximum of 112 for a small number. It is quite evident then, that the exigencies of the job give 'socialising' only peripheral importance.

2) A moot question is whether the life-styles of respondents are influenced by their class position or by their ethnic origin. Thus, while only 21 per cent were on visiting terms with their neighbours, it must also be kept in mind that 76 per cent of respondents have only white and non-Asian neighbours. Again, while 57 per cent do participate in community organisations, these are all Asian organisations.

A further point regarding the relational or status aspect is that, as far as these ethnic minority respondents are concerned, this aspect assumes a double dimension in that it becomes necessary to look at the status of the small business owner in relation to his own ethnic group, as well as in relation to the host society.

That the respondents perceive their status position within the ethnic group as considerably enhanced by entry into small business has been described in detail earlier.[21] It may also be pointed out that one of the factors to which Bechhofer and Elliott attribute the falling status of the small shopkeeper is the increasing size of communities due to urbanisation, and hence the dissociation of shopkeepers from 'big business' (1968:190). It is suggested here, that within the ethnic community, where everyone knows of everyone else, this factor is not operative, just the fact of owning a 'business' implying community acknowledgement of some elevation of status.

As far as status within the larger society is concerned, as pointed out by Werbner:

> Being in the society but - as strangers - not of it, they are freed from their hosts' frame of reference, and thus able to pursue a way of living which is, in the Pakistani case, particularly supportive of entrepreneurs (1984:167).

This appears true of the present population as well. Again as noted earlier in chapter 4, there is some degree of awareness that British society on the whole may not have as high a regard for small business as themselves:
A joke repeated quite a few times was,

> Do you know why the English are building straight roads these days? So that there won't be any corners for the Paki's to build shops on!
> Oh! They take the mickey out of us for being shop-keepers, don't they? (No.45)

> From the British point of view, the image of the shop-keeper is very tarnished. They don't think very much of us. Of course, Asians still regard shopkeeping as good. But the English, they are jealous of Asian shop-keepers. They envy us our success. (No.80)

But, there is also a belief that even the English have to respect wealth and prosperity:

> They don't know how much I have in the bank, but they see my shop, my houses, my cars, and the public,- they speak of me as 'stinking rich' - that's where the prestige lies. (No.38)

> They know I'm well off. They have to respect my wealth. (No.9)
> At the end of the day, how wealthy you are is what matters. (No.77)

> People have to respect property. They know I have a shop, houses, and a fat bank balance. (No.55)

The final point regarding the relational or status aspect concerns the political affiliation of the South Asian small business owners. Table 5.17

shows that 54 per cent of the respondents opt for the Labour Party as the party they support:

Table 5.17 Support for political parties

Percentage of respondents supporting

Labour	Conservative	Other	None	Won't Tell
54	34	2	8	2

n=94

The interesting question here, is whether the party affiliation of this petty bourgeois group is indicative of its 'true' position in the stratification hierarchy, or, whether 'ethnicity' is the dominant influence on voting patterns?

Staunch Asian support for the Labour party is a well documented fact (Anwar 1986, 1990; Heath 1991; Studlar 1978). The findings for the Oxford South Asian petty bourgeoisie appear to replicate this. But, just as well documented as the ethnic Labour vote is the Conservative affiliation of the British petty bourgeoisie (Bechhofer and Elliott 1974, 1978; Heath *et al.* 1985). Despite the general heterogeneity of the petty bourgeoisie, there is, according to Bechhofer and Elliott, a certain homogeneity in basic values in this class. Economic individualism, belief in the importance of private property as a measure of security, independence, success and upward mobility, the myth of individual success, is particularly relevant where petty bourgeois groups are concerned. Bechhofer and Elliott refer to this set of values as part of the ideological currency of Western society, and as the major reason underlying petty bourgeoisie support for the Conservative party. This set of values, however, is to be found in the South Asian petty bourgeoisie as well. The set of values and beliefs, that without ownership of property a man is worthless, that individual effort and hard work is the only route to success, that self employment provides the only chance of substantial financial prosperity, cuts across all distinctions within the South Asian group - of country of origin, religion, and social background. And yet, 54 per cent support Labour.

That there is an ethnic impact on party support cannot be denied. In fact, as against the findings of Anwar (1986), the respondents in the present survey tend to give ethnicity related reasons for Labour leanings, as can be seen from the following:

Labour is the party for ethnic minorities. (No.38)

All our people vote Labour, don't they? (No.24) (No.13)

The Tories may be supporting small business, but we are Asians. We vote Labour. (No.80)

113

I have always voted Labour. My father-in-law was here in the 1930s, and he was a staunch Labour supporter. (No.53)

Support for the Asian community comes from Labour. We don't look to the business when we vote. Labour supports our community so we vote Labour. (No.73)

Ethnicity then, appears to cut across class affiliation where political interests are concerned.

It is suggested then, that the interactional patterns and political affiliation of the small business owners should not be seen so much as indicative of lack of 'middle-classness', as a reminder of their ethnic origin.

Attitudes and values

It has been well established in earlier chapters that, normatively, the attitudes and values of the respondents, correspond to a very great extent to what Goldthorpe and Lockwood have characterised as the middle class perspective (1963:147). To recapitulate, it has been established that the respondents believe that by hard work and initiative one can make something of one's life, that success is possible with hard work, that accumulation of money is very important, that people who waste time and money get nowhere. Ideological contempt for the British working class, which relies on benefits and yet throws away money on liquor and leisure without any thought of the future, is also quite apparent.

Finally, it may noted that the middle class perspective is very evident when it comes to 'aspirations for children'. It can be seen from Table 5.18 that 36 per cent of the respondents would like their children to go into 'professional jobs' specifically those of doctors, lawyers, engineers, accountants.

Table 5.18 Choice of occupation for children

Percentage of respondents preferring

Professions	Business	What children like	Don't Know
36	7	35	22

(n=94)

To what extent are these aspirations realised? Among the respondents, 36 per cent had one child, 26 per cent a second, and 14 per cent a third child as well, in employment. Table 5.19 provides a comparison of the occupational attainments of the first three children of those respondents who had offspring in employment, with national mobility figures for the children of self-employed fathers.

Table 5.19 Class of children's occupation

	I,II	III	IV	V,VI,VII
Percentage of children of Oxford Asian petty bourgeoisie	30	24	30	16
(n=62)				
Percentage of national petty bourgeoisie children*	24	8	24	44

*source: Goldthorpe 1987:49

Though only a minority of respondents had children who were employed, 54 per cent of these children were in Class I, II, and III occupations. Comparison with national mobility results does suggest that within the petty bourgeoisie as a whole, the children of the Oxford Asians have relatively better mobility chances. They may then, be considered a relatively privileged section of the national petty bourgeoisie.

It can also be seen from Table 5.19 that 30 per cent of the employed children, are self-employed. It is generally accepted that 'if you have no qualifications, small business is best', but further, what is implicit in the respondents' conversations is that desirable though they may be, professional qualifications and professional jobs alone are not enough - together with these there should be business ownership as well. As one restaurant owner put it:

> Even if I had been able to get academic qualifications, the only sort of jobs I may have preferred to business would be those of a scientist, doctor or lawyer...but, even with this, my ambition to succeed could be met only through running my own business. (No.77)

Hence, even if children of successful businessmen acquire qualifications and professional jobs, thus fulfilling the aspirations of their parents, this does not preclude their entry into small business as well. Patel has observed that, in Bradford, the development of Pharmaceutical chemists and other service businesses is a manifestation of the utilisation of education and training to advantage in business (1987:21).

t is argued then, that the analysis of the Oxford South Asian petty bourgeoisie in terms of market, work, and status conditions, reveals that the small business owners may be seen as upwardly mobile and as a well established section of the middle class. Further, it is suggested that the continued reproduction of this class together with its increasing importance, which some have attributed to the technological changes of 'post-industrial' society, dissatisfaction with bureaucratic organisations, greater concern with the 'quality of life',[22] and so on, is also to be understood in terms of a shift in ideological support for sheer ownership of property which forms the basis of the petty bourgeoisie. In the multi-cultural societies of today, status considerations appear to be becoming increasingly fluid and greater importance being given to property. With greater convergence in life styles such that privatised and family centred living is common to a wide range of occupational groupings, the social imagery of the crass *nouveaux riches* also gets considerably diluted as actual instances of social interaction are reduced. The market and work situations then gain greater importance, and 'class' becomes increasingly determined by the property ownership criterion. And for the migrants, the people with 'projects',[23] in the context of the society of destination, 'property' and 'lack of property' do become "the basic categories of all class situations" (Gerth and Mills 1948:182), all status being seen as deriving directly from the possession of property.

Notes

1. While Angela Dale (1986) appears to see this as the basis of her claim that the increase in businesses is really only an increase in women homeworkers without capital or work autonomy, according to Goldthorpe, "Class IV, that of small proprietors and self-employed workers, has clearly grown - and further ...this growth has been greatest among self-employed workers *with* employees"(1987:262). This is certainly true as far as the Asian self-employed are concerned - 43 per cent of them fall into the category of 'less than 5 employees' as against 27 per cent with no employees (Brown 1984:210).

2. The numerically most important grouping within the petty bourgeoisie, according to Goldthorpe, is that of the small retailers (1987:42, 65).

3. See also Bechhofer and Elliot (1985), and Curran and Burrows (1986 1987).

4. See chapter 1.

5. This has been noted earlier in chapter 4, where the focus was on status considerations as a motivating force in business entry.

6. See Methodological appendix.

7. Bechhofer *et al.* admit in a footnote to their 1968 paper that, "Clearly, even the most marginal of the small businessmen enjoy considerable advantages in market and work situations if one compares them with many working class groups" (p.182).

8. See Table 3.2, chapter 3.

9. 'Better' areas of Oxford are those generally regarded as having residents of a higher class, such as North Oxford. Those areas not regarded as 'better' are the areas known to be working class areas which are generally also the areas of higher ethnic minority concentrations, such as Cowley Road and adjoining areas, St. Clements, Blackbird Leys, etc. While some support for this is to be found in the work of Collison and Mogey (1958-1959:599-605), the classification is to some extent subjective.

10. That the lack of a desire to expand existing businesses, or invest in industry, is not necessarily irrational, has been established by Fox (1973), in his study of Hindu Baniyas in a small north Indian town, and by Mines (1973), in his study of Tamil Muslim merchants of Pallavaram. Both find that the merchants are unwilling to expand their scale of operations or invest in industry due to social, political and economic factors, so that their behaviour is quite rational.

11. It is suggested here that this is part of what Scase is complaining of when he speaks of "..a neglect of the empirical dynamics whereby the petty bourgeoisie are reproduced under the conditions of monopoly capitalism. This would seem to be the result of excessively abstract analyses which focus exclusively upon positions rather than actors, that assume their progressive decline and, which fail, therefore, to study empirically present-day processes." (Scase, 1982:154).

12. See Boissevain's 'quality of life' argument (1981:23).

13. This was noted earlier, in chapter 3, where the focus was on 'the desire to be one's own boss', as a motivating factor in business entry.

14. The actual question asked was: In order to run your business competently, how important are the following factors?
Lengthy experience of this type of work
Good contacts with customers
Having a particular talent or knack for this type of work
Having good relations with other businessmen in the community

15. See Table 3.8, Chapter 3

16. See Chapter 3 and 4.

17. Goldthorpe *et al.* chose to omit the direct question on job satisfaction, and approach the matter obliquely, by asking respondents to compare their current job with others held previously, as well as, those regarded as potentially open to them (1968:10-37). In the present survey, it was decided to ask the

direct question as well as the indirect ones, as the SCELI had a direct question, and hence comparisons would be possible. The comparison with white self-employed on this question, is described in chapter 6 (Table 6.5).

18. Middle class occupations include, "the professions, businessmen, managers above the grade of foremen, most farmers, the majority of the public service, the majority of shopkeepers, a substantial number of clerks, other non-manual workers and some independent craftsmen" (Lewis and Maude 1949:17).

19. The question asked was, "What do you do in your leisure time", which often evoked responses of "What leisure time?!", "No leisure time!". This response, then, is not the same as the response of 'lack of time' to the question on the disadvantages of shopkeeping.

20. The question asked was, "Can you give me the occupations and ethnic group origins of three of your close friends?"

21. See Chapter 4.

22. The various factors of 'post-industrialism' supporting the reproduction of the petty bourgeoisie have been listed by Boissevain (1981:21-2). See also Scase (1982:150-51).

23. The concept of a 'project', according to Bechhofer and Elliott, "implies the *choice* of a particular course of action by an individual with the intention of changing his life situation; the idea of a plan for the future is critical here." (1968:201)

6 Ethnicity at work

Introduction

It has been noted in the previous chapters that a large number of South Asians are entering small business, that in Oxford they appear to be quite successful, and an explanation of this phenomenon has been attempted. It is one thing to do this, but, it is quite another thing to maintain, on this basis, that there is something ethnically distinctive about South Asian small business which separates it from small business in general. As Aldrich and Waldinger quite correctly maintain:

> We would expect *viable* business enterprises to look very much alike, regardless of ownership. Theories of ethnic businesses posit that such enterprises differ from others because of the social structure within which resources are mobilized. Researchers have focused on ethnic resource mobilization as a collective, rather than purely individual, activity, as ethnic entrepreneurs draw on family, kin, and co-ethnic relations for labour and capital. *Because so many researchers have not compared their findings to non-ethnic business operations, they have tended to overstate the uniquely "ethnic" component in resource mobilization* [1] (1990:127).

More concrete evidence, then, is required to examine the ethnically distinctive features of South Asian small business and its difference, if any, from indigenous small business in Britain. In this chapter, in an attempt to provide such evidence, the self-employed Oxford Asians are compared to a national sample of white small business owners.

Differences and similarities in the literature

The burgeoning of ethnic small businesses has almost automatically resulted in a concentration of attention on the ethnically distinctive characteristics of this activity. It is emphasized in the literature that ethnic entrepreneurs draw upon their group characteristics, or 'ethnic resources' in the context of business strategy formulation. Ethnic resources are sociocultural features of a group that coethnic business owners utilize in business or from which their businesses passively benefit (Light and Bonacich 1988:178). According to Boissevain et al., ethnic resources characterize a group, not just its isolated members, and typical ethnic resources include *predisposing factors* - cultural endowments, relative work satisfaction arising from non-acculturation to prevailing labour standards, and a sojourning orientation - and modes of *resource mobilisation* - ethnic social networks and access to a pool of under-employed coethnic labour (Boissevain et al. 1990:132). In an attempt to separate the purely ethnic from the generic process of resource mobilization, Light (1984) distinguishes between these 'ethnic' resources and 'class' resources such as private property in the means of production and distribution, human capital, money to invest, and bourgeois values, attitudes, knowledge and skills transmitted intergenerationally.

That 'ethnicity', as far as business is concerned, refers to various ethnic resources, has been noted in Chapter 1. Different aspects have been stressed by different researchers, such as,

1) an ethnic sub-market based on an ethnic group's own consumption patterns (Mars and Ward 1984:14; McEvoy et al. 1979),

2) a 'protected' market consisting of mainly Asian clientele (Aldrich et al. 1984, 1985; Boissevain 1981),

3) 'ethnic enclaves' completely dependent on cheap ethnic labour and clientele, in which Asian businesses function (Auster and Aldrich 1984),

4) ethnic strategies such as reliance on ethnic social networks for business information, start-up capital, and so on, (Werbner 1984; Light and Bonacich 1988:178; Boissevain 1990:132),

5) reliance on family and ethnic labour, (Boissevain 1990:132; Aldrich 1980),

6) ethnic business practices, such as working longer hours, not extending credit, etc., (Aldrich 1980; Cater 1984),

7) ethnic solidarity, (Cater and Jones 1987; Jones 1989).

A clear cut example of the use of ethnic solidarity to advance entrepreneurial interests, is that provided by Drake and Cayton, in their description of the 'Double-Duty Dollar' among the blacks in Chicago, according to which blacks were exhorted by the church to use their money not only to purchase whatever they themselves desired but also to 'advance the race' by making their purchases in black-owned businesses (1962:431).

It is then, maintained that in so far as ethnic entrepreneurs have access to sociocultural resources that are different from those of mainstream entrepreneurs, and utilize 'outsider' strategies, they can be distinguished from the mainstream entrepreneurs (Wilken 1979:22). In so far as ethnic or immigrant entrepreneurs utilise distinctive resources and strategies to solve common business problems such as, the acquisition of business information, recruitment of labour, management of customer relations, and acquisition of start-up capital, "...they are more than just mainstream entrepreneurs who also happen to belong to a legally, ethnically, or phenotypically distinct population subclass" (Boissevain *et al.* 1990:133)

Before this ethnic distinctiveness of Asian small business can be established, however, it must be remembered that, in the first place, the 'ethnic' characteristics cannot be presumed to exist from the mere fact of large scale ethnic entry into business. Curran and Burrows (1988), analysing GHS data to establish the relation between ethnicity and enterprise, have taken as indicators of ethnicity:

1) whether the respondent is 'black' or 'white' (as assessed by the interviewer);

2) the respondent's country of birth;

3) where the respondent's mother was born; and,

4) where the respondent's father was born.

It must, however, be stressed that all that these 'indicators' would prove is the objective fact of 'ethnic origin'. As Yinger has pointed out in relation to research in the field of ethnic studies, such research is based on the,

...single fact of an ethnic (or state origin) label, with little attention to the salience of the label, to the strength of identification with the ethnic group compared to other identities, or to the distinction between country of origin and ethnicity (1985:158).

'Ethnicity' of business activity, by definition, refers to something more than the mere fact that these business owners are of particular ethnic origins. While the GHS data is able to show that a significant number of small business owners are of ethnic minorities, it cannot in any way demonstrate the 'ethnicity' of these businesses in the sense of whether they serve their own ethnic markets, whether they are dependent on ethnic networks for finance and business information, whether they employ only ethnic labour, whether they are found only in areas of heavy ethnic residential concentration and so on. So, large numbers of ethnic minorities may go into 'enterprise activity', but this does not prove that the resulting enterprise activity is 'ethnic'.

Secondly, to establish the distinctiveness of ethnic business the approach needs to be more comparative. It can be agreed, as Jenkins has maintained:

In order to understand what, if anything, characterises the 'ethnic' business sector as in any sense different or peculiar we need to know more than we do about that with which we are comparing it. In particular...we need to know more about why people set up on their own, the marketing strategies employed by small business owners,...their labour relations strategies and the relationship between business life and the domestic domain...Clearly if we are to understand, for example, the role of the Asian extended family, or family labour in ethnic minority business generally, we must be able to bring comparative data for white-owned businesses to bear on the discussion. What might at first sight appear to be a 'cultural' phenomenon, related to family structure, might in fact be simply a characteristic feature of the organisation of small business, dictated not by kinship norms but by the economics of the enterprise (1984:235).

It is necessary, therefore, to determine whether the South Asian small business owners are significantly different from small business owners in general, and the indigenous small business owners in particular, in their functioning and resource mobilization, as well as in their attitudes, class origins, education, domestic arrangements, mobility patterns, orientation to self-employment and political affiliation.

Substantial discussion of indigenous small business owners in the UK, is to be found in the work of Bechhofer *et al.* (1968; 1971; 1974a; 1974b; 1976; 1978; 1981), and Scase and Goffee (1980; 1982). And from this work it appears that on various matters there may not be much difference between ethnic and native enterprise activity. Bechhofer and Elliot have noted that the general features of the petty bourgeoisie are much the same everywhere (1981). For instance, it has been pointed out with regard to the work ethic of the shopkeepers - the hours worked, business practices, attitudes to family, children and social life - that none of this is peculiar to ethnic minorities (Scase and Goffee 1980; 1982). It is to be noted that right from the very first sociological study of British small shopkeepers (Klingender 1951), there has been an emphasis on the long hours and constant grind that the job entails. That the small business has always been a 'family business' is quite evident from the following graphic description provided by Mills:

> As owner, manager, and worker, the marginal victim typically uses his family to help out in store, farm or shop. Economic life thus coincides with family life. In the hole-in-the-wall business, also known as a mom-and-pop store, the parents can keep an eye on each other and on the children (1951:30).

Scase and Goffee are also quite emphatic in attributing whatever economic viability small businesses have to the role of unpaid family labour (1980:90).

Again, evidence from both American and British sociological literature suggests that it is not just among the ethnic or immigrant minorities that:

> ...running a business of one's own is a cherished ideal and those from manual backgrounds who achieve it are deemed to have moved up the social scale (Bechhofer *et al.* 1971:164)[2]

Also, it is quite commonplace to regard ethnic business as a reaction to disadvantage and discrimination in the labour market. But, interestingly enough, Scase and Goffee maintain:

> ...for many of the people we interviewed, the reason for starting a business was not out of a desire ultimately to become a successful entrepreneur, but as a rejection of working for somebody else (1980:33).

As Jenkins suggests:

> If they (Scase and Goffee) are correct, white small business owners might not be too dissimilar to their black counterparts in this respect (1984:235).

Systematic comparison of white owned small businesses and ethnic minority small businesses is, then, necessary to establish the general 'non-ethnic' features of Asian small business.

Correspondingly, the salience of ethnicity for the South Asian small business owner, within the context of small business, must also be established. As Wallman emphasizes:

> Ethnicity is only one identity option, only one way of defining a community. It is structured by and dependent on other things happening. And insofar as the 'other things happening' are not fixed, the significance of ethnicity to individual or group identity must be fluid (1983:69).

Wallman maintains:

> *work* and *locality* so often override the identity potential of ethnic origin in industrial settings... (that)...identities based on work and locality may be the most important non-ethnic options. Certainly they are sometimes strong enough to counterbalance the associative and affective pull of ethnicity (1983:76-77).

Work is a setting in which ethnic identity is often irrelevant, and may even be seen as a burden.[3] Thus, where Auster and Aldrich (1984:50), emphasizing the positive role of ethnic identity, hold that relations between ethnic firms would tend towards cooperative mutual adjustment and self-regulation rather than competition, when backed by a strong ethnic economy, it would appear that it is Werbner's picture, when she speaks of Pakistani traders in Manchester competing with each other for clientele, and of ethnic identity not being the dominant consideration traders have in matters of credit (1984:186), which is more realistic. South Asian small shopkeepers may be no different from small shopkeepers as such.

It is useful here to draw attention to the distinction that Kosmin makes between the 'expressive' and the 'utility' aspects of Jewish ethnicity in work situations in Britain. The two parts of ethnicity, according to him, consist of:

> First, the specific cultural traits which can be generalised for the group and which distinguish its members from the majority of the host population. This distinctive social philosophy, the Jewish *Weltanschauung*, may be termed *the expressive factor*. Second, the using of this common culture as a focus for solidarity and identity in actual social situations. This may be termed *the utility factor* (1979:37).

It is necessary to look at both aspects of ethnicity in relation to business activity among the South Asians: their world philosophy and cultural inheritance, and their use of ethnicity as a tool or resource (cf. Wallman 1974).

It is proposed then, to consider how 'ethnic' South Asian small business really is, and whether it is at all different from the British petty bourgeoisie. The specific questions to be considered are - What is the role of ethnicity within the work sphere for the self-employed Oxford Asians? To what extent does the Asian small business owner utilize 'ethnic resources' in his business activity? Does he give significant importance to his ethnicity in his employment activity, or are there no cardinal differences in the functioning of South Asian and white small business owners? Is the success of Asian small business attributable to the ethnic distinctiveness of their businesses, and does this mean that Asian small business owners are significantly different from their white counterparts? Or, is the condition of the Asian small business owner simply a reflection of British small business as a whole?

Methodology

Some of the findings of the earlier chapters are summarized to present a profile of the Oxford Asian small business owners, which is then compared with that of a sample of white shop-keepers and restaurant owners. Comparisons are in terms of aspects of business practice, organising capacity, socio-economic background, class membership, and the orientation to self-employment in general.

The data for the South Asians has been obtained entirely from the present survey, and in all cases, N=94, which is in effect the total population of South Asian retailers and restaurant owners in Oxford as of September 1989 to May 1990, and not a sample. The data for the control group of white self-employed have been largely obtained from data sets such as the Labour Force Survey, The Social Change And Economic Life Initiative, and The General Household Survey, so that the data are nationally representative.[4] Information regarding a few variables, which were not available in these data sets, was taken from a survey of white and Asian shopkeepers in Wandsworth (Aldrich 1980).

Comparisons

Business practices

It has been argued that South Asian business success is due to culturally transmitted skills, the effects of which are to be seen in their business practices which provide a contrast to those of white small business owners. The business practices of the Oxford Asians are compared with those of white small business owners, to see if there are any cardinal differences. The results are shown in Table 6.1 below. Comparisons of Asian and white business practices are of particular interest in view of the widely held beliefs regarding them, ranging from the belief that the 'unfair' business practices of South Asians are driving white shop-keepers out of business, to the extreme one which portrays Asians as an over-ambitious, intrusive group using 'sweatshop' methods to gain a 'stranglehold' on the British economy (Billig 1978). While Aldrich, Jones and McEvoy, maintain that their survey results show that such beliefs greatly exaggerate the differences between South Asian and white shopkeepers (1984:196), the results from the present survey reveal some significant differences in business practices. The intensive competitive practices of South Asians in comparison with whites is substantiated by this study in that business practices continue to be extremely competitive.

Table 6.1 Ethnicity of owner and business practices

Variable	White	Asian****
1. Average Hours worked per week	50*	78
2. Open on Sundays (%)	55**	82
3. Making deliveries (%)	51***	11
4. Selling on credit (%)	26***	12
5. No. of part time employees(mean)	1.2*	.8
6. Total no. of employees (mean)	2.9*	1.9
7. Spouse working in business (%)	35*	64

8. Spouse paid (%)	19*	9
9. Children working in business (%)	19*	38
10. Children paid (%)	9*	7
11. Other family members working in business (%)	17*	42
12. Payment taken by respondents (%)		
According to how the business is doing	62*	15
Fixed salary	19*	32
According to need	n.a.	53

----

*   Source:SCELI (n=78)
**   Source:LFS 1989 (n=1581)
***   Source: Aldrich, 1980:399
**** n=94

It can be seen from Table 6.1 that most South Asians are open on Sundays as against just over a half of white small business owners. Asians open their establishments for longer hours than their white counterparts. They also employ very little labour as compared to white small business owners. And, fewer Asians than whites make deliveries or sell on credit.

Competitiveness in the business practices of South Asian shop owners is quite evident when they are observed at work. There were days during field work when it was not possible to get hold of any grocery owner because all had flocked to some distant 'Cash and Carry' advertising heavy discounts on certain items. Further, service is very brisk and efficient - Asians rarely have to look up the price of an item, are quick with their calculations, and carry on conversations with their customers at the same time.

While the South Asians, just as much as everyone else, are aware of the greater competitiveness in their business practices as compared to the whites - 71 per cent mention the long working hours as a disadvantage of small business - there is a willingness to work longer hours and to remain open for more days.

As a young Pakistani put it:

> You go into shopkeeping knowing its going to be like that. One is always aware of the disadvantage of long hours. But I say, if the hours bother you, don't bother doing it   (No.24)

The labour intensiveness of South Asian small business is a critical advantage which it possesses over its white competition. This is well illustrated by the following statement made by a middle aged, Indian newsagent:

> The English love their leisure too much. The Englishman from whom I bought this shop used to employ five people! I don't employ anyone. It's very hard to pay someone else, it eats up your profits (No.40)

While the mean number of employees for the Oxford Asians is only 1.9, which is considerably lower than the national white average of 2.9, it is also worth noting that 39 per cent of them have no employees at all. In view of this, it is quite surprising that Aldrich *et al.*, in their survey of Bradford, Leicester and Ealing, find no significant difference in the number employed by Asian-owned and white-owned shops and that, "Asians tend to employ more full time employees than white owners" (Aldrich Jones and McEvoy 1984:196).

Of course, the lack of employees is compensated for by the extensive use of family labour. While it may be agreed with Scase and Goffee that use of family labour is prevalent among all small business owners and not confined to ethnic minorities, the present study reveals a significantly greater utilisation of the labour of spouse, children and extended family among the Asians, a greater percentage of which is unpaid than in the case of whites. The proportion of all Asian respondents whose children help out in the business is double that of the whites, despite the fact that amongst the South Asians, 32 per cent of respondents had children who were too young to help out in the shops and restaurants. The help of spouse, children, siblings, and parents, is then crucial to South Asian business, such help being regarded as an essential part of family loyalty and unity, even when these members are employed 'outside' as well.[5] That this help should not, however, be taken as exploitation of women and children has been noted in Chapter 3. In fact, what emerges is the major role that they play in the successful functioning of the businesses. It has been noted in Chapter 4 that 22 per cent of the businesses had been started for the wives of respondents. During the initial years, which are regarded as the most difficult ones, these wives were the ones responsible for the actual running of the businesses, while the men continued with their paid employment. Even where the wives had outside employment, they had important responsibilities vis-à-vis the enterprises, as had their husbands. There was always full participation of wives in decision making, so that their role was that of equals and not the stereotypical, subservient and exploited role usually attributed to them. This equal role is quite acceptable to the men. According to the owner of a fashion wear shop in a prime location:

> A couple of years ago, I was being offered a premium of 45 grand for this shop. I was tempted to sell and start up somewhere else,

but my wife wouldn't hear of it. She kept saying 'no, this shop is better'... (No.1)

And, the owner of a grocery store maintained:

> It was my wife who kept after me to buy a corner shop. She was the one who saw the need and possibility of opening a shop. She was actually running it, deciding what to buy, etc., though I used to help out. I continued with my job in British Leyland. I got interested in the shop only later, when I saw it was doing well... (No.20)

Children, too, are trained very early to contribute effectively to the functioning of the business. It is quite normal to find school going children attending to the till, and serving customers in their spare time. This provides an opportunity to their parents to leave the premises for short periods and attend to other chores, which they would be reluctant to do with outside labour. This is never looked upon as exploitative as 'the business, after all is for the children' - a sentiment expressed so very often. The commitment of every family member to 'their' shop or restaurant, is definitely an important feature of the South Asian small business sector.

That an essential difference between the traditional mode of running a small business and more modern methods, is a decrease in the giving of credit and the making of deliveries, has been noted by Aldrich (1980:399). This would apply to both whites and South Asians alike. As the figures for the whites are from a survey conducted more than a decade before the present one, the figures applying to them can be expected to be lower than those in Table 6.1, so that differences between Asians and whites should not be exaggerated. South Asian small business owners certainly do not believe in giving credit as the following quotations demonstrate:

A very successful, Pakistani, grocery owner, speaking of relations with customers, maintained:

> You have to be friendly, but also strict at the same time - about credit for instance. If you give credit, you lose the money as well as the customer. They don't like to come back if they owe you money. Especially the Asians. They are always trying to get credit or a reduction in prices. We have learned from bitter experience not to give credit (No.20)

According to an Indian newsagent cum general store owner:

> Yes, we do give credit occasionally - its a big mistake, because you never get it back. People come to you with hard luck stories - especially Asians who say they have hungry children at home, and you feel you have to give them things on credit. But you never get your money back. As far as returning money is concerned, whites are worse than Asians. They'll never pay it back! (No.34)

128

A Sikh Off-Licensee cum Newsagent maintained:

> I never give credit. Those who ask for it are the ones who are just
> not worth giving to. There are the British with hard luck stories -
> my cat is dying, my dog is sick - and once you give them credit,
> you never see them again. You lose your money and your
> customer ...(No.30)

However, those businesses which cater to an exclusively South Asian
clientele, such as the textile shops and jewellers, do not have much of an
option - they would not be able to continue in business if they stopped
extending credit. As an elderly jeweller put it:

> It's a tradition coming down through the ages. It's difficult, but we
> have to give credit...(No.37)

Deliveries are usually confined to newspapers, but it is worth noting that
many Asian shops make occasional deliveries of groceries to old people
and regular customers. On one occasion, this researcher was left in charge
of the shop, after a fresh delivery of bread to the shop, so that the owner
could deliver a loaf to an old lady, who, he said, had come in earlier for it
and would "starve without her bread". While this is seen as a part of
maintaining good relations with customers, no strenuous efforts are made
by Asians to court custom by giving credit or making deliveries, and hence
may be slightly more competitive[6] in these business practices than their
white counterparts.

In sum, major differences may be found in the business practices of
whites and Asians, in that Asians work longer hours and are open on
Sundays. Asians also employ less labour than the whites, and ethnic
advantage is clearly evident in the greater use of family labour, a greater
percentage of which is unpaid than in the case of whites. Fewer Asians
than whites make deliveries or sell on credit, so that South Asian business
practices seem to be more competitive than those of their white
counterparts.

Ethnicity and socioeconomic background of owner

It has been maintained that ethnic distinctiveness is apparent in the
differing socioeconomic background of South Asian and white small
business owners. White small business owners are pictured in the
literature as aged, of relatively low education, and recruited largely from
blue collar employment. Asian small business owners, on the basis of the
'blocked-mobility' thesis, which posits a lack of parity between the
educational background of Asians and their occupational attainments, are
believed to be of relatively higher socio-economic background than their
white counterparts. The socioeconomic background of the Oxford Asians
is compared with that of white small business owners in Table 6.2.

As Table 6.2 shows, South Asian small business owners in Oxford
do not seem to differ greatly from the whites in age or marital status. But

the Asians have more children, which may be expected to be an asset in business in view of the greater utilisation of family labour by the Asians. Though recruitment in both groups is largely from blue collar employment, more whites than Asians were in blue collar work in the last job previous to self-employment. Again, though the proportions of the unqualified are high in both groups, the proportion of whites lacking educational qualifications is higher than that of the Asians. At the level of higher qualifications there does not seem to be much difference, which is slightly unusual as surveys of Asians in other areas (Aldrich 1980; McEvoy 1980; Wilson 1983; Lambeth 1984) have found higher proportions of Asians with degrees than of whites. Hence, though the South Asians in Oxford appear to be slightly more qualified than the whites, the differences cannot be stressed.

Table 6.2 Ethnicity and socioeconomic background of owner

Variable	White	Asian
1. Mean age (years)	44*	42
2. Married (%)	82**	97
3. Mean no. of children	2.1**	3.1
4. Educational Qualifications(%)		
No qualifications	43**	31
Secondary schooling	19**	45
A levels	8**	-
Craft or technical training	9**	9
College graduate	12**	16
5. Self-employed in last job (%)	22*	14
6. Employed in blue collar work in last job (%)	65*	47
7. Father self-employed (%)	31*	54
8. Father employed in blue collar work (%)	41*	25
9. Owning other businesses or rental property (%)	17***	61
10. percent with family members owning shops/ restaurants	31***	62

*   Source: SCELI (n=78)
**   Source: LFS 1989 (n=1581)
***   Source: Aldrich, 1980:401-404

The importance of occupational inheritance in the small business sector is quite evident from Table 6.2 in that 54 per cent of the South Asians and 31 per cent of the whites have self-employed fathers. An 'intergenerational effect', that is, a high propensity for the offspring of parents who run a business to do so themselves (Curran and Blackburn 1991), has been noted for Britain as a whole (Goldthorpe 1987; Curran and Burrows 1988; Stanworth *et al.* 1989). This intergenerational effect, though evident in both groups, appears to be far more pronounced among the South Asians than among the whites. While parents of the respondents of both groups are largely self-employed or blue collar workers, the Asians have a higher proportion of self-employed fathers and the whites of blue collar fathers.[7] It is interesting to note here that the proportion of Asians with family members who own shops and restaurants is twice that of the whites. Even while agreeing with Aldrich that:

> Many investigators in England do not seem to be aware of the high proportion of white shopkeepers who have shopkeeper relatives, as much is always made of the patterns of business ownership within Asian families as though this were somehow unique to Asians as a group (1980:405),

it has to be admitted that the pattern appears more pronounced among the South Asians.

When 'other property owned' is looked at, a significant difference is to be seen between the two groups in that 61 per cent of Asians own either another business or other rental property compared to 17 per cent of whites who do so. It is quite likely that the figure for the whites may not reveal the actual picture, a question on 'other property owned' being almost as sensitive as questions on income and turnover where small business owners are concerned. The notorious unreliability of such data has been commented on in the methodological appendix. That the reluctance to provide such information is not confined to ethnic small business owners is evident from the SCELI, where 81 per cent of white small business owners answered, 'don't know', or 'refused answer' to the question on 'net annual income'. It may well be that the present respondents were more forthcoming on the property question as no questions were asked about income and turnover. Given the historical tendency for small business owners to own multiple properties,[8] the pattern of multiple ownership may well be common to South Asians and whites, the higher proportion of Asian owners a result of their greater propensity to save and accumulate.

All in all, taking into account the occupational background of fathers, the educational attainments of the owners, and the ownership of other business or rental property, it does appear that the socioeconomic status and background of the South Asian small business owners is higher than that of the whites.

Organising capacity

'Organising Capacity' refers to the utilisation of ethnic resources available to the South Asian small business owner. Where the achievements of the white owners is seen as individual, that of the Asians is seen as collectivist, owing much to resources deriving from ethnic solidarity. Thus, Asians are perceived as obtaining start-up capital largely from family and friends within the ethnic community, relying exclusively on ethnic labour, and dependent on contacts with other Asian businessmen for the successful running of their businesses. Comparisons of Asians and whites in terms of these factors is presented in Table 6.3.

Table 6.3 Ethnicity of owner and organising capacity

Variable	White	Asian
1. Per cent who raised capital through		
family and friends	14	10
Banks or lending associations	32	81
Personal savings	26	7
Other	28	2
(more than one response possible)		
2. Per cent employing whites*	58***	68
Per cent employing non-whites*	64***	49

*** Source: Aldrich, 1980:404

* Base for these percentages is only those businesses employing labour (n=54)

It is evident from Table 6.3 that South Asians rely largely on banks and Building Societies for start-up capital, much more so than their white counterparts. This is very significant from the view point of the organising capacity of an ethnic group, demonstrating that much more than the ethnic community, it is the economic institutions of the majority group which are utilised in business start-up. In fact, as is shown in Table 6.3, a lower proportion of South Asians than of whites maintain that they raise start-up capital from family and friends. While the literature emphasizes that the most important source of capital for *all* small shopkeepers, whether in Britain or the United States, in founding a business is personal savings (Aldrich 1973; Aldrich and Reiss 1976; Aldrich 1980), only 7 per cent of the Asians claimed to have used only personal savings to start their businesses. It was generally pointed out by respondents that though to get bank loans a certain level of personal savings, whether in the form of capital or property, was essential, it would not make business sense to use personal savings only, when banking facilities were easily available.

No evidence was found of Asians experiencing difficulty raising funds through British financial institutions, and this is in accordance with the findings of McEvoy *et al.* (1979), and others, but contrasts with the findings of Allen *et al.*(1977), which established the extensive use of finance from family and friends, and very little utilisation of banking facilities. This could well be a result of the natural evolution in South Asian business practices, as Allen's Bradford study was conducted at a very early stage of Asian business activity in Britain, when Asian business ability had not yet been established. Thus, Leo, in his interviews of bank managers in London to discuss lending policies, maintains:

> ...Asians having demonstrated as a group their ability to run businesses successfully, have a head start in requesting a loan in comparison to Afro-Caribbeans. The latter have no such established reputation as a group... (1981:83-86).

There is, then, no necessity for reliance on ethnic networks for business finance.

It is usually maintained that:

> ...(an)...indicator of the extent to which an ethnic group draws upon its own resources in creating and operating small businesses...(is)...the degree to which one's own group are hired as employees (Aldrich 1980:405).

The availability of cheap ethnic labour, and the exclusive utilisation of this ethnic labour, has traditionally been regarded as an important ethnic business resource. It is found that it is here that a sharp distinction has to be made between the shops and the restaurants. This can be quite clearly seen from Table 6.4 below.

Table 6.4 Use of ethnic labour by Asian shops and restaurants*

Ethnicity of Labour	Shops(%)	Restaurants(%)
Only White	74	0
Both Asian and White	13	28
Only Asian	13	72

*   Only those employing labour; Shops n=39 as 37 shops do not
        employ labour; Restaurants n=18

Within the restaurant trade, there is a clear preference for co-ethnic labour, which is in the mutual interest of employers and employees. There is often a natural progression from kitchen hand, to waiter, to manager to owner, with most of the present owners having learned the trade in the restaurants of relatives or other co-ethnics. There is at all times an extensive use of the ethnic language amongst employees, with many old-timers in the kitchen unable to speak English.

Employment relations within the South Asian restaurant tends to be *fraternal* in that quite often a cook, a waiter, and the manager may be co-owners of the restaurant. Scase and Goffee, in their study of the self-employed in the construction industry, suggest that employers frequently adopt a fraternal strategy, abandoning overt hierarchical relations with employees and adopting an 'all workers together' strategy (1982). The strategy, then, may be dictated by the industry rather than ethnicity *per se*. Yet, ethnicity *is* of some importance among the restaurant owners in a way in which it is not among the retailers.

Even in the case of the restaurants, as can be seen from Table 6.4, though the majority employ only co-ethnics, 28 per cent of restaurants do employ at least one white person. Amongst the retailers, however, though 49 per cent of the retailers do not have employees, of those who do, 87 per cent have at least one white employee. What is even more remarkable is that 74 per cent of retailers who employ labour have *only* white employees. The employment of co-ethnic labour is then, certainly not of any importance for the shop-keepers. There seems rather, to be a growing trend towards the employment of whites among the shop-keepers, which may well be a deliberate strategy in order to underplay their ethnicity in the domain of work.

There is, as has been seen, no reliance on the ethnic community for finance, and, at least where the retailers are concerned, no reliance on ethnic labour. How important, then, did respondents consider interaction and good relations with other Asian businessmen, for the successful running of their businesses? To a direct question on this, 64 per cent did not give much importance to contacts with Asian businessmen. In fact, what emerges quite clearly from their responses given below, is the attitude of distrust towards co-ethnics in business.

According to an Ugandan Asian Newsagent:

> Asians in business just cannot get along. I just keep away from them. They'll just stab you in the back whenever they can. So I keep away. I believe in just saying 'hello' when we meet, nothing more (No.42)

A Pakistani sub postoffice owner maintained:

> ...One reason for moving from Sheffield was that there were too many of our people there, and there was too much of politics. Here too, the Asian businessmen don't want to help you - I don't have anything to do with them - I don't bother. My business is mine and I lead my own life (No.50)

According to another young Pakistani grocer, born and brought up in Oxford:

As far as business is concerned there is no support of the community. The Asians try to pull each other down instead of supporting each other. For instance, if something is not available in your shop, you try to suggest another shop to the customer, like 'try so and so, it may be available there'. But most Asian shops will never do this. They are scared that they will lose their business and that the other Asian shop will do better. A white man will do it. In business, whites are better - they don't compete all the time, and they don't grudge you your success. Asians are suspicious of each other. There is no unity among the businessmen...(No.13)

An elderly, very successful, grocer was quite emphatic:

Wherever Asians are, they are jealous of each other. I am completely separate from them. With a little brains you can work by yourself (No.26)

According to a struggling, young, general store owner:

Asians never help their own kind...Apart from a few close family friends, those Asians who are doing well look out for themselves. They are not interested in helping the less better off in any way. There are Asians here who are millionaires, with a lot of property and money in the bank, but they turn their face away from the community (No.80)

Even the 36 per cent of owners who maintain that good relations with other Asian businessmen is important for the competent running of their businesses stress that such contacts are useful in terms of business information regarding prices, demand, availability of business premises, property on the market, suitability of business location, and business strategies, rather than in terms of actual help in running the business. One or the other of these were mentioned by all those business owners who gave importance to contacts with other South Asian businessmen. According to one Indian grocer:

It helps to know other businessmen. I usually meet them in the Cash and Carry. You can find out where there are good prices available. You can discuss the customer situation, what kind of things will sell, etc. (No.57)

The gaining of business information and advice, which is essential for entrepreneurs, through ethnic channels has been stressed as an ethnic strategy by many (Boissevain and Grotenbreg 1986; Light and Bonacich 1988; Werbner 1984, 1985a, 1985b; Boissevain et al. 1990:134-136). But, to a significant proportion of the South Asian small business owners in Oxford, this is a strategy which is not of crucial importance.

A part of the superior organising capacity of ethnic entrepreneurs has been taken to be the ability to tap into ethnic markets, and to cater primarily to an ethnic clientele. It has been established in Chapter 3, in great detail, that the number of Oxford Asian businesses oriented towards the satisfaction of ethnic needs remains almost constant at six, which constitutes just eight per cent of retail outlets. Further, 80 per cent of shops and 95 per cent of restaurants report less than five per cent of its clientele as Asian. In fact, again as has been established earlier, there is a positive dislike of South Asian customers who are described as always looking for a cheap bargain, always asking for reductions on the basis of ethnic ties, and, invariably, stingy and mean. This antipathy to co-ethnic custom has been noted by many who study ethnic entrepreneurship (Boissevain and Grotenbreg 1986; Boissevain et al. 1990:145-146), and is strongly supported by the present study.

One more point needs to be made about customer relations. It has already been stated in earlier chapters, that 89 per cent of respondents stress the importance of good relations with customers for the successful running of their businesses. South Asian shopkeepers in Oxford know their regular customers by name, and always make the time to chat to them, to discuss their personal problems, to get to know their likes and dislikes in consumer goods, and to procure these goods for them when necessary. Gifts are exchanged over Christmas, and old people are often offered help of a more practical nature. All this is very reminiscent of Klingender's picture of the small shop as a social arena (1951). This social function of the small shop is treated in the literature as attenuated by the impersonal forces of urbanisation (Bechhofer et al.), so that it is very interesting to find it as important as ever in the Asian shops in Oxford. What is the role of ethnicity in this? In an earlier study of ethnic entrepreneurship in Birmingham, it has been maintained that,

> Unlike its native - British - counterpart, the Pakistani shop fulfils extra-economic functions which could not be fulfilled by the former. The specific role played by ethnic entrepreneurs in the immigrant community make the ethnic shop and the entrepreneur unique institutions in the context of Pakistani ethnicity (Dahya 1974:94)

What Dahya was talking about, however, was the ethnic shop which catered to, and was patronised by, an ethnic clientele. Such shops provided a meeting place for members of the ethnic group, where the ethnic language could be spoken, and where they could get news of the homeland, of people returning home, of available jobs, of ethnic social events, and so on. This may well have been true in Oxford as well, when retailing activity first began, as illustrated by the following statement, made by a very successful, Pakistani newsagent:

> The earliest Asian shops were all grocers. These required, one, less capital, and two, more labour ...Also, these shops had another function to perform in the early years. They were places where Asians could meet fellow Asians, get to know about who was

going back home, and if possible, send money back through them. People did not mail money, or use banks... (No.55)

Today, this newsagent, in an area known for Asian shops and Asian residential concentration, claims that "less than half a per cent" of his clientele is Asian.

In view of the fact that more than 80 per cent of the respondents have a 95 per cent white clientele, the friendly, social interaction in Asian shops and restaurants is with members of the majority group and not with Asians. Ethnicity is certainly not an important factor here, for the Asian small business owners. However, in view of the fact that such social interaction is an acknowledged strength of small shops in general, only an observational study of white shop-keepers would reveal whether there is any real difference between them and their ethnic counterparts.

To sum up, there is no evidence of reliance on ethnic networks or ethnic financial institutions for business start-up. A greater proportion of the Oxford business owners today regards contacts with other Asian businessmen as unimportant for the running of their businesses, and greater numbers today express a desire to employ white labour. In view of the fact that a large number do not employ labour, the fact that 41 per cent of all small business owners employ whites, with 31 per cent employing only whites, is very significant. Reliance on ethnic labour, apart from the family, is clearly not crucial for these Asian small business owners. And, far from a dependence on ethnic customers, it is their dismissal which is more apparent.

Ethnic distinctiveness in the organising capacity is, then, not apparent, in that Asian small business owners do not appear to utilise ethnic resources or networks to any significant degree.

Ethnicity and the orientation to self-employment

Even if greater numbers of South Asians are entering self-employment than the whites in Britain, does this necessarily mean that those Asians who go into small business are different in their orientation to self-employment from the whites who go into it? Do the Asians have ethnically distinctive reasons for entrepreneurship, or, are the reasons for self-employment not very different for Asians as well as their white counterparts? It is often implied in the literature that Asians enter self-employment for negative reasons, to avoid discrimination and disadvantage in the labour market, and that their apparent satisfaction with self-employment can only be explained in terms of cultural yardsticks. Table 6.5 presents comparisons of South Asian and white small business owners' reasons for self-employment and the extent of their satisfaction with it.

Table 6.5 Ethnicity and orientation to self-employment

Variable		White*	Asian
1.	Reasons for Self-employment(%)		
	Prefer to be own boss	41	65
	To make money	23	56
	To follow interest	17	10
	Always wanted to	27	22
	Unemployed before Self-Emplmnt	5	5
	Business with family members	22	18
	For greater prestige	-	53
2.	Satisfaction with business (%)		
	Very satisfied	74	78
	Satisfied	10	18
	Evens	9	2
	Dissatisfied	7	2
3.	Looking for paid employment (%)		
	Likely	12	7
	Evens	6	4
	Unlikely	82	89

*   Source: SCELI (n=78)

On the interview schedule, the question on reasons for entering self-employment was an open ended one, allowing for individual responses which were post-coded. The question in the SCELI, however, was a precoded one, which allowed multiple responses, but of which 'prestige' was not an available option. This could well be the reason for the difference seen in Table 6.5 between Asian and white small business owners, in that 53 per cent of South Asians as against no whites, maintain that entry provides greater prestige. However, insofar as there is an 'other' reasons for self-employment option available in the SCELI, the complete absence of this response among the whites takes on some significance.

That Asians are not unique in regarding self-employment as prestigious is borne out by the literature on small business in general. In a study of small shopkeepers and artisans in France, Mayer comments that, "To them, owning a small business amounts to a legitimate form of social 'promotion'", and that while 'being ones own boss' is the primary motivation, yet, "...above all, they aspire to social improvement for themselves and their families" (1987:40-45). Kosmin, in his study of British Jews, states that 23 per cent of pro self-employment employees desired it for the increased social status it might give them, and though 59 per cent wanted the independence self-employment offered, the concept of independence incorporated both increased earnings and independent status (1979:51-52).

Despite this similarity, the importance of prestige aspirations appears to be much greater for the Asian small business owners. As emphasized in Chapter 4, for the Asian migrants with their multiple reference groups, entry into self-employment is the one strategy which satisfies prestige and mobility aspirations within all the groups - the South Asian migrant perceives his standing within the ethnic group both here and at 'home', as well as within British society, as substantially improved by 'business' entry.

Table 6.5 shows that in both groups, that of the Asians as well as of the whites, the reason most often stated for entry into self-employment is the desire to be one's own boss. While this finding is common to all studies of the self-employed (Bechhofer *et al.* 1974; Scase and Goffee 1980, 1982; Mayer 1987; Boissevain and Grotenbreg 1987), it is easy to interpret this in the case of ethnic minorities as a desire to avoid discrimination and disadvantage in the majority labour market. Recent researchers, however, find that this is not so. Thus, Boissevain and Grotenbreg, studying the Surinamese in the Netherlands, maintain:

> We were surprised, however, that in contrast to the findings of many others (Newcomer 1961; Gans 1962; Trevor Jones 1982; Ladbury 1984), discrimination and unemployment appeared to be relatively unimportant factors in influencing the decision to become self-employed. More than two-thirds of our informants deliberately chose to set up on their own and not as a reaction to unemployment and discrimination (1987:118).

The Lambeth Council report, on Black Businesses in Lambeth, also emphasizes that most small businessmen say they set up in business for positive reasons such as to make money or for independence, and that "desire for independence specifically from white employers was not significant in the response" (1982:16). So also, a study of Indian and Pakistani shopkeepers in Glasgow, found that:

> No one in the sample gave discrimination in the place of work as a reason for leaving...A large percentage of Indians (62%),...voiced

the 'pull' effect of wanting to own their own business... (Krcmar 1984:99).

That this is certainly true of the Oxford Asian entrepreneurs as well has been emphasized in Chapter 4. In their desire for independence then, there is little difference between the South Asians in Oxford and their white counterparts.

What of satisfaction with self-employment? Bechhofer *et al.*, writing about white shopkeepers in Edinburgh, maintain:

> ...rather more than 50 per cent indicated that they would like to get out of retailing. Thus, like men in a great many other jobs a sizeable number continue in the occupation because they are 'trapped' (1974:112).

That the Asian small business owners in Oxford are well satisfied with their employment, has been established not just through self-assessment of job satisfaction, but by considering their desire for change to paid employment as well as liking for alternative jobs.[9] Does this mean that satisfaction with small business is restricted to the South Asians because of "internal sources of satisfaction" and motivation "by goals separate and distinct from those of the majority society" (Jones 1982:471)? As the SCELI did ask the self-employed the question 'All things considered, how satisfied or dissatisfied are you with your present job overall?', as well as, 'Over the next three years how likely are you to look for a job working for someone else as a paid employee?, and as the present study had asked identical questions, the responses of the Oxford Asians to these two questions are compared to those of the whites. As can be seen from Table 6.5, there is a remarkable similarity in the proportion of South Asians and whites who are 'very satisfied' with their jobs, as well as in the proportions who maintain that they are unlikely to be looking for paid employment.

In sum, consideration of the attitudes towards self-employment in the two groups of white and Asian self-employed reveals that in both groups, the reason most often given for entry into self-employment is the desire to be one's own boss. It must, however, be recognised that this desire on the part of the Asians may well be largely due to the perceived improvement in prestige and standing through self-employment, which does not appear to be an important consideration for the white sample. Both groups, however, have very high proportions claiming to be very satisfied with their employment, bolstered by the fact that in both groups the vast majority maintain that it is very unlikely that they will be looking for paid jobs in the future. The difference between the Oxford Asians and whites, in their orientation towards self-employment, appears to lie mainly in the prestige aspirations of the South Asians.

Ethnicity and class membership

If the South Asian small business owners in Oxford do not utilise ethnic resources to any significant degree in their business activity, and do not differ very much from their white counterparts in their orientation to self-employment, can they then be regarded as part of the British petty bourgeoisie? Or are there significant differences in the class attributes of the Asian and white small business owners? The Asians and whites are compared in terms of house and car ownership, aspirations for children, as well as voting patterns, all of which are regarded as significant indicators of class position. It is also seen if the expected associations between class and voting is reflected in the Asian and white small business owners' self-assessment of their class position. The results are shown in Table 6.6.

It is immediately apparent from Table 6.6 that figures for house as well as car ownership are unusually high for both Asian as well as white small business owners. As Bechhofer *et al.* point out, such figures would be high even for professional groups. And, yet, such patterns of consumption have been generally noted for the petty bourgeoisie (1974:108). So, within this petty bourgeois group at least, there is nothing ethnically distinctive about high levels of Asian house ownership. In fact, the similarity in the proportions of Asians and whites who own cars and houses is quite remarkable.

Table 6.6 Ethnicity and class membership

Variable		White	Asian
1.	Housing Tenure (%)		
	Owner Occupation	88*	85
	Rented from Council	3*	6
	Rented Privately	9*	9
2.	Cars Owned (%)		
	No Cars	11**	4
	1 Car	41**	49
	2 Cars	37**	46
	3 or more Cars	11**	1
3.	% respondents with children in selective, fee-paying schools	25****	17

4.   Choice of Occupation for Children

Professional/white collar	25***	36
Business	n.a.	6
Other	n.a.	3
"What they like"	67***	32

5.   Which Vote (%)

Conservative	56*	25
Labour	7*	47

6.   Self assessed class membership (%)

Upper Class	-	4
Middle Class	18*	48
Working Class	10*	43
No Class	69*	5

*   Source: SCELI (n=78)
**   Source: GHS (n=333)
***   Source: Aldrich 1980:402
****   Bechhofer *et al.* 1974:122

Again, higher aspirations for educational and occupational attainments of one's children is regarded as an important element of class situation, one in fact which distinguishes the petty bourgeoisie from the class of manual workers, or the 'traditional working class perspective' from the 'middle class' one (Goldthorpe *et al.* 1969). As Table 6.6 shows, educational aspirations are high in both groups, with Bechhofer *et al.*, finding that within their sample of white shop-keepers, half of those with children desired some kind of selective, fee-paying secondary schooling, and that 25 per cent did attend such schools (1974:122). Amongst the South Asians in Oxford, it was found that while 63 per cent did not want their children to continue with small business, the reason most often given was that they would like their children to get a better education than themselves and enter a professional or white collar job. A lot of emphasis was placed on obtaining a good education for children, as that was something they themselves had been unable to do.
According to a 40 year old Pakistani grocer:

When I first came, my father wanted me to study. But I refused - I asked my father if I had come all the way to Britain to study. I had come to earn money, to become rich, and that was what I was going to do. So I started working as a waiter...I'd like my children to study, but if they don't, the business is always there (No.49)

According to another 36 year old, Pakistani, general store owner:

I regret my lack of qualifications. I never got round to it in England. I spent two years learning English, but all the people my age were interested in working, earning money and accumulating it. So I messed around with education. I would rather my children studied and got professional qualifications. I have now started classes in Book-keeping and Accountancy... (No.32)

Yet another Pakistani grocer, 26 years old, who had come to England at the age of 10, maintained:

I regret I did not pay more attention to my studies - I would have been able to get a better job then...My father has never forgiven me for not studying. I want my children to study, become doctors, lawyers... (No. 18)

And, as shown in Table 6.6, 17 per cent pay very high fees to educate their children in the exclusive, private schools of Oxford. This appears to be a growing trend, as many of the shopkeepers, as well as restaurant owners with young children, expressed a desire to register their children in the prestigious, private schools of Oxford. There is, thus, not much difference between the white and South Asian small business owners in this respect.

When it comes to specific job expectations for their children, Table 6.6 shows that 32 per cent of the Asians are willing to let the children take up whatever occupations they like, though 63 per cent had earlier expressed a desire for educational attainment and professional or white collar jobs. A possible reason for this could be that 60 per cent of the respondents had children too young to be working, so that their education, rather than their occupation, was the immediate preoccupation.

The figure for the whites saying 'what they like' is, however, considerably higher, and the proportion desiring professional jobs for their children, lower, than that for the Asians. These figures for the whites have been obtained from Aldrich's survey, and he himself comments that he is unable to explain the lack of accord between his findings and those of Bechhofer and Elliott, who found that white shopkeepers in Edinburgh were ambitious for their children and that their male offspring had done remarkably well in occupational mobility (Bland *et al.* 1978:241-244).[10] In the light of this, differences in white and South Asian aspirations for their children may not need to be stressed. As far as actual occupational attainments are concerned, that the Oxford Asian children appear to be in a better position than petty bourgeoisie children in general has been established in chapter 5.

A signal feature of the petty bourgeoisie is its conservative vote (Heath *et al.* 1985; Bechhofer and Elliott 1974, 1978). It is here, however, as Table 6.6 shows, that the South Asian small business owners can be seen to differ considerably from their white counterparts. While only seven per cent of the white small business owners intend to vote Labour, a majority of 47 per cent of the Asians say they will vote Labour 'if there is a general election tomorrow'. The Conservative vote of the petty bourgeoisie is usually attributed to its 'bourgeois' attitudes and values such as a belief in the importance of private property, and of individual success through hard work. As already established earlier,[11] these values which, according to Bechhofer and Elliott, are part of the ideological currency of Western society and the major reason underlying British petty bourgeois support for the Conservative party (Heath *et al.* 1985:17; Bechhofer and Elliott 1978:57-88), is to be found in the Asian petty bourgeoisie as well. That they still vote Labour is then indicative of ethnic affiliation taking precedence over their work and class identity, in a way in which it seldom does in other areas of work. In as much as there is no difference in basic values, the difference in voting patterns is indicative not so much of difference between the South Asian and white small business owners as of a similarity between the Asian petty bourgeoisie and the rest of the South Asian community in Britain[12] - a result, in fact, of the Asian migrants' involvement in the different systems of stratification of his own ethnic group as well as of the host society, which has been discussed in Chapter 4.

Hence there are considerable similarities between the Asian and white small business owners where class attributes such as house and car ownership, and educational and occupational aspirations for children, as well as the attitudes underlying them are concerned; however, where voting patterns are concerned the hold of ethnicity remains strong.

Summary and conclusions

The comparisons show that though the business practices of both South Asian and white small business owners involve working long hours and the use of family labour, the Asians exploit these strategies to a much greater extent than the whites. It is the fact that Asian small businesses can be seen to be open longer, open on Sundays and manned by various members of a family at different times, which makes it observably different from the white small businesses. But, apart from this there are no significant differences in the business practices of the Asians and the whites.

The Asian small business owner appears to have a slightly better socio-economic background than white owners. Whether this in any way contributes to the supposedly greater success[13] of the Asians must remain an open question. That higher educational qualifications could contribute to success has been pointed out by Werbner, who maintains, "It does seem, however, that a university degree however irrelevant it may be, has a radical impact on the expansion of businesses" (1990:21).

There are no significant differences between South Asian and white businessmen in their 'organising capacity', in that Asians in Oxford do not appear to utilise ethnic resources such as culturally specific economic institutions, or other ethnic sources of credit. They are not dependent on ethnic clientele or ethnic labour, or the support of the ethnic business community so that ethnicity is certainly not a dominant consideration in the running of businesses.

As far as the orientation to self-employment of the two groups is concerned, the stated reasons for entrepreneurial entry are similar in both groups, drawing attention to the positive reasons for Asian entry rather than just the negative ones of discrimination and disadvantage in the labour market. The major difference, however, lies in the satisfaction of status and prestige aspirations through business entry for the Asians, as a result of the greater importance of 'business' in the stratification hierarchy of the ethnic group. It is this Asian involvement in different systems of stratification which results also in the major difference in the class attributes of the Asian and white small business owners - the Labour leanings of the Asian group.

It would then, appear that the Asian small business owners in Oxford may be regarded as fairly representative of the British petty bourgeoisie, with ethnic distinctiveness honed down to what can be seen as a darkening or a deeper colouration of certain attributes commonly found within the petty bourgeoisie - the use of family labour, long working hours, and the use of business entry as a route to success. To the non-Asian, the ethnicity of the Asian enterprise is of some significance in that there is a recognition of the contrast in styles of entrepreneurship - the Asian retailer works longer hours, stays open all week, and utilises the labour of all his family members. But, to the Asian retailer himself, this is all part of the job, and of family commitment. In so far as collective ethnic resources are not utilised, and strategies are other than ethnic, in his actual work situation, the South Asian small business owner today does not appear to function within the ethnic dimension.

The significance of South Asian ethnicity in the entrepreneurial situation then, appears to lie in what Kosmin has referred to as the 'expressive factor' - the distinctive Asian philosophy of hard work, family commitment, prestige and mobility aspirations, accumulation and deferred gratification; the 'utility factor' of ethnicity appears to take a secondary place. As Clark (1979) has argued, it is not 'ethnic group consciousness' as much as it is pre-existing habits of organisation which should be given importance in understanding ethnic business enterprise. In the actual work situation of the Asian small business owner, his ethnic identity not only does not constitute a significant resource any more, but may even be regarded as a liability to be overcome, for instance by the employment of white labour. That the Asian small business owner in Oxford often attempts to play down his ethnicity is apparent in the general decor of the shop or restaurant. Dahya, speaking in 1971, could maintain that:

Pakistani shops and cafes are distinguished from their native counterparts by means of Urdu signs and notices on the fascias and shop-windows...pictures of famous Muslim shrines...and the Muslim calendar are displayed inside the shops and cafes. Consequently, some of the streets...acquire a peculiar character and remind the immigrants of their ethnicity... (1974:91).

While this is still true of certain known areas of South Asian shopping such as Southall, Manchester, and Birmingham, in Oxford today there is nothing distinctive about the Asian shop. In the early years of business activity in Oxford,[14] Asian shops and restaurants did carry ethnic posters, and notices of ethnic cultural events, and even the names of shops were a reflection of ethnicity - Asian shops being identifiable by their names. Today, Asian shop-keepers prefer non-Asian names for their shops. Thus, in Oxford, you now have 'Tip Toes', 'Lace-Ups', 'Continental Grocers', 'Globe Newsagents', while 'Muhammed Stores', 'Khan and sons', 'Raja Brothers' and similar names, are largely a thing of the past. Being Asian and being seen to be Asian is no longer regarded as necessary for business success. For the South Asian small business owner, in Oxford today, within the context of work, ethnicity is not useful and does not manifest itself.

Notes

1.   Italics present writer's.

2.   See also, Goldthorpe, Lockwood, Bechhofer and Platt, 1968:131-6; Lipset and Bendix 1959:173; Chinoy 1955; Mills 1951:24).

3.   In his work on 'Ethnicity and Opportunity in Urban America', Hannerz points out that ethnic minority status is frequently a handicap as minority members attempt to gain access to the more attractive niches controlled by white Protestants. The best strategy in such situations is most likely to try not to involve ethnicity at all in the advancement of individual interests, and this is indeed the line of action frequently chosen. But the decision to define ethnicity as irrelevant cannot always be made unilaterally; one still has to take into account white Protestant conceptions of ethnicity...(1974:60).

4.   See methodological appendix.

5.   See also chapter 3.

6.   'Competitive practices' is here being used in Aldrich's sense which refers to the practices that facilitate the successful operation of a small business, rather than to competition between businesses for custom (1980:398-400).

7.   The proportions of white shopkeepers whose fathers were either self-employed or in blue collar work was quite similar to those in

Aldrich's survey, McEvoy's study as well as the study of shopkeepers in Edinburgh conducted by Bechhofer and Elliott, which lends support to our findings.

8. That ownership of multiple properties insured for relatively small sums was common among small producer tradesmen in Birmingham in the 18th century has been well brought out by Maxine Berg in her study of Artisans and Factory systems in the Industrial Revolution (1991). Thus, a watchchainmaker left 5 houses and a brewhouse to his dependents and a hammermaker had 11 properties, including houses, shops, coalhouses and brewhouses. Further, according to Berg, accumulation appeared to proceed through the addition of further small premises rather than through amalgamation into larger scale premises" (1991:26-27). The story appears very familiar.

9. See chapter 5.

10. The precise figures for occupational aspirations could not be found in Bechhofer and Elliott's work.

11. See chapter 5.

12. This may well be why the Asian business community is being wooed by the British Conservative Party. According to the Independent on Sunday, 12th Jan. 1992, "John Major chose to celebrate his first anniversary as Prime Minister in November with a most unusual dinner party. Seated round the Downing Street table were more than a dozen of the UK's most important business leaders...The prime minister was giving long-overdue official recognition to the growing importance of the Asian business community...Mr Major was also, no doubt, seeking to win over a traditional Labour constituency to his own party..."

13. Whether South Asian small business owners are actually more successful than the white ones would depend on the definition of success. Here, it is just the fact that greater proportions of Asians than whites appear willing to adopt the entrepreneurial route to success that contributes to their image of greater success.

14. As related by some of the older respondents and early settlers.

7 Assimilation and ethnicity

Introduction

Chapters 5 and 6 have established that the self-employed South Asians in Oxford may be viewed as participating effectively in the economic life of Britain, as a well entrenched section of the British middle class in terms of their market and work situations, and that in their economic activity ethnicity is not regarded as salient. What impact does this economic 'integration' have on the general interaction of this group with the host society on the one hand, and on the nature of their 'ethnicity' on the other? As noted in chapter 1, economic integration in the sense of success in employment and economic security, has been regarded as a necessary, if not a sufficient, condition of social integration. Also, the work place is the very first arena of immigrant-host interaction, and though social integration at the work place need not necessarily lead to general social integration (Wright 1968:13; Patterson 1968), it may be regarded as the first essential step towards it.

　　The further question which arises is whether, in encouraging integration, entrepreneurial entry also results in a weakening of ethnic identity and ethnic affiliation. Assimilationist theories often predict that as minority groups climb the social ladder towards some measure of parity with the majority group, there would be a corresponding decrease in ethnic identification and solidarity (cf. Tajfel 1978). Thus, as mentioned in chapter 1, a study of Jews (Rosentraub and Taebel 1980), found evidence of declining ethnic collectivism, solidarity and patronage among prosperous Jews. Other studies, however, do not support this. Driedger (1976), for instance, found that Jews of the highest socio-economic status in Winnipeg manifest a high level of ethnic identity. And, a further study of American Jews discovered a trend towards increasing polarisation, i.e., while a large section of the group is attempting assimilation, a section of this community which is inclusive of young people, is active in maintaining and perpetuating Jewish traditions and customs (Himmelfarb 1979).

　　It is proposed, therefore, to see what effect successful entrepreneurship has on the 'ethnicity' of the South Asian small business owners in Oxford. An attempt is made to draw a profile of this occupational group in terms of its degree of assimilation as well in terms of the nature and salience of its ethnic identity. In order to do this, a theoretical analysis of the concepts of assimilation and ethnicity is first attempted.

The concept of assimilation

'Unilateral assimilation' or 'Straight Line Theory'

Over the years, 'assimilation' has been conceptualised in various ways. According to an early and widely quoted view:

> Assimilation is a process of interpenetration and fusion in which persons or groups acquire the memories, sentiments and attitudes of other persons or groups, and by sharing their experience and history, are incorporated with them in a common cultural life (Park and Burgess 1921:735).

This definition was further elaborated by Fairchild (1924), who argued in terms of a biological analogy, that just as foodstuff becomes an integral part of the organism that ingests it, assimilation of immigrants involves "such a complete transformation and unification of the new constituents that all sense of old and new disappears". Assimilation was then, a one way process, and involved identity between immigrant and host. It was understood to mean complete adaptation by the minority group or by individual members of it, to the values and patterns of the receiving society; such complete adaptation is accompanied by complete acceptance of the assimilating group of individuals on the part of the hosts (Patterson 1965).

These definitions would seem to be in accord with what Gordon (1964:88-99) refers to as the ideology of Anglo-conformity - the fever of 'Americanization' which gripped America during World War 1. The emphasis was on stripping the immigrant of his native culture and attachments to make him into an American along Anglo-Saxon lines. In Britain, however, as late as 1965, Patterson appeared to accept a similar concept of assimilation in her analysis of Britain's *Dark Strangers* (1965). Accepting a consensus model of society for Britain, she evidently felt that the onus of assimilation was on the immigrants not the hosts. Playing down considerably the 'discrimination-prejudice axis', she assumed that through various stages of varying difficulties a process of assimilation was possible and desirable. The in-built assumption that assimilation in this sense is the natural or desirable goal is subject to criticism as the anticipated adjustment is rather one-sided, with the migrants being expected to take on the values and norms of the receiving society. The desire by migrants and their descendants to maintain their original culture is underestimated, and the potential of their own cultural contributions overlooked.

149

'Reciprocal fusion' or 'The Melting Pot'

With the recognition of some impact of immigrant culture on that of the hosts - Berry (1951), for instance, provides a long list of products such as Grimm alfalfa, Tokay grapes, spaghetti, and so on, which have been introduced into America by immigrant groups and accepted by 'native' Americans - 'assimilation' began to be looked at from the point of view of the 'Melting Pot'. Thus, 'unilateral assimilation', the process in which one group relinquishes its own beliefs and behaviour patterns and takes over the culture of another, is distinguished from 'reciprocal fusion', in which a third culture emerges from the blending of two or more cultures, and also from various intermediary levels of assimilation.

But, as Glazer and Moynihan (1963 1975), have pointed out, the point about the melting-pot was that it did not happen. Entrance by the descendants of migrants into the social structure of the existing Protestant white society did not lead to the creation of new structures, new institutional forms, and a new sense of identity (Gordon 1964:127). The invitation to 'melt' could only result in the loss of group identity for the immigrants and acculturation on Anglo-Saxon lines. Though massive acculturation did take place, the American scene was one of 'multiple melting pots' or 'pluralism'. According to Bernard:

> The fact of the matter is that the U.S. has not assimilated the newcomer nor absorbed him. Our immigrant stock and our so called native stock have each integrated with the other...This concept of integration rests upon a belief in the importance of cultural differentiation within a framework of social unity. It recognizes the right of groups and individuals to be different so long as the differences do not lead to domination or disunity (1956:2)[1].

This leads to the third approach to Assimilation.

'Ethnic pluralism'

The existence of 'unassimilated' groups[2] is, according to Eisenstadt (1954), inevitable, in that, in the short run the receiving society cannot completely obliterate the distinct cultures of immigrant groups. What usually develops is a society composed of different groups maintaining some degree of separate identity, that is, a 'pluralistic' structure. The existence of a group with different patterns of behaviour, values, and attitudes, is not in itself a negative index of absorption.[3] What is more important in gauging the level of assimilation is the extent of 'institutional dispersion', that is, "the extent of the immigrants' dispersion or concentration within the various institutional spheres of the society" (Eisenstadt 1954:13), which as Gordon emphasizes, pinpoints a significant dimension of the assimilation process (Gordon 1964:67).

Gordon (1964) goes on to present a multidimensional model of the assimilation process. This model distinguishes seven assimilation dimensions:

1) Cultural or behavioural assimilation;

2) Structural assimilation - large scale entrance into cliques, clubs or institutions of host society on primary group level;

3) Marital assimilation - large scale inter-marriage;

4) Identificational assimilation - development of sense of peoplehood based exclusively on host society;

5) Attitude receptional assimilation - absence of prejudice;

6) Behaviour receptional assimilation - absence of discrimination;

7) Civic assimilation - absence of value and power conflict.

The hypotheses advanced about the relationship of these variables were first, that in majority-minority group contact, cultural assimilation or acculturation would occur first. Second, that acculturation may take place even when none of the other types of assimilation has occurred; and this situation of 'acculturation only' may continue indefinitely; and third, that if structural assimilation occurs along with or subsequent to acculturation, all other types of assimilation will inevitably follow. All groups, according to Gordon, go through a process of acculturation; however, there is a critical divide between acculturation and structural assimilation, in as much as acculturation means adopting the externals while structural assimilation means adopting the internals.

Structural assimilation, then, rather than acculturation, is held to be the keystone of the arch of assimilation. The price of such assimilation, however, is the disappearance of the ethnic group as a separate entity and the evaporation of its distinctive values (Gordon 1964:81). Gordon clearly expected this complete assimilation to take place at some time, and while this expectation is itself subject to criticism, from the point of view of this study, the more serious shortcoming is the fact that Gordon does not consider economic integration at all in his theory. His dimension of 'structural assimilation' could be broadened to include entry into economic institutions as a first stage. Thus, Yinger (1981), suggests looking at structural assimilation as a continuum ranging from acceptance into the workforce through to membership of 'cliques and clubs'. This would lead to a further modification, this time in Gordon's sequence of change - structural assimilation need not necessarily result in other types of assimilation - and the possibility of regression, as in the case of Jews in Nazi Germany, cannot be overlooked. It is this recognition of 'uneven assimilation' which Borrie emphasises when he speaks of the necessity of seeing the process of adjustment:

...as one which is generally accompanied by sub-groups being accommodated within the total framework, while wholly or partially absorbed in various sectors or isolates of that framework. Hence there may be economic absorption but cultural pluralism; cultural absorption at some levels (e.g. clubs, societies), yet cultural differentiation and isolation at others (e.g. family customs, diet, etc.)...and so on through many permutations which arise because of variations in the social systems brought into contact through immigration (1956:94).

One other challenge to Gordon's theory which may be mentioned is that put forward by the social psychologist, Richardson, who believes that a certain measure of 'satisfaction' with his new life is an essential pre-requisite for an immigrant's identification with and even acculturation (in the sense of 'optional acculturation' relating to attitudes and values, rather than 'obligatory acculturation' to language, food, etc.), into the host society (1967:3-30).[4]

Gordon's analysis of American society revealed that though large-scale acculturation did take place, structural separation of racial religious groups, and to some degree national origins groups, still remained. Gordon applied the term 'structural pluralism' to this picture of ethnic and racial relations. This analysis contributed to the growing realization among those studying race and ethnicity that the initial optimism of sociologists concerning the inevitable assimilation or 'melting' of American minority groups into some common framework which would bring about their disappearance was quite unwarranted and that in the words of Glazer and Moynihan, "the persisting facts of ethnicity demand attention, understanding and accommodation" (1975:84-85).

The concept of ethnicity

With the evolution of the concept of assimilation from its initial meaning of the final stage of an inevitable race relations cycle, to an almost never attainable end-point of an ethnic continuum, the emphasis shifts to 'ethnicity', the character or quality of an ethnic group. Ethnic groups, expected to be modified by the process of assimilation, are now recognised as revitalising themselves in various ways rather than succumbing to assimilatory pressures. According to Glazer and Moynihan, there is in 'ethnicity', the emergence of a new social category in as much as there has been a pronounced and sudden increase in tendencies by people in many countries and in many circumstances to insist on the significance of their group distinctiveness and identity and on new rights that derive from this group character.

The term 'ethnic group' has been expanded to refer not only to subgroups or minorities but to all the groups of a society characterized by a distinct sense of difference owing to culture and descent (Glazer and Moynihan 1975:2-5). According to Gordon, the two functional characteristics of the ethnic group are: first, it serves psychologically as a source of group self identification, as the locus of the sense of intimate peoplehood, and second, it provides a patterned network of groups and institutions which allow an individual to confine his primary group relationships to his own ethnic group, throughout all the stages of his life-cycle. A third characteristic is that there is the possibility of cultural diversity, in so far as the ethnic group refracts the national culture through the prism of its own cultural heritage (Gordon 1964:38). This third characteristic points to the general view that ethnicity is not identical with culture and is not usefully conceived of as a 'primordial sentiment' (Hechter 1974:1151-1178). Ethnicity, according to Hechter, refers to the sentiments which bind individuals into solitary groups on some cultural basis. Ethnicity, therefore, alludes to the quality of relations existing between individuals sharing certain cultural behaviour. This distinction has an important methodological consequence: cultural variables cannot be used to indicate the strength of ethnic solidarity. Thus, changes in a group's cultural practices have no necessary bearing on changes in the extent of its ethnic solidarity. The study of ethnic change cannot, therefore, rely upon evidence concerning cultural change (Hechter 1974:1152). Subjective definitions of ethnicity necessarily place critical emphasis upon "the ethnic boundaries that define the group, not the cultural stuff it encloses" (Barth 1969). If the boundaries between members and non-members is maintained, the ethnic group continues over time even if the distinctive physical and cultural traits that define it objectively change sharply (Pettigrew 1978:26). Barth suggests:

> ...the focus of investigation should, therefore, shift from the cultural factors exemplified by the group to the process of persistence and maintenance of ethnic boundaries and the 'continuing' dichotomization between members and outsiders (1969:14-15).

Parsons, using a term of David Schneider's, refers to the 'desocialization' of ethnic groups: the 'culture content' of each ethnic group in the U.S., seems to have become very similar to that of others, but the emotional significance of attachment to the ethnic group appears to persist (1975:66). Thus, Bell is quite emphatic that ethnicity is best understood *not* as a primordial phenomenon in which deeply held identities have to re-emerge, but as a strategic choice by individuals, who, in other circumstances, would choose other group membership as a means of gaining some power and privilege. The attachment to ethnicity may then flourish or fade very quickly depending on political and economic circumstances (1975:171). This appears a little doubtful - even if the overt expression of ethnicity waxes and wanes, the attachment, which, as Bell himself has admitted, includes an affective element, surely does not fluctuate. Glazer and Moynihan point out in a similar vein, that ethnic groups are increasingly being defined in terms of interest, as 'interest groups'. According to them, the weight of conflicts regarding language, religion, and other cultural characteristics, has shifted from an emphasis on culture, language, religion, as such, to an emphasis on the interests broadly defined of the members of the group (1975:8). They also speak of the 'strategic efficacy of ethnicity' as a basis for asserting claims against government, and the fact that government, too, employs ethnic categories as a basis for distributing its rewards. The paradox, according to Bell, is that with more syncretism and intermingling, formal ethnic attachments may weaken, yet, if one wants to, one can now identify oneself more readily, and without losing esteem, in ethnic terms, and make claims on the basis of that identity (Glazer and Moynihan 1975:171).

The view that modernization would break ethnic attachments is now countered with its antithesis - sub-societal, culturally and ancestrally defined groups persist; they may even be strengthened by the competitive forces released by modernization (Rex and Mason 1986:39). It becomes necessary to look on 'ethnicity' as assuming different forms in different circumstances, ranging from 'primordial', to 'symbolic', to 'affective', to 'interest based' ethnicity.

The strength of ethnic attachments will no doubt vary widely. In Toronto, North America's most ethnically heterogeneous city, Weinfeld (1977), discovered that ethnic preferences as reflected in choice of residence, spouse, friends, language, and community participation, decline with each generation and with greater educational attainment. But, he found that this assimilationist model does *not* fit the two psychological variables of self identification and support for cultural pluralism. Weinfeld labels this psychological component 'affective ethnicity'; it is this element that is the persistent core of North American ethnicity that effectively resists assimilationist pressures. While Gordon had predicted that the sense of 'peoplehood' would necessarily lessen when significant structural entry is made, Weinfeld's Toronto results question this. Close boundary convergences among the affective, cultural, and social components of ethnicity should not, then, be assumed.

Pettigrew emphasizes that the most lasting core of ethnicity may be its affective basis (1978:31). Yinger holds that neither the assimilationist thesis nor the persistence-of-ethnic-difference antithesis is adequate. The synthesis according to him would recognize the wide variation and explore the conditions under which societies fall along various points on the range. In some societies, ethnic and racial identities are the most powerful, while in other societies, the lines separating ethnic groups are thin; intermarriage is quite common and assimilation has been extensive. 'Affective ethnicity' in Pettigrew's sense, continues but cross-cutting contacts and memberships predominate. This 'ethnic continuum' has to be recognized if a powerful theory of ethnicity is to be developed (Rex and Mason 1986:39).

Further, with the recognition of this continuum there is a paradigmatic shift in conceptualisation: the integration of immigrant groups into the larger society does not necessarily require a loss of ethnicity. The awareness of this is reflected in definitions, some rather early, which clearly distinguish between assimilation on the one hand and integration and acculturation on the other. Thus, according to Krausz (1972):

Whilst assimilation implies changes that bring about the disappearance of the minority group, acculturation is regarded as the process whereby the minority becomes more akin to the dominant group, although it continues to exist as a separate entity.

And, according to London (1967), integration implies:

Interaction between the minority group and the host society with a resultant change in the cultural amalgam, but without loss of cultural identity.

Hence, where previous assimilationist theories required the eventual elimination of all expressions of ethnicity, 'integration' and 'acculturation' give the ethnic group the freedom to maintain its ethnic identity, while acquiring a competence in the ways of the majority group. To recognise this is to recognise that a single continuum with ethnicity and assimilation at its poles is no longer adequate in understanding inter-group relations. There is a need for two continua, one measuring high and low ethnic identification and the other high and low identification with the majority group. Hutnik (1985), therefore, provides a 'quadrapolar paradigm' for the study of ethnic minority identity and styles of cultural adaptation. According to Hutnik:

Most of the earlier research has measured degrees of assimilation and/or degrees of dissociation by placing these concepts at the opposite ends of a single continuum...it is necessary to introduce a second continuum. A person adopting a dissociative style finds great enjoyment in using the ethnic language, wearing ethnic clothes, viewing ethnic films, listening to ethnic music - but so too does a person adopting an acculturative style. The crucial difference is their level of enjoyment of aspects of the majority culture. The acculturative individual is high on this continuum, whereas a dissociative person scores low. Similarly, assimilative and acculturative individuals look remarkably alike if one measures their appreciation of their majority group culture. The critical difference between these two types of cultural adaptation lies in their appreciation of the ethnic minority culture, with the assimilative person wanting to deny, forget, break ties with the culture of his origin, whereas the acculturative person is happy to be immersed in the ethnic culture.

It is therefore necessary to treat ethnic minority individuals' identification with the ethnic minority group and their identification with the majority group as two separate (although not necessarily independent) continua, in order to arrive at an accurate portrayal of their style of cultural adaptation (1991:128-29).

The analysis requires to be carried a step further, to draw attention to the fact that whatever the type of ethnicity that survives despite assimilatory

155

pressures, it is itself capable of fragmentation, in that ethnic group members are able to *compartmentalize* their ethnic identification, restricting its salience to certain areas of their life and regarding ethnic identity as completely non-salient in other areas. As Peach maintains:

> ...ethnicity is a transactional rather than categorical dimension...Because ethnicity is many layered and because the ethnicity of others is many layered, the degree to which ethnicity is displayed depends in part on the other actors...I may be Welsh in England, British in Germany and European in Thailand...Ethnicity, in other words, is a category which is in part a product of what it confronts (1983:123).

And, as Wallman points out:

> No one - not even the members of visible or beleaguered ethnic minority groups - consistently identifies himself or is always identified by others in ethnic terms. Ethnicity is only one identity option...and the significance of ethnicity to the individual must be taken into account (1983:69).

She goes on to say that:

> while there are many new instances of ethnicity persisting among immigrants, reviving in their children, and burgeoning among natives all over Europe, there are also signs of the growth of identities based on other social groupings and defined by other kinds of boundary. Among these, identities based on work and on locality may be the most important non-ethnic options[5]...(1983:77).

Khan, in a similar vein, speaks of 'the elasticity of ethnic affiliation'. According to her:

> For some purposes, notably those related to marriage and family visiting, it is the narrowest ethnic affiliation which regulates interaction. For other purposes, such as job-seeking, the boundary is extended to envelop a wider network of affiliation...(1979:133).

The questions to be considered in this chapter, then, refer to the nature and relevance of the ethnicity that is to be found among the members of South Asian groups who occupy petty bourgeois positions in Britain. In which of the areas regarded as significant for assimilation, are ethnic factors salient, and how salient are these factors?

The concepts operationalized

As has been noted earlier, Gordon, in his revision of his 1964 seminal model (1975), proposed that the seven indicators of assimilation should not be considered as having a necessary chronological sequence, but should be regarded as variables, such that any group could occupy differential positions on each of them. A group, for instance, could have a high degree of identificational assimilation with low exogamy. For purposes of research economy, Gordon suggests that the seven variables be reduced to four main areas - those of structural assimilation, acculturation, amalgamation through inter- marriage, and identification (1975:90). Yinger (1981) in his theory of assimilation and dissimilation suggests various amplifications and clarifications of Gordon's theory, notably, as mentioned earlier, that structural assimilation should be seen as a continuum ranging from acceptance into the workforce through to the membership of the same clubs and cliques. He is, however, in full agreement with Gordon in the delineation of the four major areas of assimilation. Fixing the position of a minority group in each of these areas would give us a profile of the group which identifies the essential features of its position in the society at a given time (Gordon 1975:60).

Arbitrarily trichotomising each of the variables into high, moderate and low, it would, according to Gordon, be possible to give a group scores on each of the variables and then combine the scores to provide a score of total assimilation. In line with this, Robinson (1982), ranks 12 sub-groups within the Asian minority in Blackburn on each of the variables, such that a high rank indicates tendencies towards assimilation and a low rank tendencies towards encapsulation. A profile of each group is provided by combining scores, so that a particular group, for instance, is "consistently assimilated on all criteria", while another is "highly acculturated and structurally integrated...(with)...absence of exogamy", and so on (1982:162-64).

Robinson's indicators are as follows:

Identificational assimilation - 'remittances to the home country', 'desire for return migration' and 'ethnic language transmission to children';

Acculturation - 'wearing of traditional dress by adults', 'wearing of traditional dress by children', 'capacity to speak and write English';

Structural integration - 'occupational concentration' and 'residential segregation';

Amalgamation - extent of exogamy.

Hutnik points out, however:

...Attempts at quantifying cultural adaptation have...measured either the degree of identification with the ethnic group *or* the degree of assimilation into the majority group. One example of this, the Ethnic Identity Questionnaire (Masuda *et al.* 1973) measures liking for Japanese food, movies, etc. The implicit assumption here is that high identification with the minority group precludes high identification with the majority group. Such measures tell only a partial truncated story of cultural adaptation...both the acculturative and the dissociative individual should have high levels of identification with the ethnic minority. It is their pattern of identification with the majority that makes the crucial difference in their styles of cultural adaptation. The two dimensions - ethnic minority identification and majority group identification - *must* be used in conjunction with each other, in order to arrive at an accurate understanding of the various styles of cultural adaptation (1991:158).

The two dimensions in conjunction give rise, according to Hutnik, to four patterns of identification as well as styles of cultural adaptation. Her model is reproduced in Figure 7.1.

Figure 7.1 Styles of adaptation*

High
Identification
with majority group

'Assimilative'   'Acculturative'

Low   High
Identification   Identification
with ethnic group   with ethnic group

'Marginal'   'Dissociative'

Low
Identification
with majority group

*   Source: Hutnik 1991:158

It is suggested here that Hutnik's fourfold schema may be effectively extended to each of the four areas of identificational assimilation, cultural adaptation, structural assimilation and amalgamation. That is, an attempt will be made to see if the South Asian entrepreneurs in Oxford are 'assimilative', 'acculturative', 'dissociative', or 'marginal', in each of these areas. The choice of indicators of each of the dimensions of assimilation, is derived from previous research as found in a review of the relevant literature, and an attempt has been made to select a good mix of attitudinal and behavioural variables. The variables used are as follows:

Identificational assimilation: 'satisfaction with employment in Britain', 'desire for return migration', 'visits to country of origin', 'remittances to country of origin', 'political participation in Britain', and 'intention to remain in Britain'.

Acculturation: 'reading of Asian newspapers', 'watching Asian films', 'desire to preserve Asian culture', 'desire to transmit Asian languages', 'speaking of Asian languages by children', 'desire to adopt British culture', 'wearing of traditional dress', 'capacity to speak English'.

Structural assimilation: 'importance of Asian business contacts', 'participation in community organisations', 'having only Asian friends', 'desire to keep apart from the English', 'residential segregation', 'relations with neighbours', 'participation in elections'.

Marital assimilation: 'choice of spouse for children', 'objections to marriage outside the ethnic group', 'outmarriage of children'.

Identificational assimilation

As mentioned earlier, a certain level of satisfaction with the situation in the host country has been regarded by Richardson (1967), as the basic pre-requisite for identification to even begin.

The interviews clearly revealed that the present respondents, as members of the petty bourgeois group, have a very high level of satisfaction, primarily with what they see as their occupational and financial success, and because of that, with life in general. As mentioned in chapter 5, the responses to the question, 'How satisfied are you with your present job? Please mark yourself out of ten', were very positive. Though self assessment of job satisfaction is highly suspect, it is given some consideration in view of its consistency with the responses to three related questions asked at different places in the interview schedule. These questions were, 1) 'Would you consider the alternative jobs available to you to be better or worse than the present one?' 2) 'If you had a choice between your present job and being a paid employee with a higher income, which would you prefer?' 3) 'Over the next three years how likely are you to look for a job working for someone else as a paid employee?'

As the tables for the responses to these questions are to be found in chapter 5, the results are merely summarized here. Ninety three per cent of respondents gave themselves 7+ out of a possible 10 for job satisfaction, 85 per cent considered the alternative jobs available to them as worse than their present one, 75 per cent held that they would prefer self-employment to being an employee, and 85 per cent considered it very unlikely that they would look for paid employment over the next few years. Levels of satisfaction, then, appear to be very high.

Most respondents see Britain as a land of opportunity, providing means of economic advancement inconceivable in their home countries, and hence are quite satisfied with life in Britain despite racial prejudice and discrimination. A Pakistani woman, waxing eloquent in her eulogy of Britain maintained:

> Great Britain is really great, that's why its called so. Nowhere else can people have such an opportunity to rise. In India and Pakistan, the rich remain rich and do not allow the poor to rise. How can a poor person even think of starting a business there? The rich and powerful will see to it that he does not succeed...Here, in Britain, the people are very honest. Of course there are dishonest people even among them, but generally the British are more honest than us... (No.44)

This satisfaction does not appear to be much affected by the experience of racial prejudice and discrimination, which is largely accepted as a fact of life in Britain, but which does not directly affect them, and which should not in any case be allowed to stand in the way of economic betterment. The general attitude is summed up by a 35 year old post-office cum grocery owner:

> Of course there will be some discrimination and prejudice...We have to learn to adjust to it and not let it affect us. We have to handle it light. I don't care if people say anything to me - I know how to handle it. And in the majority of cases it is best to ignore it - how does it hurt you? (No.50)

It comes as no surprise then that 67 per cent of respondents answered 'yes' to the question, 'Do you feel that people of Asian origin should just ignore prejudice?'

Does the high level of satisfaction encourage identificational assimilation? Do these 'satisfied' entrepreneurs identify with their host country, or does their identification remain 'ethnic'? Crucial to the question of identification has been the celebrated 'myth of return'(Robinson 1982; Anwar 1979; Brooks and Singh 1979; Dahya 1974 1972; Desai 1963) - the unrealised and unrealisable intention to return to the home country which moulds the attitudes, aims and behaviour of migrants. If migrants regard themselves as transients in Britain, it is difficult to see them as identifying with the British. Thus, it has been argued that if migrants plan to return 'home', send money back for investment as well as for the needs of the extended family, and make visits to the home country on a regular basis, the attachment to the area of origin is not merely a sentimental or nostalgic link, but a definite 'ethnic' identification. There were direct questions[6] in the questionnaire on number of visits to home country, year of last visit, remittances, and plans for return. That identification with the home country remains strong is evident from the fact that visits are still made on a regular basis. Table 7.1 shows that 59 per cent of respondents have gone back at least once in the last five years. Thirty six per cent have actually made the last visit within the last two years.

Table 7.1 Visits to home country

Number of Visits from 1958-1990	Year of Last Visit			Row Total
	pre 1979	1980-1985	1986-1990	
0				9
1	4	4	2	10
2-5	4	17	36	57
6-9	1	-	8	9
12-26	-	-	9	9
Column Total	18	21	55	94
Per Cent	19	22	59	100

It is of some interest that eight out of the nine respondents who have never visited the home country are African Asians whose links with the sub-continent have become attenuated through 'double migration'.

While respondents were not very forthcoming about the amounts of money sent back, 33 per cent were sending money to families on the subcontinent on a regular basis, both for investment purposes (usually for the mutual benefit of respondents and family members) such as buying land, building houses, or starting businesses, as well as for the personal use of family members. Forty five per cent claimed that only occasional remittances were made, usually for festivals, weddings, deaths and other emergencies, but the amounts spent were often quite heavy. For instance, one respondent had "got eleven girls in the family married", many had got houses built for their families and provided other improvements and amenities, and no one visited home without carrying a huge quantity of merchandise as gifts. While one respondent quite frankly claimed that the demands of the 'biraderi' or the extended kinship group, could ruin a man, others looked on it as an exercise in benevolence which served to increase their power and prestige 'back home'. Table 7.2, which provides the percentage of remitters, also reveals that 22 per cent of respondents *never* remit money, though gift-giving on visits is regarded as an inevitable part of visiting the home country.

Table 7.2 Remittances to country of origin

Percentage of respondents sending remittances

Regularly	Occasionally	Never
33	45	22

n=94

It appears then, that remittances to the sub-continent continue as do the periodic visits. Can this be looked at as an effect of the 'myth of return'? It must first be considered whether there is at all a myth of return. A direct question was asked on plans to return to the home country. The answers, as set out in Table 7.3, reveal that while 21 per cent claim intention to return, 44 per cent hold that though 'return' is an attractive proposition and though they would like to go back, they cannot see themselves as being able to do so. A further 35 per cent state that they do not want to go back. For the vast majority of 79 per cent,[7] then, it may be maintained that there is no longer a 'myth of return'.

Table 7.3 Desire to return

Percentage of respondents saying

Will Return	Wish to, but Cannot	Do Not Wish
21	44	35

n=94

Table 7.4 Effect of myth of return on remittances

Percentage of Respondents

	Regular Remittance	Occasional Remittance	No Remittance	Row Total
Will Return	13	7	1	21
Will Not Return	21	36	22	79
Column total	34	43	23	99

n=94

That the lack of the intention to return may not affect other links with the home country can be seen from Table 7.4 where 'intention to return' and 'remittances to country of origin' are cross tabulated.

It is seen from Table 7.4 that while those who never remit money is largely made up of those who do not intend to return, of those who do remit regularly, a larger proportion falls into the non-returning group. The largest proportion of respondents is to be found in the category of those who do remit occasionally, but who do not intend to return. It appears then that remittances continue even without any intention of return.

Along the same lines visits to the home country continue regardless of intention of permanent return. Thus 71 per cent of those who have made at least one visit home in the last five years, do not intend returning permanently.

In view of the fact that 79 per cent of respondents plan to remain permanently in Britain, it may be suggested that some measure of identification with this country as well should be recognised. Further indicators of British identification may be views regarding involvement in the political life of Britain as well as actual political behaviour. Attitudes towards political involvement may be gauged by answers to the question, 'Should people of Asian origin join political organisations alongside white people?'

A majority of 80 per cent answer this question in the affirmative. Most of the responses were an emphatic 'yes'. According to a 36 year old Pakistani grocer:

> Definitely we should join - not separate parties of our own. We should join the political parties here and try to get our people elected. (No.32)

Other responses included the following:

> Yes, definitely, otherwise how will we get a voice? (No.30)

> We *should* join, because we live in this country and we must participate. (No.80)

This positive attitude is reflected in behavioural patterns as well, in that 93 per cent support the main national political parties, and 92 per cent claim regular participation in elections. If intention to remain in Britain and political participation are taken as indicators of British identification, it is clear that identification is not unidimensional, in that ethnic identification does not rule out the possibility of British identification as well. Dual identification fits quite easily into the Hutnik model described earlier.

To fit the above data into this model, a score for 'Ethnic Identification'[8] is computed by combining the scores for the three variables 'desire to return', 'visits to country of origin' and 'remittances'. Similarly, a score for 'British Identification' is computed by combining scores for 'desire to stay', 'political participation' and 'job satisfaction'. Ethnic identification and British identification are then cross tabulated in Table 7.5. The cross tabulation shows 69 per cent of respondents exhibiting high identification with both the ethnic group and Britain, that is, the 'acculturative' mode of identification.

Table 7.5 Identificational assimilation

Percentage of respondents

| | British Identification | | |
	High	Low	Row Total
Ethnic Identification			
High	69	21	90
Low	10	-	10
Column Total	79	21	100
n=94			

On the grounds that the group as a whole appears to have a high identification with both the ethnic group as well as the majority group, their identification appears to be of the acculturative kind.

Acculturation

'Acculturation', according to Gordon, "is used to designate one factor or dimension in the meeting of peoples: cultural behaviour"(1965:62). Changes in cultural behaviour, ranging from the apparently trivial such as dress, food, manner, which Gordon has called the 'extrinsic' traits, to the more basic ones of religious beliefs and practices, ethical values, language and literature, termed 'intrinsic' by Gordon, have been regarded as the first to take place.[9] While a certain level of acculturation is inevitable, it need not lead to any other kind of assimilation, the stage of 'acculturation only' carrying on indefinitely. According to Richardson, what occurs at an initial stage is only what he calls 'obligatory acculturation' or 'advantageous acculturation', in that an immigrant may, even if dissatisfied, learn some English, acquire some elementary economic and geographical facts and adapt to some extent to the food and dress habits of the local population. But, what is significant is 'optional acculturation', which relates to those attitudes and behaviours on which the host society exerts no pressure on the migrants to conform, and this, Richardson holds, takes place only much later, when the migrant has achieved some measure of satisfaction with life in the host country (1967:3-30). In addition the distinction made by Robinson, between 'substitutive acculturation' where one trait is replaced by another, and 'additive acculturation' when new forms of behaviour supplement the old, must also be noted (1982:154). Where Robinson regards use of the English language by Asian migrants as an additive extrinsic trait, and giving up of traditional dress for western clothes as a substitutive cultural trait, present evidence suggests that most acculturation is *additive*, in that respondents move freely between the two cultures as far as dress, language, food, entertainment, and even observance of religious festivals are concerned. Thus, it is not enough to consider just the extent of traditional dress and language retention, but also the extent of acceptance of the majority culture. Again, a useful model to follow here is that provided by Hutnik in her study of styles of cultural adaptation, which is set out in figure 7.2.

Figure 7.2 Styles of cultural adaptation*

	Rejects Culture of Origin	Retains Culture of Origin
Rejects Majority Culture	Marginal	Dissociative
Retains Majority Culture	Assimilative	Acculturative

*Source: Hutnik, 1985:196

In order to place respondents into one of these four categories, their responses to a number of attitudinal as well as behavioural questions are considered.

Respondents were asked specific questions relating to reading of Asian newspapers, watching of Asian videos and T.V. programmes. The answers are summarized in Table 7.6 below.

Table 7.6 'Do you read Asian newspapers, watch Asian videos and Asian T.V. programmes?'

Percentage of respondents

	Reading Asian Newspapers	Watching Asian Films/Videos	Watching Asian T.V. programmes
Often	44	64	26
Occasionally	30	33	71
Never	26	3	3

n=94

Videos of Asian films are an important source of entertainment, which includes the whole family and is thus also a significant source of socialization into the traditional culture for the children. The latest film releases from the subcontinent are readily available on video, and are an important means of language transmission, as well as providing information on the latest fashions in dress. While it is not always possible

165

for respondents to watch the Asian programmes on T.V. due to the time constraints imposed by long hours of work, there are no such constraints on video-watching, and as can be seen from Table 7.6, only three per cent of the sample maintain that they never watch Asian films.[10]

Respondents' attitudes towards the preservation of ethnic culture and the transmission of traditional skills such as the ability to speak the language of the country of origin, were also considered. One of the questions asked was, 'Would you say that people of Asian origin should try to preserve as much of their own way of life and culture as possible?' Seventy five per cent answered 'Yes, definitely' to this question.

A few of those who made this positive response also voiced the belief that, together with preservation of ethnic culture, British culture should be rejected, falling into the dissociative category. One of these responses was that of a 40 year old, African Asian grocer, according to whom:

> The children are growing up here and going to British schools. They will not feel the difference between Indians and British. They won't have the feeling that the British are different, so it is for the parents to educate them in their own culture. This calls for a lot of dedication. But it is better that Asians should take the trouble to preserve their own culture. The British culture is too different and causes a lot of problems. (No.57)

Along similar lines, a 45 year old Muslim grocer maintained:

> Very important that they do so. Look at the West - they are fed up with their culture and are always seeking peace - either through drugs, alcohol or sex. They should learn from Islam. We can continue to teach our children our way of life, it only requires a little organisation of time...We must make sure that our children know our ways of behaviour, our culture (No.73)

The responses of the remaining 25 per cent, interestingly, were not so much against the preservation of traditional culture as for a certain flexibility in its retention. As a 30 year old Pakistani woman, owner of a sub-postoffice, stated:

> Asians should retain their own culture, but should be more flexible and broadminded about it. There is no point in trying to preserve the Asian culture of 25 years ago. They should try to change. The idea is to be open to change in one's own culture which does not mean adopting a different one completely (No.72)

According to an Indian restaurant owner:

> It is important to keep our culture but we must not be too conservative. You should not show to the Europeans that you are a stubborn Asian (No.87)

The desire for cultural flexibility can be seen even more clearly in the responses to another question, 'Do you feel that people of Asian origin should try to adopt the way of life and culture of white people?' Forty seven per cent of the respondents believed that there were features of the British culture which were 'good', worthy of emulation and which Asians should try to adopt. Some of the responses are given below:

> We should take the good things from the Western society - like their general behaviour, politeness, honesty. Their outlook is not suspicious like ours. (No.58)

> We should take the good things from them - honesty, helpfulness etc., not the liquor and gambling and going out with women. (No.17)

> If Asians want to live here they must adapt to the British environment. (No.5)

A 38 year old Indian sub-postoffice owner, was quite emphatic that to lose one's cultural language was to lose one's identity. Though he was educating his sons in an expensive private school, he was at the same time teaching his sons Hindi at home. According to him:

> ...you can't really live separate from British life and culture. Some things you have to adopt such as the clothes, the food, the language - we even celebrate Christmas because if we didn't it wouldn't be fair on the children, they would feel left out. (No.52)

The duality in respondents attitudes' to culture preservation is then evident. While the majority do maintain that preservation of ethnic culture is important, this does not necessarily imply any sort of cultural encapsulation or dissociation, in that nearly 50 per cent also maintain that acceptance of certain aspects of British culture is an essential part of living in Britain.

The same duality is evident in attitudes towards language as well. The belief in the importance of traditional language retention is unswerving - 95 per cent maintain that it is very important to be able to speak the language of the country of origin.[11] The Indian shop-keeper referred to above, who took time off from his busy schedule to teach his three sons Hindi, waxed eloquent on the need to know the language of origin:

> The mother tongue, together with the mother, and the mother land are three things you should worship... without it you lose your identity. Your language is your culture... (No.52)

Only five per cent maintained that they would try to retain their mother tongue 'as far as possible' but would not consider it of crucial importance.

To what extent is this linguistic attachment reflected in actual behaviour? One way of testing this is by looking at the level of transmission of traditional language skills to the children. The importance that respondents give to their children's ability to speak their mother tongue has been taken as an indicator also of the parents' attitude towards the socialisation of their children into their own group culture (Robinson 1982:152). Robinson asked interviewees whether they considered it important that their children should be able to speak their mother tongue, framing the question in a hypothetical form for those without children, and, not surprisingly, found that 90 per cent considered it important. The question asked in this survey was, 'Do your children speak any of the Asian languages?' The results are quite impressively in favour of ethnicity.

If the 'not applicable' category, which includes those without children or with young babies, is excluded, 74 out of 86, that is 81 per cent of respondents have children who are able to speak the language of their ethnic group. Evidently, the commitment of respondents to the transmission of their linguistic cultural heritage is very strong.

However, this does not in any way detract from the importance given to the English language, which is adopted in addition to the mother tongue, and is thus, clearly an additive extrinsic trait. That attitudes towards the learning of English are very favourable is quite clear from the unanimous reply - a clear 100 per cent response - to the question, 'Should people of Asian origin learn to speak English?' Respondents appeared surprised by the question, and usually answered, 'Yes, of course', 'it is very important', 'how can you manage without English?'

Does this attitude translate into an actual ability to speak and write English? Though it was not possible to make any sort of objective test of ability, interviews were conducted for the most part in English. Respondents occasionally used Hindi or Punjabi to emphasize or reinforce a point, but questions were asked and answered in English. And observance of the respondent and family members in their interaction with their white clientele, provided a good understanding of their ability to speak English, if not to write it. The fluency with which English was spoken by the shopkeepers was very impressive, in view of the fact that the same people were definitely not of the class of people on the subcontinent who would be likely to speak English in general interaction.[12] The accent, intonation, and phraseology made it quite clear that the language had been picked up after migration. The point to be emphasized here is that it was not a case of just knowing enough English to get by on, but of being able to communicate effectively and easily in the language. Only two women, spouses of the respondents, admitted to some difficulty in speaking English, but were fairly confident of improvement.

Among the restaurateurs, however, some exceptions were found. There were surprisingly, a few men who spoke only Bengali, and who were, therefore, confined to work in the kitchen. These were not just 'workers', as, because of the peculiar ownership structure of the South Asian restaurant, even a cook could share part ownership of the restaurant, together with a waiter or a manager. Those who worked 'in the front' were, however, quite fluent in the language. The small business owners then, were for the most part, quite comfortably bi-lingual.

While there are clear signs of the acceptance of many extrinsic cultural traits of the majority society, there are no indications whatever of any inclination to move away from the ethnic culture.

Previous research which had looked at specification of religious faith in order to gauge the extent of intrinsic acculturation, has concluded that no intrinsic acculturation had taken place on this indicator (Robinson 1982:157). Where the intrinsic trait of religious beliefs is concerned, changes were neither expected nor found by the present study. In fact, adherence to the original religion appears to be very strong, as also the feeling of closeness to people who share the same faith. To the question, 'How close do you feel towards people of the same religious faith as you?', 55 per cent maintained that they 'feel close', and only five per cent held that they do not feel any closeness on the basis of religious faith. Religious festivals are celebrated with great *éclat*, with the families of respondents taking an active part in the celebrations, though respondents themselves are often not able to take time off from work. While the ethnic festivals are collective affairs, respondents claim that, on an individual family basis, they also celebrate the religious festivals of the majority group, such as Christmas and Easter. Many hold that such celebration cannot be avoided because of the young children who would otherwise feel left out of the general festivity. Others see it as part of their business activity - gift giving to old and regular customers being a normal practice for many shop keepers.

In an attempt to operationalise the scheme proposed by Hutnik, a measure of 'acceptance of majority culture' is computed[13] by combining scores for the following variables:

1) Importance given to the speaking of English;

2) Views on Adoption of British Culture; and

3) Wearing of Western clothes.

Again, the following variables are combined for a measure of 'retention of culture of origin'[14] :

1) Speaking of Asian Language by Children;

2) Reading of Asian Newspapers;

3) Watching of Asian Films;

4) Importance given to the preservation of ethnic culture; and

5) Importance given to the retention of Asian languages.

Cross tabulating the two combined variables, it is found that the majority of respondents follow an 'acculturative' style of cultural adaptation, that is, both accepting the majority culture as well as retaining the culture of origin. This can be seen from Table 7.7, which also reveals that only a very small minority can be termed 'assimilative' in their style of cultural adaptation.

Table 7.7 Styles of cultural adaptation

Percentage of respondents

	Majority Culture	
	Accepts	Rejects
Culture of Origin		
Accepts	59	31
Rejects	8	2

n=94

Structural assimilation

It has been customary to look on structural assimilation, defined by Gordon as entry into the primary groups, clubs and cliques of the host society, as the most significant step towards complete assimilation. As stressed earlier, in so far as it is now rightly felt to be necessary to look on entry into occupational structures as entry into the structural institutions of the host country, and in so far as such entry does not necessarily lead to any further assimilation, structural assimilation is looked upon as just another continuous variable in the assimilation profile of a migrant group.

A widely used indicator of structural assimilation has been the extent of occupational dispersion of the group as a whole. If any migrant group is assumed to start its work history at the bottom rungs of the occupational ladder, it can be expected over time to move upwards, and towards an occupational structure similar to that of the majority. A comparison of its occupational structure with that of the majority group would then directly indicate the extent of similarity and consequently the extent of structural assimilation (Duncan and Lieberson 1959; Lieberson 1961; Taeuber and Taeuber 1964). This indicator, however, is not available here as the present study is looking at one particular occupational group rather than the minority group as a whole. However, in as much as this group is one which has successfully moved into a middle class occupation, it may be looked upon as having achieved substantial integration into the economic structure of the host society.

It has, however, also been argued that concentration of minority groups in particular occupations could lead to increased ethnicity and ethnic solidarity, or what Yancey *et al.*, refer to as 'emergent ethnicity'. On the grounds that ethnicity is not so much based on cultural heritage or primordial sentiments as on contextual conditions such as a group's position on the stratification hierarchy, it has been argued that solidarity is more likely to develop among occupationally specialized ethnic groups (Hechter 1978; Yancey Ericksen and Juliani 1976; Hannerz 1974; Cohen 1969; Barth 1969). Some of the reasons advanced for the development of group identity and solidarity are that similarity of occupational status is likely to be accompanied by similarity of economic status and thus similarity of life styles. Again, similarity in occupation provides common social and economic interests. Occupational status is also linked to consciousness of class, and thus, group solidarity (Yancey Ericksen and Juliani 1976:393).

As mentioned in chapter 3, the South Asian business community in Oxford clearly has a coherent structure, in that generally, each person knows of everyone else within it, his creditworthiness, trustworthiness, how well he is doing, even whether he has a Swiss bank account. But, when it comes to actual business activity, the orientation of the ethnic shop-keeper continues to be what Goldthorpe and Lockwood (1963), characterised as 'radical individualism'. As noted in chapter 3, 64 per cent of respondents believe that contact with other Asian businessmen is not very important in order to run their business well, and this includes 25 per cent who dismiss it as entirely unimportant. The 36 per cent who believe that contact is important stress that its importance lies in the business information available through such contact, and not in the sense of any practical help.

Thus, a 20 year old, Pakistani grocer believed:

It is good to be on good terms with everybody, but, if I'm in trouble, they are not going to help me, are they? It is only my immediate family, my parents and brothers and their wives who are important to me. (No.24)

A 60 year old Indian sub-postmaster, resident in Oxford for 29 years, said:

...there has always been distrust in the Asian community, and there will always be. But sometimes we can rise above the differences and unite for a cause. (No.54)

A 57 year old, successful Pakistani businessman maintained:

I stopped associating with the Oxford people[15] long ago. The Asians here are jealous of my wealth and success. (No.55)

An East African Asian, recently turned shop-keeper, stated quite bluntly that he did not believe in the importance of the Asian community:

I just keep away from them. They will stab you in the back whenever they can. So I keep away. Asians in business just cannot get along. (No.42)

Commonality of occupation, then, does not result in ethnic solidarity of any kind. Is this lack of solidarity restricted to the pursuit of economic interests, or does it extend to the social sphere as well? Respondents were asked whether they were members of any community organisations, and what the extent of their participation was. These community associations, according to Rex, are to be seen as social structures through which the wider community life of migrant groups is expressed. The various functions of such associations include:

> ...acting as a kind of community trade union and negotiating on its behalf with the larger society, overcoming the social isolation of individuals, affirming beliefs and values, and ministering to the needs of individuals and families...Of particular importance is the role of the associations in...offering of beliefs to the individual about himself, that is to say identity options... (1986:132).

To what extent does this hold for the present respondents? Forty three per cent of respondents did not belong to any community organisation. While 57 per cent were members of organisations such as the Hindu Mandal, the Pakistani Welfare Association, the Nirankari Mission, and so on, only 22 per cent participated regularly in the activities of these associations; 35 per cent maintained that they attended very occasionally and only if time permitted. Participation in these community associations was evidently not an important aspect of the social life of these self-employed Asians.

It must be remembered, however, that by the very nature of their occupations, the self-employed lead very restricted social lives - it is generally maintained that 'there is no leisure time' - and to the question on the ethnic origins and occupations of close friends, 28 per cent answered that they did not have close friends, all interaction being within the family. There is then, little evidence of reliance on ethnic solidarity amongst the entrepreneurs, or of the enhancement of solidarity as a result of their business activity.

Identity options for the self-employed do not appear to stem from ethnic group participation so much as from occupational activity which forms the major preoccupation of their lives. There is, amongst the small business owners, a certain consciousness of sharing a relatively high status within the Asian group as a direct result of their entrepreneurial activity,[16] from which the non-self-employed are excluded. Further, of those respondents who said that they did have friends, 56 per cent maintained that these friends belonged predominantly to the business community.

However, 67 per cent of respondents do claim a certain closeness to people from the same area of origin as themselves. And, in response to the question on the actual ethnic origins of close friends, 59 per cent maintained that all their close friends were Asian, with only a minority of 13 per cent claiming both Asian and white friends.[17] A certain consciousness of ethnicity is evidently there but not to the extent of a definable collective solidarity.

Some evidence that this ethnic consciousness does not involve encapsulatory tendencies may be found in the answers to the attitudinal

172

Some evidence that this ethnic consciousness does not involve encapsulatory tendencies may be found in the answers to the attitudinal question, 'Do you feel that people of Asian origin should keep themselves apart from white people?' Just two per cent answered in the affirmative. A further 12 per cent felt that they 'should keep themselves apart to some extent', but the overwhelming majority of 86 per cent said 'no', with reasons ranging from, 'why should we?', to 'it wouldn't be right', to 'even if we wanted to, it wouldn't be possible - we would have to make separate colonies for ourselves!'. So also, the response to the question, 'Should people of Asian origin have white friends whom they see outside of their workplace?', was largely positive, in that 79 per cent answered 'yes', with a further 12 per cent qualifying their 'yes' with '...if the white people will be friends!'. Nine per cent believed that they should not have white friends.

One variable which is often taken as an important indicator of structural assimilation, is that of patterns of residence. Along the lines of Park's (1926) relationship between physical and social distance, it has been argued that the extent of residential segregation of a minority group may be taken as indicative of its social distance from the majority group, in as much as there is less likelihood of involvement in the primary groups and associations of the majority. Also, residential segregation would result in heightened ethnicity, as:

> Insofar as minority people are forced to live together, communal ethnic ties will be strengthened by daily interaction. Even if the minority workers were to form alliances with their white peers in the work place, such unity would not be fostered by residential community life, as was the unity of the workers in traditional working class communities whose neighbourhood life served to reinforce ties at work (Rex 1986:71).

What is the nature of the residential location of the self-employed South Asians in Oxford? Areas within Oxford are characterised as 'Asian' or 'non-Asian' on the basis of accepted notions among Oxford residents regarding ethnic concentrations.[18] Thus, areas around Cowley Road, St. Clements, and Abingdon Road, are known to be areas of heavier concentrations of Asians, while areas in North Oxford or Headington have few Asians. Fifty three per cent of respondents are residentially located in areas which are clearly 'non-Asian', in that the proportion of Asians living in these areas is negligible. Forty seven per cent of the population do, however, live in areas which may be characterised as areas of 'ethnic concentration'. This does not in any way imply segregation of any kind, insofar as in an area such as Oxford, even in the areas characterised as 'Asian', the Asians would definitely be living amidst whites rather than just Asians. This may be illustrated by Table 7.8 where residential location of respondents and the ethnic group of the immediate neighbours are cross tabulated.

173

Table 7.8 Residential location and neighbours' ethnic group

Percentage of respondents (n=94)

| Residential Location | Ethnic Group of Neighbours | | | Row Total |
	White	Asian	White + Asian	
'Asian' Area	31	2	14	47
'Non-Asian' Area	45	2	6	53
Column Total	76	4	20	100

It is clear from Table 7.8 that regardless of the area that they live in, 76 per cent of the self-employed have only white neighbours, and only four per cent have only Asian neighbours.

The basis of choice of residential location can be seen from Table 7.9 where 'Residential Location' is cross tabulated with 'Reasons for Choice of Location'.

Table 7.9 Residential location and reasons for choice of location

Percentage of respondents

Reasons for Choice of Location

Residential Location	Business Opportunity	Chance Area	Asian	'Good' Area	Row Total
Above shop + Asian area	12	5	4	-	21
Above shop + Non Asian area	22	7	-	3	33
Away from shop + Asian area	12	8	3	3	26
Away from shop +Non Asian area	2	5	-	14	21
Column total	48	25	7	20	100

It can be seen from Table 7.9 that only seven per cent of the population chose the location of their residence specifically because they wanted an

Asian area. To live among Asians is no longer a priority, the choice of residence being largely determined by 'business opportunity', either in the sense of wanting the residence to be close to the shop or restaurant, or the house being above the shop. If those choosing non-Asian areas are considered, 17 per cent of respondents give as the reason for their choice their belief that these areas are 'good areas'. That the criteria of 'goodness' are universalistic, and may include a desire to maintain a certain distance from South Asians in general, can be seen from the following remarks made in connection with the choice of residential location:

According to a 30 year old, Pakistani woman:

> I would hate to live among the old-fashioned, conservative Pakistani migrants - all living close together, in and out of each other's houses, gossiping about each other. I prefer to live away from the crowd. And North Oxford is a very good area, an upper class locality, and the people are very nice. (No.72)

This attitude was quite wide-spread, with many respondents holding that living close together with other Asians was what caused problems. According to a 35 year old African Asian, he chose his shop cum house in North Oxford, because he "preferred something outside Cowley." (No.7)

However, the lack of physical distance should not be equated with greater social interaction with whites and thus, greater social assimilation. In fact, Rex and Moore (1967), have shown that proximity may give rise to greater competition and conflict. While this does not appear to be true for the Oxford self-employed, their busy and essentially privatized life-style does not allow for much interaction with neighbours, whichever ethnic group the neighbours may belong to. The majority of 70 per cent maintained that while they knew their neighbours, and were on 'good terms' with them, all interaction was limited to casual chatting when they happened to meet outside their houses. That the nature of interaction may not be determined by the ethnicity of the neighbour can be seen from Table 7.10, where 'interaction with neighbours' is cross tabulated with 'neighbours ethnic group'.

It is worth noting from Table 7.10 that 19 per cent of those respondents who are on visiting terms with their neighbours, have only white neighbours, so that this close interaction is effectively with the majority group. The nature of interaction with neighbours, then, appears to be independent of ethnicity.

Table 7.10 Ethnic group of respondents' neighbours' by respondents' interaction with neighbours

Percentage of respondents

	Casual chatting	Hardly know them	Unfriendly	Visiting terms
		Nature of Interaction		
Ethnic Group of Neighbours'				
White	50	5	1	19
Asian	2	1	1	
White + Asian	18	1	1	
Column total	70	7	1	21

n=94

In an attempt to draw the various strands of structural assimilation together, a measure of 'involvement in Ethnic Structures' is computed[19] by combining the following variables: 1) Participation in Community Organisations, 2) Ethnicity of Close Friends, and 3) Contact with other Asian businessmen. Similarly, a measure of 'involvement in British Structures' is computed by combining the variables 1) Residential Location, 2) Relations with Neighbours, 3) Living apart from the British, and 4) Participation in elections. Cross tabulating the two combined variables in Table 7.11, it is found that 64 of the 94 respondents, i.e. 68 per cent, fall into the 'assimilated' category of high involvement in British structures and low involvement in Asian structures. It can also be seen from the table that the 'dissociative' and 'marginal' categories are extremely small. Twenty two per cent, however, maintain high structural involvement with both groups, falling, then, into what has been described as the 'acculturated' category.

Table 7.11 Structural assimilation

Percentage of respondents

	Involvement in British Structures		
	High	Low	Row Total
Ethnic Involvement			
High	22	5	27
Low	68	5	73
Column Total	90	10	100

n=94

A high level of intermarriage between members of minority and majority groups has been regarded as a conclusive indicator of assimilation insofar as it leads to biological amalgamation and is expected to occur only after significant acculturation and structural integration have taken place, as well as a significant reduction in prejudice and discrimination. Considerable evidence is also produced for a negative association between exogamy and ethnic identity, ethnically endogamous groups being less open to inter-ethnic interaction than exogamous groups. It is, then, generally agreed that the ultimate measure of the salience of ethnic boundaries is endogamy (Hechter 1978:304). While levels of intermarriage continue to have an important place in the testing of assimilation and ethnicity, it is now recognised that there are certain limitations to this criterion which must be noted.

First, it is possible for immigrants to intermarry with the indigenous group without any significant acculturation or structural integration or identification having taken place. An instance of this is provided by Tamil refugees to Denmark, who intermarry despite discrimination, and disadvantage and in the face of antagonism from the indigenous group (Steen 1992).

Secondly, interracial marriages do not necessarily lead to assimilation for the individuals concerned or for their offspring. Benson, in her study of interracial unions in Brixton, has argued that while at one extreme there will be those who seek and obtain incorporation into mainstream white society, at the other extreme there will be those whose social world is that of the minority group, with those at the centre straddling two social universes, both black and white (1981:148). Further, the offspring of mixed marriages generally identify with one of the groups to which their parents belong and do not become a wholly assimilated group. Objectively, the precise status of this group remains ambiguous. For example, government statisticians regard those of ethnically mixed descent as part of the West Indian, African or Asian groups from which one of their parents is drawn, though, as an Immigrant Statistics Unit publication points out:

> ...there is no firm basis for defining people of mixed descent as part of an ethnic minority: some of those of mixed descent will be identified with or will themselves identify with the ethnic minorities while others will be associated entirely with those of wholly UK descent (OPCS 1979:26).

Finally, intermarriage as a measure of assimilation has been criticised by Marcson, who argues that a minority group, such as the Scots-Irish, say, have persisted as a distinct group, with a pronounced tendency to in-marry, not as an unassimilated immigrant group but as a group of persons with considerable family, economic and religious affinities who naturally marry amongst themselves; but they cannot be styled 'unassimilated Americans' in any meaningful sense (1951:75-8).

Despite these difficulties, the level of intermarriage may be regarded as giving us some information concerning the assimilation profile of an ethnic group. As far as the present respondents are concerned, the rate of intermarriage with the white majority is negligible. There were a few who had formed liaisons with white women during the earlier stages of migration but who were legally married to women from their own communities at the time of the survey, and one who had been married to a white woman, by whom he had children, but who was divorced and remarried to a woman from his own ethnic group.

The picture changes, however, when patterns of marriage among the respondents' children are considered. Seven per cent of respondents have at least one child who has married a white. While this still appears to be low, it must be noted that 75 per cent of the respondents do not have married children. If only those who do have married children are considered, the proportion of respondents with exogamous children rises to 29 per cent.

Though in actual fact the proportion of children marrying out appears to be increasing, attitudes towards ethnic group exogamy remain fairly negative. To the question 'Would you object to your children marrying outside the ethnic group?', 68 per cent of respondents maintained that they *would* object. While 25 per cent of respondents say that they would not object to children marrying out, that they would prefer that children married within the group is brought out by the following responses: according to a 38 year old Indian post-office owner:

> No, I wouldn't object because there is nothing you can do if they want to marry out. There is no use losing your son as well. (No.52)

And, according to a 53 year old Sikh shop-keeper:

> No, I wouldn't object, but the way they have been brought up I don't think they would. I hope they will not. (No.21)

The sentiment that 'white and coloured people cannot mix together' and settle down in a lasting and permanent marriage was very widespread. There was an innate dislike of intermarriage, and the hope that their Asian upbringing would prevent children from wanting to marry out, and yet a certain pragmatism in handling possible or actual intermarriages because of the primacy of kinship bonds over antipathy to exogamy.

Thus, a 35 year old Pakistani maintained:

> Yes, I would object, but you cannot force children to do what you want. If they insist, you have to allow it. (No.50)

Similarly, according to a very successful, 47 year old Pakistani shop-keeper:

Yes, I do object. My eldest son has an English girl friend whom he wants to marry. We are not happy, but we do not want to oppose it and force our son in any way, as that could lead to more trouble. We have nothing against the girl as such, but no marriage outside the culture is a success. I have never known a mixed marriage to last - among the highly educated and those who have lived away for many years, maybe. But, my son has been brought up in an Asian way, and sometime or other the differences in the culture will break up the marriage and that is what upsets me. But there is nothing I can and will do about it. We allow the girl to come to the house and are on visiting terms with the parents as well. (No.38)

The preference for ethnic group endogamy is quite apparent in the responses to the question, 'If you were looking for a spouse for your son or daughter, which factors would you consider important?' As can be seen from Table 7.12, 76 per cent of respondents give importance to the ethnic group, though a half of them would also give consideration to the class factors within the ethnic group. Only seven per cent of respondents believed that social class preferences would take precedence over ethnic group membership.

Table 7.12 Significant factors in choice of spouse for children

Percentage of respondents

Ethnic Group	Ethnic Group and Social Class	Economic/Social Class	Don't Know
38	38	7	17

n=94

Crosstabulating 'outmarriage of children' with 'preference for ethnic endogamy'[20], it is found that the largest number of respondents fall into the 'dissociative' category of those who would prefer to confine themselves to the ethnic group where marriage is concerned. This can be seen from Table 7.13, which also reveals that six out of the seven respondents who do have children married out would have preferred them to marry within the ethnic group. Only one respondent, then, is truly assimilative where marriage is concerned. It is essential, however, to remember that the likelihood of this picture changing is quite high as 75 per cent of respondents' children are not married as yet.

Table 7.13 Marital assimilation

Percentage of respondents

Preference for Endogamy	Child Outmarriage		
	Yes	No	Row Total
Yes	6	76	82
No	1	17	18
Column Total	7	93	100

n=94

The crucial element of Asian ethnicity amongst the Asian self-employed in Oxford, then, appears to be ethnic endogamy, though there is a also a growing resignation to the probability of it weakening in the next generation.

Synthesis and conclusion

Drawing together the conclusions regarding the position of self-employed Oxford Asians on the four main assimilation variables, the assimilation profile that presents itself is of a group that has achieved considerable structural assimilation[21] insofar as they participate effectively in the economic and political structures of British society. They are economically successful, satisfied with their occupational mobility, and by the nature of their occupations, not heavily involved in the ethnic community. Their total preoccupation with their work, which is to them a whole way of life, precludes any significant interaction or involvement in 'cliques and clubs', whether of the host society or of the ethnic group. They believe in mainstream political participation and support the main political parties.

In the spheres of identificational assimilation and cultural assimilation, there is a certain dualism, in that identification with the host country does not necessarily imply lack of identification with the country of origin. Neither does taking on the secondary culture of the host society involve giving up the culture of the ethnic group. Thus, respondents are 'acculturative' in both their identification and their cultural adaptation.

Where marital assimilation is concerned, however, the tendency is towards 'dissociation' from the host society, there being a strong preference for marriage within the ethnic group. This appears to be the one sphere where the hold of ethnicity and ethnic cultural traditions continues.

What is, then, the nature of the ethnicity to be found in this self-employed group? Milton Singer, in describing the reconciliation of modern industry with the traditional Hindu ethic in South India, speaks of the adaptive process of *'compartmentalization'* of the two spheres of conduct and belief. According to Singer:

> The physical setting for the traditional religious sphere is the home, where many of the traditional ritual observances of Sanskritic Hinduism are performed. The physical setting for modern practices is the office and factory; there English is used. Western dress is worn, contacts with different castes and communities are frequent...The differences in behaviour indicate a culturally recognized difference in the two physical settings: The home is categorized as the domain of one's family, caste, religion, and language community; the norms appropriate to these groups are in operation there. The office and factory, on the other hand, are categorized as a domain that includes nonrelatives, other castes and communities, and even foreigners; the norms of behaviour there will accordingly be very different from those prevailing in the home (1972:321).

Compartmentalization, according to Singer, "represents a *heterogenetic* cultural change that seeks a mutual adaptation between the indigenous and the foreign", and this adaptation involves, "permitting new patterns and groups to be formed outside the old by setting them aside and labelling them as 'new' or 'foreign'..." (1972:324).

It is argued then, that it is the strategy of 'compartmentalization' that is adopted by the self-employed Oxford Asians in reconciling the demands of ethnicity and assimilation. They participate effectively in the economic and political structures of the country of adoption. Within the work environment, in the shop and the restaurant, ethnicity is largely forgotten - there is close interaction with the English clientele, Western clothes are worn, very often by the spouses as well, and the language spoken is English. In the domestic domain, however, ethnic values are upheld, there is considerable use of the ethnic language, and where food, dress, entertainment, intra-familial interaction, and marriage are concerned, ethnic culture takes precedence. It is, then, a 'compartmentalised ethnicity' that is to be found among the South Asian self-employed in Oxford today.

Notes

1.   Also quoted in Gordon (1964:68), and Borrie (1959:93-4).

2.   That maintenance of cultural heritage need not lead to lack of adjustment in relations with the host society, has been brought out by Useem and Useem in their study of Norwegian immigrants in a Prairie town. Useem and Useem show that it was the lack of assimilation or superficial integration with the out-group that allowed the Norwegians to retain their culture without conflict (1945).

3.   Though Eisenstadt prefers the term 'absorption', the sense in which it is used appears interchangeable with 'assimilation'.

4.   The importance of psychological and power variables is recognised by Gordon in his revised model (1975), where he emphasises that the seven indicators of his 1964 model should be seen as variables without any fixed chronological sequence, such that any group may have varying positions on each of the assimilation variables.

5.   This has been considered in chapter 6, where the significance of ethnicity for the Asian small business owners, within the specific context of work was examined.

6.   The questions were spaced out and asked in different contexts to avoid linked responses.

7.   This has been noted in chapter 3 in the discussion of the 'sojourner attitude'.

8.   Details of the computing of variables are provided in the appendix.

9.   Price has rightly pointed out that what counts as intrinsic and extrinsic traits would depend on the central value systems of particular groups, as traits such as dress and music may be of intrinsic importance to certain groups and not to others (1969:221-222). Gordon's point, however, holds that as long as traits basic to a group remain unchanged, assimilation cannot be considered to have taken place.

10.   It is interesting to note that Indians, Pakistanis, Bangladeshis and even the African Asians, who in Oxford, are largely Gujerati speaking, watch Hindi movies on video on quite a regular basis. One Gujerati speaking African Asian, who does not speak Hindi, says he watches at least two Hindi films on Sundays.

11.   The question asked was, 'Is it a good thing to be able to speak the language of your family's area of origin?'.

12.   The *Asian Business* magazine of 13th March-9th April 1992 reports 'Asian retailers prefer their trade magazine in English' as that is the language used all the time in the shop. The general response was: "we would not have risked investing our life savings....if we did not feel able to conduct our businesses effectively , and on equal terms with our English colleagues." Several went so far as to say that they felt offended at the thought of being patronised by trade magazines in Indian languages (p.11).

13.   Details of computation provided in appendix.

14.   Details of computation provided in appendix.

15.   That is, the Asian people in Oxford.

16.   As noted in chapter 4.

17.   The remaining 28 per cent claimed to have no friends, as noted earlier.

18.   This was later found to be supported by the 1991 Census results, according to which, as noted in chapter 3, St. Clements, East and South wards are the wards of heaviest concentrations of Asians.

19.   Refer to appendix.

20.   Computed by combining scores for 'objections to outmarriage of children' and 'factors of importance in marriage of children' - refer to appendix.

21.   It must be remembered here that 'structural assimilation' is used not in Gordon's sense of entry into the cliques and clubs of the host society, but in the wider sense which includes entry into economic institutions as the first step. Robinson, using 'diversification of occupational structure' and 'residential concentrations' as indicators of structural assimilation in this wider sense, describes the 'East African Gujerati Muslim' groups in Blackburn, as having achieved a high degree of structural assimilation (1982:162-165).

8 Summary and conclusions

The general approach

The focus of this book has been on the nature and development of a petty bourgeoisie among the South Asian minorities in Britain and within the city of Oxford in particular. However, before an attempt is made to draw any conclusions or even summarize the argument, it is necessary to stress an important point. This is that both from the point of view of the city itself and the characteristics of its South Asian inhabitants, Oxford should not be regarded as a case study which is 'typical'. The study does not claim any national or even regional universality either for its findings or its conclusions. Oxford is among the more prosperous areas of Britain, with very low rates of unemployment. It is not a large conurbation and does not suffer from the sort of housing shortages which afflicts many inner city areas of Britain. With its South Asian ethnic minorities constituting just over 4.5 per cent of its resident population, it is not among those areas in Britain which are known for their high concentrations of Asians. It is also likely, though there is no way of testing this objectively, that white hostility towards these minorities in Oxford, as in the Midlands and the South East of the country, may be less than in certain other areas of Britain. Once all this is understood, the question of typicality need not affect the weight to be given to the findings and conclusions. It is hoped that this Oxford study may provide a detailed description of the nature of South Asian entrepreneurship, and the attitudes and behaviour of the Asian entrepreneurs, in one of the types of cities which has seen the establishment of a sizeable immigrant retail and catering sector over the last two decades.

This leads to the further caveat that in as much as the approach is a case study one, it only aims to provide insights into the theoretical questions raised. While no case study can establish a general truth, it can, quite clearly refute accepted generalities (cf. the refutation of the embourgeoisement thesis by Goldthorpe *et al.* 1968 1968b 1969), and that this book does attempt to do. The perspective is, however, essentially a framework for future research, to be validated or falsified by further studies of a similar type.

Caveats aside, the aim of this enquiry has been to clarify the antecedent and consequent factors underlying South Asian entrepreneurial entry. An attempt has been made to bring together a diverse and scattered literature on ethnic minority entrepreneurship as well as the assimilation of immigrant outsiders into the established population. To this has been added an in-depth survey of the entire population of shop-keepers and restaurant owners of South Asian origin in Oxford. Through this review of both the theory and the empirical research related to the field, the effort has been made to throw some light on a few conceptual difficulties and to establish some empirical generalisations regarding South Asian entrepreneurship and its effect on the 'assimilation' of these entrepreneurs into British society.

Summary

While a summary has been provided at the end of each chapter, an attempt is here made to draw them together. The book began by highlighting the issues arising from the increasing entrepreneurial entry of those minorities in Britain of Indian sub-continental origin. To determine the significance of this business entry it was necessary to look first at the reasons behind it. That is, were the South Asians constrained to adopt the self-employment option owing to discrimination and disadvantage in the white labour market, or were they exploiting opportunities presented by the market using culturally determined resources encouraging business ownership? The second issue was that of the consequence of business entry. Did it imply an improvement in their economic and social position or were these Asians merely exchanging one form of drudgery for another, without any significant upward social mobility for themselves or their families? The third issue was that of the nature of the business activity. Whatever the motivations underlying business entry, were the Asian business owners significantly different from their white counterparts? What was the salience of their ethnicity within the sphere of their work? Having looked at the reasons underlying business entry, the economic and social consequences of this entry, and the nature of the activity itself, the fourth and final issue was the effect of all this on the process of 'assimilation' of these minority entrepreneurs into the majority society. In what ways were they integrated into British society and what was the nature of their ethnic identity?

Chapter 2 went on to describe the research setting, that is, the City of Oxford. The start of South Asian labour migration into Oxford was shown to fit quite well into the 'replacement labour' framework provided by Peach (1968). The first significant movement of South Asians into Oxford during the mid-1950s coincided with the drawing away of indigenous labour from the poorly paid, unskilled and semi-skilled jobs in the hospitals, transport and construction industries into the better paid car factory jobs. The mid-1960s, however, saw the widening of occupational opportunities and the start of South Asian retailing. Within two decades a thriving Asian small business sector had been established within the prosperous economy of Oxford, an economy which had consistently maintained low unemployment levels and alternative occupational opportunities. Only five per cent of the small business owners had been unemployed or made redundant immediately prior to self-employment. It was also established that, while at the start of retailing activity shops and restaurants were located within the areas of South Asian residential concentration, there was a gradual dispersion so that at the time of the survey more than half of the small businesses were located outside these areas.

With the theoretical, methodological and empirical background to the study established, chapter 3 went on to discuss the first substantive issue, that of the reasons underlying business entry. Beginning with a review of the literature on sociological explanations for minority entrepreneurship, it attempted to assess them in the light of the survey evidence. The aim was not to provide any definitive evaluation of the theories reviewed, but to see whether some of the characteristics essential to these theories were present in the population studied.

The data analysis revealed that while ethnic solidarity, culturally specific economic institutions such as 'Rotating Credit Associations', and a protected ethnic market, may have been cultural resources utilised at an earlier stage for business entry, they did not appear to be operative any longer. There was more evidence of competition and rivalry within the ethnic business community than of solidarity; Rotating Credit Associations had been relegated to the women's sphere and were not perceived as generating enough capital to be of use in business activity. Furthermore, South Asians in Oxford had certainly gained access to wider markets and wider opportunities than that provided by the ethnic community. While the restaurants had always targeted the non-Asians in Oxford, the shops too, had grown beyond the provision of ethnic groceries to an ethnic clientele, to catering for a mainly white clientele even where ethnic foods were concerned.

The ethic of hard work, in the case of owners as well as family members, definitely appeared to be a strength which was well utilised in small business activity. It was noted, however, that as far as hours of work go, where the South Asians were concerned, the hours worked in the shop or restaurant were not much longer than what they would attempt to work when employed.

Business entry could no longer be attributed to the 'sojourner attitude' in as much as there was no evidence for a 'myth of return' amongst the majority of respondents. And, it was found that the constraint of blocked opportunities in the labour market is not really operative for this population, in so far as there is no real lack of fit between their qualifications and the jobs held by them before the start of self-employment.

The desire to be one's own boss was very evident. It was not, however, a simple desire for independence, but quite closely associated with considerations of finance and social prestige. It was only by working for oneself that it was possible to really make money and to count for something in society.

Chapter 4 then went on to produce evidence for a central claim made by this book: that South Asian entry into small business is to be seen as a strategic choice for the satisfaction of mobility aspirations. And it was further contended that these mobility aspirations must be placed in the context of the three systems of stratification within which the South Asians in Britain may be seen as functioning - that of the British society, that of the ethnic group within Britain, as well as that of the country of origin. It appeared that an important consideration influencing South Asian business entry was the improvement in status it brought about, both within the ethnic group in Britain as well as 'back home'.

Chapter 5 went on to consider whether entry into self-employment had brought about any real improvement in the class position of these small business owners. Analysing class position in terms of their 'market', 'work', and 'status' situation, it was shown that the economic position of these entrepreneurs is quite secure. They were seen to be pursuing a policy of rational capitalism in diversifying rather than expanding existing businesses, so that the small shop or restaurant was not necessarily synonymous with a low economic level of living. Self-employment, in overcoming the constraints of the employee situation, and in providing some measure of control in relations with the white majority, was seen to afford considerable satisfaction to the small business owners. Their status situation contained a certain discrepancy in that while the middle class status of the occupation itself, in terms of its non-manual character, could not be denied, in the relational aspect of styles of life, interactional patterns did differ from the accepted British middle class ones as did political attitudes. It was, however, pointed out that the Labour leanings of this group as well its low levels of social interaction could be attributed to the influence of ethnicity, rather than to a lack of 'middle classness'. All in all, the South Asian small business owners in Oxford could be considered a well established section of the local middle class.

Chapter 6 changed the angle of approach to compare South Asian small business activity with that of the indigenous white small business owners. It was maintained that large scale entry into entrepreneurship and successful business activity need not necessarily imply that there is anything ethnically distinctive about Asian small business which separates it from small business in general. To establish this, data on white shop-keepers and restaurant owners from large scale national data sets, were compared to the survey data on the Oxford Asians. Comparison revealed that while the longer hours worked by the South Asians, including the opening of shops on Sundays, and the extensive use of family labour, may be what makes the Asian business observably different from white-owned ones, there were no other significant differences. In as much as the Asian small business owners did not make use of collective ethnic resources, and business strategies were other than ethnic, the salience of ethnicity within the actual work situation appeared to be limited. It was the 'expressive factor' of ethnicity, rather than the 'utility factor', which was more apparent within the entrepreneurial situation. The situation of work did not appear to be one in which South Asian small business owners chose to assert their ethnic identity.

Chapter 7 attempted to draw together the evidence of the preceding chapters to gauge its effect on the 'assimilation' of the South Asian small business owners into British society. If these South Asians were entering the business sector more by choice than by constraint, if they were successful in their business activity, if they were not restricted to an ethnic market for clientele or for labour, but were catering to the white majority, and if within the sphere of work they did not choose to exercise the ethnic option, did it mean that they could be considered to be assimilated? Did that also mean that their identification with their ethnic group was no longer relevant?

Analysing the literature on assimilation and ethnicity, it was first established that there was a need for reconceptualisation, such that 'assimilation' did not necessarily call for a loss of 'ethnicity'. Effective adjustment to the country of adoption did not require minorities to forfeit all allegiance to their ethnic group, so that it was possible for groups to exhibit not merely more or less of either 'assimilation' or 'ethnicity', but also, more of both or less of both. Following Hutnik (1991), the four styles of adaptation were labelled the 'assimilative', 'acculturative', 'dissociative' and 'marginal'. It was further contended that the style of adaptation need not be uniform across all the major areas of assimilation. Thus, a group may be assimilated in the structural sphere, but dissociative in its identification, and so on. Using this theoretical framework, the adaptational style of the Asian small business owners was tested in each of the four areas generally characterised as major areas of assimilation, namely, identification, acculturation, structural assimilation and amalgamation. Analysis revealed that this petty bourgeois group may be seen as exhibiting a certain dualism in both its identification and acculturation. The majority of its members fall into the category of those who identify with both the country of origin and of destination, and also accept the extrinsic culture of the host society while retaining the culture of origin as well. The sphere of amalgamation is the one sphere where the group remains dissociative, not desiring even to consider marriage with out group members. In as much as members may be seen as participating effectively in the economic and political structures of British society, while not very involved in the structures of the ethnic group such as the community organisations and friendship groups, the group appears to have achieved a certain measure of structural assimilation. The nature of the ethnicity exhibited by this petty bourgeois group is therefore, described as a compartmentalized one, members showing considerable dexterity in juggling the demands of both majority and ethnic groups.

Conclusions

The more general conclusions of this book have, in many ways, been pre-empted by the preceding summary and the conclusions at the end of each chapter. It is, however, worthwhile to attempt an overall synthesis of the more significant conclusions. In view of the fact that the overall findings of the study were positive to a degree which may appear surprising in the face of earlier studies of South Asian entrepreneurship in Britain,[1] a word must be said about their reliability. Experience of in-depth research brings with it the awareness of the fact that people when interviewed, are likely to present their actions in the best possible light. Another danger is that of conclusions being influenced by the empathy and liking for their subjects which qualitative researchers do tend to develop. Yet, after all allowances are made, it does appear that the conclusions are soundly based.

The evidence from the survey appears to cast in doubt earlier theories regarding South Asian entrepreneurship as mainly a consequence of constraints faced by the Asians in the British labour market. While a small number of respondents did mention lack of promotional avenues owing to discrimination, only five per cent were actually unemployed immediately prior to self-employment. The general trend was to continue with paid employment at the start of business activity, some choosing to give it up once businesses were established, others choosing to continue with it alongside self-employment. There does not appear to be a mismatch between the educational qualifications possessed by the Oxford Asian entrepreneurs and the jobs held by them before business entry. A more positive theory of entrepreneurial entry is therefore advanced, which takes into account the attitudes and values, as well as the aspirations for prestige and status, among the South Asian population. Business entry is seen to have important implications for social standing within the South Asian community in Britain as well as within the communities in the South Asian countries of origin, the latter remaining an important reference group for the migrants even today. In view of this the positive reasons for business entry need to be recognised - the pull of high aspirations being more significant than the push factors of unemployment and racial disadvantage in the labour market.

The important role that women play in the start up, as well as the successful running of small businesses has been highlighted in this book. Business entry enables the utilisation of the labour power of South Asian women whose entry into the open labour market has been limited by educational disadvantages as well as cultural restrictions on work outside the home. The substantial role played by South Asian women in the running of the businesses, and the significant levels of responsibility undertaken by them, serves to contradict the stereotype of the downtrodden and submissive Asian female.

Where business entry has been regarded as a result of discrimination and disadvantage, it has also been held that the small business sector is a marginal one, which does not afford much upward social mobility. This book contends, to the contrary, that the small shop and restaurant has brought considerable financial security as well as status enhancement to the Oxford Asians. Far from subsisting on the fringes of the economy, their healthy economic position appears to indicate that ownership of a small shop or restaurant may no longer be indicative of marginality.

That the small business sector today is not to be dismissed as marginal is being increasingly recognised. A major retailing trend recently identified by Shell (Asian Business 22nd May 1992), highlights the growing reliance on regular 'top-up' shopping trips, in addition to less frequent 'stock-ups' at supermarkets and hypermarkets. The trend in retailing appears to have come full circle with convenient, accessible, local shops being seen as putting pressure on the supermarkets that were previously looked upon as threatening their existence. As one British sociologist puts it:

> We may like to think of ourselves as primarily supermarketing people, but in reality we now use small convenience stores with almost the same sort of frequency that we formerly used local shops before those big supermarkets came along (Taylor 1992:8)

Indeed, it is being argued that there is likely to be an increased scope for small retail units as more large stores are built (Kirby 1980). This stems from the polarisation theory which assumes that because the large stores will be widely spaced out, a substantial trade vacuum will emerge at the local level (Davies 1983:162). As evidence of this, Kirby cites the experience of the United States where the so-called modern convenience store has been the fastest growing of all retail developments in recent years (1976).

In the vanguard of this regeneration of the convenience store as a retailing concept is the South Asian small business owner. Thus the *Asian Business* magazine of 22 May 1992, noting that for many years the Asian small business sector was regarded as limited in its prospects for success, argued:

> Now, however, the picture has changed and Asian independent retailers have established their businesses as amongst the fastest-growing in the retail sector ...irrespective of the backdrop of economic recession and a fall in consumer spending, these businesses have managed to ride the recession and not only survive but continue their extraordinary record of growth...(p.5)

Arguing that it is the multiples which are being adversely affected by the recession, and that the independent sector may have actually benefited from the recession which forces consumers to shop sporadically and carefully, it is maintained that:

> ...anyone who is convinced that the independent trade cannot hold its own in the marketplace needs to think again (Asian Business 23 May- 19 June:5)

The Oxford Asian small business owners appear to fit into this pattern quite well.

While the bite of recession was, of course, being felt in the years after the survey, especially by those retail units which were not convenience stores, the vast majority managed to ride the recession, so that there appears little doubt that the South Asian business sector in Oxford will survive and prosper.

When it is remembered that not all Jewish businesses are a Marks and Spencer or a Tesco, the success of the South Asians may well be likened to that of the Jews. It has been argued that the danger of lauding this success is to lay the responsibility for success or failure at the feet of the South Asians themselves and to deny the need for action against discrimination. It is, however, suggested here that to recognise the success of the entrepreneurial group is not so much to deny the presence of discrimination as to raise the image of the South Asians in Britain, to give to them a certain measure of respect that is well deserved, and to begin regarding them as something other than a 'problem'. Instead of decrying the achievements of the South Asian small business owners by dismissing it as illusory or by attributing it to the exploitation of self and family, it is time that their tenacity, grit, and determination to succeed economically, whatever the obstacles, be recognised. With this, hopefully, would also come the recognition of their positive contributions to British life.

Notes

1.   Studies of small business owners in other countries, for instance, the Netherlands and Australia, appear to be far more positive than those done in Britain (cf. Boissevain and Grotenbreg 1987; Lever-Tracy *et al.* 1991).

Appendix I

Reasons for primary research

The decision to undertake primary research, that is, an intensive case study of one city - Oxford, was based on the following grounds:

1)   It was felt that while secondary analysis of existing national data sets, such as the Labour Force Survey (LFS), or the General Household Survey (GHS), would provide some information about South Asian small-businesses, information about the ethnically distinctive characteristics of South Asian businesses, as well as other detailed information regarding such things as attitudes, aspirations, and patterns of social interaction, could be obtained only through primary research.

There have been attempts to analyse GHS data to establish the relation between ethnicity and enterprise (Curran and Burrows 1988). While the GHS data is able to show that a significant number from ethnic minorities are small business owners, it cannot in any way demonstrate the 'ethnicity' of these businesses in the sense defined in Chapter 1. 'Ethnicity' of business activity, by definition, refers to something more than the mere fact that business owners are of particular ethnic origins. Any information on this aspect of ethnic businesses would, then, require primary research.

2)   Specific surveys of South Asian businesses have, of course, been conducted in various places, beginning with the survey of 29 Asian businesses in Bradford, conducted by Allen and associates in 1966 (Allen *et al.* 1969), and of 74 Asian businesses, in the Wandsworth borough of London, conducted by Aldrich in 1975 (Aldrich 1980).   Subsequently, surveys were carried out in Bradford (McEvoy *et al.* 1979; Rafiq 1988), Leicester and Ealing borough of London (McEvoy *et al.* 1979), Croydon borough of London (Mullins 1979), Manchester (Patel 1989), Birmingham (Patel 1989), and Brent (Wilson 1983; Patel 1989).   It is interesting to note that all these surveys were carried out in areas especially chosen for their heavy concentrations of Asians. These places, with a heavy concentration, and residential segregation of Asians, are likely to be

'institutionally complete' in Breton's (1965) sense of the term, and thus, to have different patterns of retailing and business growth, as well as different levels of ethnic solidarity, and assimilation, from smaller cities without a heavy concentration of Asians, but a significant number of Asian shops and restaurants - of which Oxford is a good example. A study of cities like Oxford, then, could be expected to help balance the picture presented by the numerous studies of cities like Bradford, Birmingham, Leicester, etc.

3)   The most recent survey of Asian entrepreneurs, that conducted by Patel (1991), in Birmingham, Manchester, and Brent, had been carried out in 1986. Changes in the economic situation since then was likely to have brought about changes in the causes and patterns of retailing activity.
        It was moreover within the years that had elapsed since this last survey that a great many of the shops in Oxford had sprung up.[1] It was likely that the picture of retailing in places where the ethnic infrastructure developed quite early, such as Bradford and Birmingham, would be different from that in places like Oxford, where the spurt in retailing activity was a far more recent phenomenon. A survey of Oxford, could relate the different patterns of growth in ethnic retailing activity in different cities to stages of the migration process.

4)   Previous surveys had concentrated on the business and business practices of the Asian entrepreneurs, and no serious attempt had been made to get a more general picture of this group in British society. It was felt that certain questions had been overlooked in previous surveys, such as:

    a) The nature of the small business owners' relations with the host society in the course of their employment activity.

    b) Their social attitudes and way of life in terms of family and friendship patterns, leisure-time activities, etc.

    c) The extent of their intergenerational and intra-generational mobility.

    d) Their subjective perceptions of their class position.

    e) The degree of ethnic solidarity among these entrepreneurs.

    f) Their attitudes towards racism and assimilation.

    g) Their voting patterns.

Some questions on these topics were included in Brown's PSI survey, but the information given was for Asians as a whole, so that there was no specific information on the small business owners alone.
There appeared to be strong reasons then, for collecting primary data on Asian small business owners in Oxford.

The population: sample vs census

Once it was decided to conduct a survey, the next issue was the methodological one of data collection, which according to Moser and Kalton, involves the three problems of, "...from whom to collect the information, what methods to use for collecting it, and how to process, analyse and interpret it" (1971:53). The first of these was the question of the coverage of the enquiry, that is whether the survey should be a *complete* one, in the sense of covering all the units in the population under study, or, whether it should be a *sample-survey*, studying only a part of the population selected by accepted statistical methods.

In either case the first requirement was a complete list of all South Asian businesses in Oxford, which at the outset of this study was not available. Whereas previous researchers in other cities, had been able to get some help from the administrative records of Economic Development Units, investigations by community relations officers of various boroughs, or ethnic business development councils, it was found that in Oxford, interest in ethnic businesses was just beginning, with the local authorities inviting applications only in January 1990, for the post of Ethnic Business Outreach Worker who was to look into the nature and extent of ethnic business development, and to encourage the establishment and growth of small businesses by members of the ethnic minorities in Oxfordshire. No list of ethnic businesses was thus available with the local authorities.

A possible way of compiling a list was by going through the Local Authority's Rate Valuation List, and listing the commercial properties registered under South Asian names. This would have provided valuable information about the worth of the businesses as well, in terms of the rates paid. But as there was no separate list for commercial properties, it was felt that going through the list would be too time consuming.

Directories, such as *Thompsons* and *The Yellow Pages*, were consulted, but were not able to provide complete lists, as only a fraction of the shops were listed in them.

As there was no sampling frame at the start, and it was felt that waiting to compile a complete list before beginning the survey would be a waste of time, it was decided to start with an initial list based on the Directories, personal contacts among the shop-keepers, and direct observation of the commercial activity on the streets of Oxford. Once the survey began, more shops were added to the list by asking each respondent about other Asian shops in the vicinity. This process is described by Kish as follows:

> *Snowball sampling* is the colourful name...for techniques of building up a list or a sample of a special population by using an initial set of its members as informants (1965:408).

In cities or areas that are not too large - like Oxford, South Asian shop-keepers and restaurant owners tend to know about each other so that the probability of inclusion of all business owners is very high. The initial list of 50 shops had increased to 75, by the time 54 interviews had been conducted. At this stage, a list of ethnic businesses in Oxfordshire was obtained from the Cooperative Development Agency. But this list, too, did not lay any claim to completeness, and it was found that while all of the Asian shops on this list were on the researcher's list, many of the shop owners already interviewed were not on the Agency's list. While there were 164 businesses on the list, these included Chinese, Afro-Caribbean, and other ethnic businesses as well. It was thus decided to rely on the list personally compiled by the researcher.

The obvious problem with compiling the list in this way is that there is no way of knowing how complete the information is, though 'diminishing returns', in the sense of no more new shops coming to light, is a good indicator of near completion. Also, it was hoped that using a combination of sources in the compilation of the list as mentioned above, would minimize this drawback and that the list ultimately obtained, would provide a more or less complete enumeration of businesses in Oxford. An absolutely complete list would be hard to get because of shops closing down, others changing location, and new ones starting up. For the last two months of the survey, that is, during April and May 1990, the number of shops on the researcher's list remained stable at 83. It was decided to take this list as the final one.

This list did not include the restaurants. The list of South Asian restaurants was relatively easier to obtain as they were more centrally located than the shops, and also much fewer in number. There were found to be 22 restaurants in Oxford, at the time of the survey. It must, however, be kept in mind that here, too, the start up and closure rate is quite high.

The inability to obtain an exhaustive list at the start of the survey made any sort of systematic sampling difficult. The dangers of incorrect sampling had been clearly brought out by McEvoy *et al.*'s (1979) research, in which the sample of Asian businesses was taken from only five out of the 30 electoral wards of Bradford. These wards were chosen for their high concentrations of the Asian population. It was hardly surprising then that McEvoy *et al.* found that Asian shops and even restaurants relied heavily on an Asian clientele. Rafiq, in his survey of Bradford in 1983, gave far more emphasis to correct sampling, and arrived at very different conclusions. The 30 wards were reduced to 22 by amalgamation, and a 15 per cent sample was taken from each area using a scientific sampling procedure.

But, given the delay in obtaining a suitable sampling frame in Oxford, as well as the small number of businesses, it was felt that the representativeness of a *sample* would be vitiated, and that any sort of survey should attempt a complete coverage of the entire population. Also, the limited number of shops and restaurants made such a project quite feasible - it *was* possible for a single researcher to complete the research without too much expenditure of time or money. It was thus decided to collect information from all the shop-keepers and restaurant owners willing to co-operate.

Method of data collection

When it comes to the actual collection of data, various methods of data collection, such as mail questionnaires, telephone interviews, personal or face-to-face interviews, observation, may be used (Moser and Kalton 1971). The efficacy of each would depend on the nature of the information required, the educational level of the respondents, the type of questions, etc.

In a survey such as the present one, where a large amount of information was sought and where it was imperative that the response rate be high as the population was not very large, the only appropriate method appeared to be the face-to-face interview. The point in favour of the mail questionnaire was that a busy shop-keeper could answer it at his own leisure. But the usual response rate for mail questionnaires is around 30-40 per cent (Moser and Kalton 1971:268), and even lower for lengthy questionnaires. Moreover, mail surveys also depend on a high literacy rate among the respondents. And previous surveys of South Asian shop-keepers had shown that a substantial percentage of them had low educational levels.

Telephone interviews were also felt to be inappropriate, as the probability of non-completion for lengthy and complex questionnaires is found to be high.

Another drawback of both these methods was that they precluded the opportunity to supplement the respondent's answers with observational data. An interviewer can observe the respondent's attitude to the survey, his reactions to questions, his manner and appearance, and in the present survey, the shop or restaurant and its neighbourhood, the type of customers served and the nature of the relations between shop-keepers or restaurant owners and their customers. All this is valuable background material, which can be obtained only through personal face-to-face interviews.

Response rates for face-to-face interviews are usually high, at around 70 per cent, and lengthy questionnaires do not present much of a problem during direct contact. The literacy of the respondent, too, is not an issue. Hence, the method of data collection decided upon was that of personal or face-to-face interviews.

As all interviews were to be conducted by the researcher, it was decided to combine formal and informal methods of interviewing. The formal interview, with set questions and answers recorded on a standardised form, which is the norm in most surveys, was felt to be necessary in the interests of uniformity. Comparability between interviews was important for statistical analysis of data, so that conclusions regarding the characteristics of the aggregate could be arrived at, rather than information of the individual. Hence a large number of closed questions were included in the interview schedule, regarding occupational and educational background, work history, type of business, business practices, residence, ethnicity, family size, children's occupations and educational qualifications. But, a large number of questions were open-ended, to allow for lengthier and more individual responses.

It was also decided to ask additional questions, to explore and probe where necessary, and to allow the respondent to impart whatever information he wished to regarding hopes and aspirations, attitudes and opinions, experiences of racial discrimination and harassment, and so on. It was felt that these responses could be treated satisfactorily through post-coding.

The type of interview, then, was to be partly structured and partly unstructured.

It was not decided at this stage whether the researcher should write out the answers on the interview schedule or record the interviews on tape. This decision is largely determined by the nature of the respondents as well as the subject of interview. Previous experience had demonstrated that students being questioned on their subject choices and career aspirations were quite willing to have their interviews tape recorded, as also housewives talking about their problems and life situation. But the same enthusiasm for speaking on tape was not apparent in the case of university employees being questioned on their job conditions and work satisfaction. This decision was therefore, to be taken during the pilot survey.

The pilot survey

The pilot survey was carried out during October 1989. Since the number of Asian shops in Oxford was limited, and it was not considered advisable to use up these cases, the pilot was carried out mainly in the Islington Borough of North London. As representativeness is not an issue in a pilot, as long as respondents are similar to those who will be interviewed in the main survey, shops were approached casually, and no systematic sampling was attempted. The high refusal rate was a signal of the need for personal introductions to the respondents. The size of the pilot survey depends on the size of the main survey sample. A pilot sample of between five and 10 per cent of the main sample usually suffices (Moser and Kalton 1971)). Though the main sample size was expected to be about 70, 12 shops were interviewed in the pilot as questions were changed after the first three or four interviews.

Piloting of interviews was regarded as essential for a variety of reasons, the most important of which was testing the adequacy of the questionnaire. Improperly worded questionnaires are held to be a more important source of error than bias in sampling, or errors in the methods of questionnaire administration (Payne 1951:5). The pilot survey was very useful in highlighting the ambiguities in questions. Many questions were simplified and rephrased in easier and more colloquial form, making them both easier to ask and easier to answer. Inadequacies in the structure of the questionnaire were also revealed by the pilot. It was found that it was best to start with innocuous questions regarding the shop and business practices as these generally put the respondents at their ease. Personal details were kept for later. Certain questions regarding income and turnover were found to generate hostility to the survey, despite changes in wording and order of asking. In many instances respondents required reassurance right at the beginning of the survey that it did not include questions on income or profit. It was thus decided to cut out these questions altogether rather than jeopardise the survey. In view of this uniform reaction, the reliability of information regarding turnover and profit in previous surveys was cast in doubt.

The pilot also revealed the need for an introductory talk, emphasizing the confidentiality of the survey, and explaining its aims and objectives. Respondents were told that the survey was for purely academic reasons and did not have any practical implications. It was explained that the large scale entry of South Asians into self-employment had excited academic interest in the reasons for entry and in the socio-economic background of those who were small-business owners. Despite this, it was found that respondents were more co-operative when the interviewer was introduced by a common acquaintance.

This was a useful lesson taught by the pilot and assiduously adhered to in the actual survey.

Given the reluctance of respondents to air their views and the emphasis on confidentiality, it was decided not to record the interviews on tape but to write out the answers on the schedule and to make extensive notes on whatever was said. This was done as unobtrusively as possible and later written up and attached to the schedule.

The time required for the completion of the questionnaire was also established by the pilot. It was found that the minimum time required was 45 minutes, with a really good interview extending to two hours. While care was taken to fix up appointments at times when shops were expected to be less busy, occasionally, if the shop-keeper did not have any help, and there was a sudden spurt in custom, interviews could take up to three hours. The timing of the interview was thus found to be important. While the interviewer's time could not be considered wasted, as she was able to observe retailer-customer interaction, and look around the shop, the respondent was likely to get distracted.

It was reassuring to find that language did not present a problem during the pilot. All shop-keepers were able to speak English fluently, and to understand the questions posed in English. Responses were occasionally made in Hindi, often to emphasize a point.

The actual survey

As Denzin maintains:

> ...the research act first comes alive during the interview, when the researcher is forced to confront his observational units on a direct face-to-face basis. He must convince persons they should be interviewed, get them to set time aside for the interview, and keep them conscious of what the interview is about (1970:2).

The interviewing of the actual population was begun in November 1989, with the majority of interviews being conducted in December 1989 and early January of 1990. As some shops were widely scattered and not easily located, and restaurant appointments were difficult to fix, field-work continued till the end of May 1990.

Except for a few shops, where owners were willing to be interviewed immediately, the others had to be visited twice. On the first visit, the purpose of the survey was explained to the shop owners, and their co-operation sought. Owners were asked to indicate a time convenient to them, for the interview. While a few preferred to be interviewed after shop hours, or on Sundays, others indicated times when the shop could be expected to be less busy than usual.

Uninterrupted interviews were obtained, even during shop hours, from shops selling textiles, crafts and jewellery. Most of the shops, however, were grocers and newsagents, where a constant stream of customers could be expected to interrupt the interview. A few shop-keepers, in such circumstances, chose to hand over charge to an employee or their spouse, and concentrate on the interview. Others carried on their retailing activity, while answering questions. This was not as disruptive as it was expected to be as it gave both the interviewer and respondent time to think about the responses and questions respectively. It also provided the researcher with a first hand picture of retailer-customer relations. This was one of the reasons for preferring to conduct interviews in the shop itself rather than in the shop-keepers' house.

Invitations to the house were always extended, and very often, where the house was above the shop, a brief visit to the house was made, where typical South Asian hospitality was extended to the researcher. The researcher's South Asian origin was definitely felt to be an advantage in the establishment of interviewer/respondent rapport. Respondents felt free to express themselves in Hindi/Urdu, and Punjabi, to a fellow Asian who could understand all these languages.

Restaurant owners were all interviewed in the restaurant, but during the hours when the restaurant was not open to the public. As week-ends were always busy, and owners took a day off during the week, appointments were difficult to fix, and interviews were spread over many weeks.

The interview was directed at the owner of the shop or restaurant. Where husband and wife were partners in business ownership, though information was sought from both, the respondent was the male owner. In most shops, both were usually present, so that it was possible to talk to both husband and wife. Where older children were helping out in the shop, they often participated, with the consent and approval of the parents. In a very few shops, the owner and active manager was a woman, and it was only here that the respondent was female.

The restaurants were generally owned by more than two partners. Here, the partner responsible for the managerial work was the one interviewed.

Response rate

As there was no official backing for the survey, and it was not mandatory for the small business owner to impart any information, co-operation was on a purely voluntary basis. Despite this the response rate was unusually high. One hundred and five small businesses were approached, and 94 consented to the interview. Only nine shops and four restaurants refused to participate in the survey. This is a response rate of 90 per cent. It was possible to obtain this high rate of response because most of the shops and restaurants were approached through some person known to both researcher and shop or restaurant owner. Despite this, on occasion, even after initial agreement had been given, respondents evaded or refused interviews. After a reasonably large number of interviews had been obtained, the remaining business owners, for whom no contacts were found, were approached without introductions. The fact that the researcher had already obtained such a large number of interviews proved to be an asset here, as the fact that so many fellow Asian business owners had consented to being interviewed helped to make the remaining respondents more comfortable with the idea of divulging information.

Editing, coding, and tabulation

The initial editing of questionnaires prior to the coding of responses did not present much of a problem as each schedule had been checked by the researcher for completeness and accuracy soon after the interview. Notes were written up after each interview, and it was possible to complete any questions left unanswered and to resolve inconsistencies during the writing up. As Moser and Kalton point out:

> ...editing a whole questionnaire facilitates viewing the individual case *as a whole*, noting the relationship between answers to the different questions and detecting inconsistencies. It also ...enables one to get on with the editing as the questionnaires come in, instead of having to wait until the fieldwork is complete (1971:413-414).

Coding the answers, or classifying them into meaningful categories, so as to summarize the data and bring out the essential patterns, was a more difficult task. Attempts at pre-coding had been made, but, while the coding frames for background information such as sex, religion, ethnic group, and so on, presented no problems, it was found that answers to some questions did not always fall into the categories coded, and that some of the categories were superfluous and could be omitted. There were also a number of open-ended questions which, necessarily, had to be post-coded.

As wealth of detail is a strength of small-scale surveys, it was decided to allow for detailed grouping in the coding and thus retain as much information as possible. It was felt that it was:

...advisable to retain more rather than less detail in the coding since it is easier to amalgamate groups in later analyses (particularly if a computer is used) than to split one group into several when they have been coded alike (Moser and Kalton 1971:415).

While many of the coding frames were developed with the specific aims of the survey in view, in the interests of comparability, certain existing frames were also used. For instance, in coding occupations as an indicator of social class, the frame used was that of *Goldthorpe's Revised Class Schema, 1983 based on OPCS, Classification Of Occupations, 1980.* Employment status codes are those used in the 1972 mobility inquiry based on OPCS.

1. Self-employed with employees, 25+

2. Self-employed with employees, 25-

3. Self-employed without employees

4. Managers in establishments with 25+ employees

5. Managers in establishments with 25- employees

6. Foremen and Supervisors

7. Employees, including family workers, apprentices and trainees.

The class schema is in the ten-category version reported in Erikson and Goldthorpe (1987).

Class	Code	Brief Description
I	1	Professional, Administrative, Managerial (higher)
II	2	Professional, Administrative, Managerial (lower)
IIIa	3	Routine non-manual - higher
IIIb	4	Routine non-manual - lower
Iva	5	Small proprietors - 1-25 employees
Ivb	6	Small proprietors - no employees
Ivc	7	Farmers and Smallholders
V	8	Supervisors of manual workers

VI	9	Skilled manual
VIIa	10	Semi- and unskilled manual
VIIb	11	Agricultural workers

Once the code book was ready, it was fairly simple to enter the data into the computer, using the Data Entry programme of the *Statistical Package for the Social Sciences* (SPSS).

Use of secondary data

Since it had not been possible to interview white shopkeepers, it was decided to use data on white shopkeepers collected by other surveys for purposes of comparison. Wherever possible, national and other large scale data sets such as the *Labour Force Survey* (LFS), *The Social Change And Economic Life Initiative* (SCELI), and *The General Household Survey* (GHS), have been used so that the data would be nationally representative. As the sample of the Asian self-employed in Oxford included only shopkeepers and restaurant owners, only those whites who were similarly self-employed were selected from the LFS, GHS and SCELI. The 'white' sample is, thus, not representative of all white business owners, but only of those of similar size and type of South Asian businesses studied.

The SCELI has a separate section on the self-employed, which looks at many variables important to the present study for purposes of comparison, such as the reasons for entering self-employment, sources of start-up capital, nature of labour employed, payment criteria, parental occupational background, marital status, age, number of children, self-assessed class membership, satisfaction with self-employment, likelihood of taking up paid employment, housing tenure, voting patterns, etc. Though six different areas have been surveyed in the SCELI, previous analyses of data have suggested that it can reasonably be used as a quasi-national sample. The six areas are thus combined to obtain the required sample. It is possible to separate out the retailers and restaurant owners, and this provides a sample size of 78, where the SCELI is used.

Data regarding a few variables, such as the educational qualifications of the white shopkeepers and restaurant owners, their jobs previous to self-employment, and whether they hold a second job, were obtained from the 1989 Labour Force Survey, which provided a sample size of 1581. The 1989 General Household Survey provided information regarding ownership of consumer durables by white shopkeepers and restaurant owners, their number in the GHS being 333.

As information regarding certain variables was not available in these data sets, the possibility of using data for the white entrepreneurs available from previous small scale surveys of small business owners, conducted at different times in different urban areas such as the London boroughs of Wandsworth, Lambeth, and Ealing, as well as Bradford, Leicester, Glasgow and Edinburgh, was considered.[2] However, as all the variables not available in the national data sets were to be found only in the survey of Asian and white shopkeepers in Wandsworth conducted in 1975 by Aldrich (1980), the figures for the whites for these variables are taken from this study.

Snapshot view

The survey is essentially concerned with providing a picture of Asian retailing in a specific location, at a particular period of time. While longitudinal or time series analysis would have been useful, no reliable data were available. Some researchers have used *Kelly's Trade Directories* to trace the growth of retail and catering units. The Kelly's directories for Oxford, however, were not found to be reliable for this purpose for the following reasons:

> 1)   Not all the Asian shops find a mention in the directories - the 1971 trade directory, for instance, mentions only two Pakistani grocers, whereas there were many more shops known to exist.[3]
> This does not hold true of the record of restaurants, and it is quite possible to chart their development through the directories.

> 2)   The only way of identifying the Asian shops in the directory is by their Asian names,[4] and by the 1970s Asian shops did not always have Asian names.

Hence, while anecdotal evidence of growth and change is utilized for descriptive purposes, the picture presented in the survey is essentially that of Asian shops and restaurants in Oxford, during 1989-90.

Analysis and interpretation

The data were analysed using the SPSS. Taking into consideration the small-scale nature of the survey, the emphasis was on obtaining descriptive statistics, rather than attempting any sophisticated quantitative analysis. However, since a good deal of data had been collected, 183 variables were utilized, and this provided detailed frequency tables and cross tabulations to back up the theoretical arguments.

Though quantitative comparisons have been made, as in chapter 5, between the Oxford Asian small business owners and a sample of their white counterparts, no statistical tests of significance have been used. The justification for this is to be found in Lipset, Trow, and Coleman's clear statement of why such tests may be irrelevant to exploratory studies in the social sciences. In their analysis of the inside politics of the International Typographical Union, they maintain:

> This study, like many in social science, is an exploratory study, not a confirmatory one, while statistical tests of hypotheses are designed for confirmation. Chi square tests of independence are

designed to confirm and consolidate what is already believed to be true. A study like the present one is designed to find out what was not even guessed at before. That this new knowledge is not fully confirmed is no great cause for concern. Further studies upon different organisations will constitute more reliable confirmation, for they test the hypotheses in a different population, which a chi square test used on this data could never do. It is probably better to place one's faith in further studies to confirm hypothesized relationships than to place it in chi square tests (1956:430).

It is similarly maintained that this study only seeks to suggest hypotheses, not confirm them, and that confirmation is best achieved by replication of the study in other areas and with other populations, rather than by tests of significance.

But what of the quantitative description of the Oxford group? Statistical tests are usually used to indicate the precision of a descriptive statement about a population. When a random sample of a population is measured in terms of some attribute, then the sample distribution is used to make a statement about the population distribution. Such a statement is, however, subject to sampling error as only a sample of the population was measured, and hence statistical tests become necessary to specify the confidence with which the statement may be made. What must be emphasized here is that in this study the group studied is the *entire population* of shop-keepers and restaurant owners in Oxford, and not a sample of this population. Also, as noted earlier, the response rate was very high (90 per cent). Clearly then, tests of significance are not required.[5]

Research validity

However sophisticated the techniques of analysis may be, they are of secondary importance for, it is on the validity of the data that the success of a social survey depends. In this study, the survey data were supplemented by in-depth qualitative research, in as much as a considerable amount of time was spent in observing and interacting with the respondents. This was possible both within the precincts of the shop and restaurant, as well as in their homes in the case of some respondents. There were also social occasions, such as weddings and religious festivals, when observation and interaction were possible. As pointed out by Vidich and Shapiro:

> ...the techniques of participant observation and the sample survey are not competitive, but, in the well conducted community study, will be complementary. The survey provides representative information which is given meaning by the anthropological observer (1970:522).

The present study utilizes both methods, and in the use of both, care has been taken to apply the test of internal consistency, described by Vidich and Shapiro, as follows:

> The careful anthropologist, for example, will cross-check the reports of one informant against those of another, and will pay careful attention to discrepancies between avowals in one context and facts which are allowed to "slip out" in another...In a very similar fashion, careful survey technicians check the results they receive on one attitude question by comparison with results on a different question which is supposed to measure the same variable (1970:513)

They go on to say that:

> One valuable way of testing the external validity of both methods is to examine the degree to which their results correspond to one another in areas where the two methods can be made to yield comparable data (1970:513).

This study attempts to do this by presenting quotations together with quantitative data wherever possible. The use of this type of multiple research strategy, termed 'theoretical triangulation' by Denzin (1970:472), may then be seen as the basis upon which the validity of this study rests.

Notes

1.   Evidence for this is provided by the survey.

2.   The relevant surveys are as follows:

Author	Date of survey	Area	Types of business	No. of interviews Asian	White
Bechhofer *et al*	1970	Edinburgh	Retail	398	
Aldrich	1975	Wandsworth	Retail	74	47
McEvoy *et al*	1978	Bradford	Retail and	100	100
		Leicester	Services	100	100
		Ealing		100	100
Lambeth Council	1982	Lambeth	All Kinds	70	100
Krcmar	1984	Glasgow	Retail	50	43

3. On the basis of information from respondents and early Asian settlers in Oxford.

4. In the early years of Asian business, it was usual to name the shop after the owner (Khan and sons, for instance), or give the name an ethnic flavour (e.g. Asian grocers), so that Asian shops were identifiable by their names.

5. For a comprehensive discussion of why significance tests in survey analysis are either too strong, too weak or irrelevant, see Lipset, Trow, and Coleman, (1956) *Union Democracy*, pp. 427-432.

Appendix II

Identification

The variable 'Asian Identification' (ASIANID) is computed by summing the scores for the following three variables:

1) DESRETA (whether respondents will return to country of origin), those who will return =0 and, those who will not return =1

2) LSTVST (When last visit to country of origin was made), those who had made the last visit 10 years ago, i.e., before 1982 =0, and those who had made it after 1982 =1 and,

3) SENDMONY (whether money is sent to country of origin), those who do send money =1, and those who do not =0.

ASIANID is then further collapsed into two categories of high=1 (scores of 2 or 3) and low =0 (scores of 0 or 1).

Then, the variable BRITID (British Identification) is computed by summing the scores for the following variables:

1) DESSTAY (whether respondents will stay in Britain), those who will stay =1, and those who will not stay =0.

2) JNPOLORG (the political participation of respondents), those who do participate =1, and those who do not=0, and

3) JOBSAT (satisfaction with employment), those with low satisfaction =0, and those with high levels of satisfaction =1.

BRITID is further collapsed into high =1 (scores of 2 or 3) and low=0 (scores of 0 or 1).

Finally ASIANID and BRITID are cross tabulated to give the four categories of 1) High BRITID + High ASIANID = Acculturative Identification, 2) High BRITID + Low ASIANID = Assimilative Identification, 3) Low BRITID + Low ASIANID = Marginal

Identification, and 4) Low BRITID + High ASIANID = Dissociative Identification.

Acculturation

The variable 'Retention of Asian Culture' **RAC**, is derived by summing the scores for the following five variables:

1) RDASNWSP - whether Asian newspapers are read, yes=1; no=0,

2) PRSCULT - whether Asian culture should be preserved, yes=1; no=0,

3) ASFLMWCH - whether Asian videos watched, yes=1; no=0,

4) SPKASLNG - whether Asian language should be spoken, yes=1; no=0,

5) CHDSPLNG - whether children speak Asian language, yes=1; no=0.

Similarly, the variable 'Acceptance of Majority Culture' **AMC**, is derived by summing the scores for the following three variables:

1) DRESS - those wearing only traditional clothes = 0; those wearing western clothes as well as traditional =1,

2) ADTBRCLT - whether British culture should be adopted, yes=1; no=0,

3) ENGSPK - whether English spoken, yes=1; no=0.

The two derived variables, RAC and AMC, are then recoded into the two categories of 'high' and 'low', and then cross tabulated to give the four categories of 1) CULTURAL ASSIMILATION = high 'acceptance of majority culture' + low 'retention of Asian culture'.   2) ACCULTURATION = high 'acceptance of majority culture' + high 'retention of Asian culture'. 3) DISSOCIATION = low 'acceptance of majority culture' + high 'retention of Asian culture'. 4) MARGINALITY = low 'acceptance of majority culture' + low 'retention of Asian culture'.

Structural assimilation

The variable ETHSTRC - Involvement in ethnic Structures, is computed by summing the scores for the following variables:

1) ASBIMPTC - whether contacts with Asian businessmen are considered important for the running of the business, yes = 1; no = 0.

2) ORGPART - whether there is participation in the community organisations, yes = 1; no = 0.

3) CLSFRNDS - whether close friends only Asian, yes=1; no=0.
ETHSTRC is further collapsed into two categories of 'high'=1 (scores of 2 or 3) and 'low'=0 (scores of 0 or 1).

The variable BRITSTRC - Involvement in British structures, is computed by summing the scores for the following variables:

1) APTBR - whether Asians want to keep apart from the British, yes=0 no=1.

2) RESLOC - whether residential location in area of heavier concentrations of Asians, yes=0 no=1.

3) VISWHTNB - whether on neighbourly terms with white neighbours, yes=1 no=0.

4) ELECPART - whether they participate in elections, yes=1 no=0.
BRITSTRC is further collapsed into 'high' (scores of 3,4,5) and 'low' (scores 1,2)

The two derived variables are then cross tabulated to give the four categories of 1) Structural Assimilation = High BRITSTRC + Low ETHSTRC; 2) Structural Acculturation = High BRITSTRC + High ETHSTRC; 3) Structural Dissociation = low BRITSTRC + High ETHSTRC; 4) Structural Marginality = Low BRITSTRC + Low ETHSTRC.

Marital assimilation

The variable ENDOGAMY is computed by summing the scores for the following two variables:

1) MRGFCTS - those giving primary importance to ethnic group membership in choice of spouse for children =1; those not giving primacy to this =0.

2) OTMRGOBJ - objections to marriage outside the ethnic group, yes=1; no=0.

ENDOGAMY is then recoded into high and low, and cross tabulated with CHDOTMRG - those whose children have married out=1, those whose children have not married out =0.

The cross tabulation gives us the four categories of   1) Marital Assimilation = High CHDOTMRG + Low ENDOGAMY. 2) Marital Acculturation = High CHDOTMRG + High ENDOGAMY. 3) Marital Dissociation = Low CHDOTMRG + High ENDOGAMY. 4) Marital Marginality = Low CHDOTMRG + Low ENDOGAMY.

Bibliography

Aldrich, H. (1975), 'Ecological succession in racially changing neighbourhoods: a review of the literature', *Urban Affairs Quarterly*, vol.10, March.

------. (1980), 'Asian Shopkeepers As A Middleman Minority: A Study Of Small Businesses In Wandsworth', in Evans, A., and Eversley, D. (eds.), *The Inner City: Employment and Industry*, Heinemann, London.

Aldrich, H., Jones, T., and McEvoy, D. (1984), 'Ethnic Advantage and Minority business development' in Ward, R., and Jenkins, R., (eds.), *Ethnic Communities in Business* (1984) Cambridge University Press:Cambridge.

Aldrich, H., Cater, J., Jones, T., and McEvoy, D. (1981), 'Business Development and Self Segregation: Asian Enterprise in three British cities' in Peach, C., Robinson, V., and Smith, S. (eds.), *Ethnic Segregation in Cities*, Croom Helm, London.

Aldrich, H., Cater, J., Jones, T., McEvoy, D., and Velleman, P. (1986), 'Asian residential concentration and Business development: an analysis of shop-keepers' customers in three cities' *New Community* Vol.xiii, No.1., pp 52-64.

Aldrich, H., and Reiss, A. (1976), 'Continuities in the Study of Ecological Succession: Changes in the Race Composition of Neighbourhoods and their Businesses', *American Journal of Sociology*, Vol.81, pp.846-66.

Aldrich, H., and Waldinger, R. (1990), 'Ethnicity and Entreneurship', *Annual Review of Sociology*, vol.16, pp.111-135.

Allen, S., Bentley, and Bornat (1977), *Work, Race and Immigration*, University of Bradford.

-------. (1981), Business Activity and the Self-employed', in Braham, R., and Pearn (eds.), *Discrimination and Disadvantage in Employment: The experience of Black Workers*, Harper and Row, London.

Allen, S., and Smith, C. (1974), 'Race and Ethnicity in Class Formation', in Parkin, F. (ed.), *The Social Analysis of Class Structure*, Tavistock, London.

Anwar, Muhammad. (1979), *The Myth of Return: Pakistanis in Britain*, Heinemann, London.

-------. (1980a), *Vote and Policies*, Commission for Racial Equality, London.

-------. (1986), *Race and Politics*, Tavistock, London.

-------. (1990), 'The Participation of Asians in the British Political System' in Clarke, C., Peach, C., and Vertovec, S. (eds.), *South Asians Overseas: Migration and Ethnicity*, Cambridge University Press, Cambridge.

Ardener, S. (1964), 'The Comparative Study of Rotating Credit Associations', *Journal of the Royal Anthropological Institute*, Vol.94, pp.201-229.

Auster, E., and Aldrich, H. (1984), 'Small Business Vulnerability, Ethnic Enclaves and Ethnic Enterprise', in Ward, R., and Jenkins, R., (eds.), *Ethnic Communities in Business* (1984) Cambridge University Press:Cambridge.

Ballard, R., and Holden, B. (1975), 'The Employment of Coloured Graduates in Britain', *New Community* IV

Ballard, R., (1976), 'Ethnicity: Theory and Experience', *New Community*, v, 3, pp.196-202.

Ballard, R., and Ballard, C. (1977), 'The Sikhs: The Development of South Asian Settlement in Britain', in Watson, J. (ed.), *Between Two Cultures*, Basil Blackwell, Oxford.

Banton, M. (1983), *Racial and Ethnic Competition*, Cambridge University Press, Cambridge.

Barth, F., (1963), 'Introduction', in Barth, F., (ed.), *The Role of the Entrepreneur in Social Change in Northern Norway*, Universitetsforlaget, Bergen.

-------. (1969) (ed.), *Ethnic Groups and Boundaries*, Universitetsforlaget, Bergen.

Baquer, S. (1965), 'The File of Regrets', in Tajfel, H., and Dawson, J. (eds.), *Disappointed Guests*, Oxford University Press, London.

Bechhofer, F., and Elliott, B. (1968), 'An Approach To A Study Of Small Shopkeepers And The Class Structure', *European Journal of Sociology*, vol.9, pp 180-202.

Bechhofer, F., Elliott, B., Rushforth, M. (1971), 'The Market Situation of Small Shopkeepers', *Scottish Journal of Political Economy*, vol.xviii, pp.161-180.

Bechhofer, F., Elliott, B., Rushforth, M., and Bland, R. (1974) 'The Petits Bourgeois In The Class Structure: The Case Of The Small Shopkeepers', in Parkin, F. (ed) *The Social Analysis of Class Structure*, Tavistock, London.

-------. (1974b), 'Small Shopkeepers: Matters of Money and Meaning', *Sociological Review*, vol.22, pp.465-482.

Bechhofer, F., and Elliott, B. (1976), 'Persistence and Change:The Petite Bourgeoisie in the Industrial Society', *European Journal of Sociology*, xvii, pp.74-79.

-------. (1978), 'The voice of Small Business and the Politics of Survival', *The Sociological Review*, vol.26, No.1, pp.57-88

-------. (1981), (eds.), *The Petite Bourgeoisie: Comparative Studies of the Uneasy Stratum*, Macmillan, London.

-------. (1985), 'The Petite Bourgeoisie in Late Capitalism', *Annual Review of Sociology*, pp.181-207.

Bell, D. (1975), 'Ethnicity and Social Change', in Glazer, N., and Moynihan, P. (eds.), *Ethnicity: Theory and Experience*, Harvard University Press, Cambridge, Mass.

Benson, S. (1981), *Ambiguous Ethnicity: Interracial Families in London*, Cambridge University Press, Cambridge.

Berg, M. (1991), 'Artisans and Factory Systems in the Industrial revolution', Warwick Economic Research Papers, No.379.

Berger, S. and Piore, M. (1980), *Dualism and Discontinuity in Industrial Societies*, Cambridge University Press, Cambridge.

Bernard, W.S. (1956), 'The Integration of Immigrants in the United States', Unesco (mimeo).

Berry, B. (1951), *Race Relations*, Houghton Mifflin, Boston.

Billig, M. (1978), 'Patterns of Racism:Interviews with National Front Members', *Race and Class*, vol.20, pp.583-594.

Blalock, H.M. (1967), *Towards a Theory of Minority Group Relations*, New York.

Bland, R., Elliott, B., and Bechhofer, F. (1978), 'Social Mobility in the Petite Bourgeoisie', *Acta Sociologica*, vol. 21, pp.229-248.

Blauner, R. (1960), 'Work Satisfaction and Industrial Trends in Modern Society', in W. Galenson and S.M. Lipset (eds.), *Labour and Trade Unionism*, New York.

Boissevain, J. (1981), *Small Entrepreneurs in Changing Europe:Towards a Research Agenda*, European Centre for Work and Society, Masstricht.

Boissevain, J., and Grotenbreg, H., (1988), 'Culture, Structure and Ethnic Enterprise: The Surinamese of Amsterdam', in Cross and Entzinger (eds.), *Lost Illusions*, Routledge, London.

-------.(1986), 'Culture, Structure and Ethnic Enterprise: the Surinamese of Amsterdam', *Ethnic and Racial Studies*, 9, pp.1-23.

-------. (1987), 'Ethnic Enterprise in the Netherlands', in Goffee, R., and Scase, R. (eds.), *Entrepreneurship in Europe*, Croom Helm, London.

Boissevain, Jeremy *et al.* (1990) 'Ethnic Entrepreneurs and Ethnic Strategies', in Roger Waldinger, Howard Aldrich, Robin Ward and Associates (ed.), *Ethnic Entrepreneurs: Immigrant Business in Industrial Societies*, Sage Series, Race and Ethnic Relations Vol I.

Bonacich, E. (1973), 'A Theory of Middleman Minorities', *American Sociological Review*, vol.38, pp.583-594.

Bonacich, E., and Modell, J. (1980), *The Economic Basis of Ethnic Solidarity: Small Business in the Japanese American Community*, University of California Press, Berkeley and Los Angeles.

Borjas, G. (1986), 'The Self-Employment Experience of Immigrants', *The Journal of Human Resources*, Vol.xxi, No.4, pp.485-506.

Borrie, W. (1959), *The Cultural Integration of Immigrants*, UNESCO.

Bose, M. (1989), *Independent Magazine*, 11th November.

Breton, R. (1964-65), 'Institutional Completeness of Ethnic Communities and the Personal Relations of Immigrants', *American Journal of Sociology*, vol.70, pp.193-205.

Brooks, A. (1983), 'Black Businesses in Lambeth: Obstacles to Expansion', *New Community*, Vol.11, pp.42-54.

Brooks, D., and Singh, K. (1979), 'Ethnic Commitment versus Structural Reality: South Asian Immigrant Workers in Britain', *New Community*, vol.7, pp.19-30.

Brown, C. (1984), *Black and White Britain: The Third PSI Survey*, Policy Studies Institute, Heinemann, London

Bunzel, J. (1955), 'The General Ideology of American Small Businessmen', *Political Science Quarterly*, Vol.70, pp.87-102.

Butler, D., and Stokes, D. (1971), *Political Change in Britain*, Macmillan: London.

Carchedi, G. (1975), 'On the Economic Identification of the New Middle Class', *Economy and Society*, vol.4, no.1.

Castles, S., and Kosack, G. (1985), *Immigrant Workers and Class Structure in Western Europe*, Oxford University Press: London.

Cater, J. (1984), 'Acquiring premises: a case study of Asians in Bradford', in Ward, R., and Jenkins, R., (eds.), *Ethnic Communities in Business* , Cambridge University Press:Cambridge.

-------. (1984), *Immigration, Segregation and Retail and Service Sectors in a Northern City: A Case Study of Bradford*, Ph.D thesis, Liverpool Polytechnic.

Cater, J., and Jones,T. (1987), 'Community, Ethnicity and Class among South asians in Britain', Paper presented to the Conference on South Asian Communities Overseas, Mansfield College, Oxford, 26th-28th March 1987.

-------. (1978), 'Asians in Bradford', New Society, no. 810, pp. 81-2.

Census Report for Oxfordshire, 1961, 1971, 1981.

Cheng and Bonacich (ed.), (1984), *Labour Immigration under Capitalism*, California.

CBI, (1980), *Smaller Firms in the Economy*, Confederation of British Industry, London.

Chinoy, E. (1955), *Automobile Workers and the American Dream*, Random House, New York.

Clark, D. (1979), Politics and Business enterprise:Limits on the scope of Ethnicity, in Wallman, S., (ed.), *Ethnicity at work*, Macmillan, London.

✳ Clarke, C., Peach, C., and Vertovec, S. (1990), (eds), *South Asians Overseas*, Comparative ethnic and race relations series, Cambridge University Press, Cambridge.

Cohen, A. (1969), *Custom and Politics in Urban Africa*, Routledge and Kegan Paul, London.

-------. (1974a), 'The Lesson of Ethnicity', in Cohen (ed.), *Urban Ethnicity*, Tavistock, London.

-------. (1974b), (ed.), *Urban Ethnicity*, Tavistock, London.

Coleman, D. (1982), *Demography of Immigrants and Minority Groups in the United Kingdom*, Academic Press, London.

-------. (1984) 'The Demography of Ethnic Minorities,' *Journal of Biosocial Science Supplement*, 8, pp. 43-87.

Collison, P. (1963), *The Cutteslowe Walls: a study in social class*, Faber and Faber, London.

------. (1959-60), 'Occupation, Education, and Housing in an English City', *American Journal of Sociology*, Vol.65, pp.588-597.

Collison, P., and Mogey, J. (1958-59), Residence and Social Class in Oxford', *American Journal of Sociology*, Vol.64, pp.599-605.

Cross, M., and Entzinger, H. (1988), 'Caribbean Minorities in Britain and the Netherlands: Comparative Questions', in Cross and Entzinger (ed.), *Lost Illusions*, Routledge, London.

Cross, M. (1992), 'Editorial', *New Community*, vol.19, no.1, October.

-------. (1988) (ed.), *Lost Illusions*, Routledge, London.

Crossick, G. (1977), *The Lower Middle Class in Britain*, Croom Helm, London.

Curran, J. (1981), 'Class Imagery, Work Environment and Community:Some Further Findings and A Brief Comment', *British Journal of Sociology*, vol.32, No.1.

Curran, J., and Burrows, R. (1986), 'The Sociology of Petit Capitalism: A Trend Report', *Sociology*, vol.20, No.2, pp.265-279.

------. (1987), 'The Social Analysis of Small Business: Some Emerging Themes', in Goffee, R., and Scase, R. (eds.), *Entrepreneurship in Europe*, Croom Helm, London.

------. (1988), 'Ethnicity and Enterprise: A National Profile', Paper presented at the Eleventh Small Firms Policy and Research Conference, Cardiff Business School.

Curran, J. and Blackburn, R. (1991), (eds.), *Paths of Enterprise: The Future of the Small Business*, Routlegde, London and New York.

------. (1991), Changes in the context of enterprise: some socio-economic and environmental factors facing small firms in the 1990s', in Curran, J. and Blackburn, R. (eds.), *Paths of Enterprise: The Future of the Small Business*, Routlegde, London and New York.

Dahya, B. (1974), 'The Nature of Pakistani Ethnicity in Industrial Cities in Britain', in Cohen (ed.), *Urban Ethnicity*, Tavistock, London.

------. (1988), 'South Asians as Economic Migrants in Britain', *Ethnic and Racial Studies*, vol.ii, No.4.

Dale, A. (1986), 'Social Class and the Self-Employed', *Sociology*, vol.20, No.3.

Davies, J. (1991), *Aspects of Health Beliefs and Practices of Bangladeshi Women Living in Oxford*, M.Sc. Dissertation in Medical Anthropology, Dept. of Human Sciences, Brunel, The University of West London.

Davies, R.L. (1983), 'Retailing', in Pacione, M. (ed.), *Progress in Urban Geography*, Croom Helm, London.

Davison, R.B. (1966), *Black British*, Oxford University Press, London.

Denzin, N.K. (1970), (ed.), *Sociological Methods*, Butterworths, London.

Desai, R. (1963), *Indian Immigrants in Britain*, Oxford University Press, London.

Despres, L.A. (1975), (ed.), *Ethnicity and Resource Competition in Plural Societies*, Mouton Publishers, The Hague.

217

------. (1975), 'Toward a theory of Ethnic Phenomena', in Despres, L.A. (ed.), *Ethnicity and Resource Competition in Plural Societies*, Mouton Publishers, The Hague.

Drake, St C., and Cayton, H. (1962), *Black Metropolis: A Study of Negro Life in a Northern City*, Harper and Row, New York.

Driedger, L. (1976), 'Ethnic Selfidentity: a comparison of ingroup evaluations', *Sociometry*, 39(2), pp.131-41.

Dummett, A. (1973), *A Portrait of English Racism*, Pelican, England.

Duncan, O.D., and Lieberson, S. (1958-59), 'Ethnic Segregation and Assimilation', *American Journal of Sociology*, vol.64, pp.364-374.

Duncan, O.D. (1968), 'Inheritance of Poverty or Inheritance of Race,' in Moynihan, P. (ed.), *Understanding Poverty*, Basic Books, New York.

Eisenstadt, S.N. (1954), *The Absorption of Immigrants*, Routledge and Kegan Paul, London.

Elliott, B., and McCrone, D. (1982), 'The Social World of Petty Property', in Hollowell, P. (ed.), *Property and Social Relations*, London.

Emmerich, M., and Lewis, J. (1991), *Unemployment in Oxfordshire*, Final Report of the Oxfordshire Unemployment Research projectCherwell District Council, Heart of England TEC, Oxford City Council and Oxfordshire County Council, Oxford.

Erikson, R., and Goldthorpe, J. (1992), *Constant Flux: A Study of Class Mobility in Industrial Societies*, Clarendon Press, Oxford.

Ethnic Minority Business Service, Strategic Plan, (1990), Oxford.

-------. Newsletter, (1992), April, Oxford.

Evans, M.D.R. (1989), 'Immigrant Entrepreneurship: Effects of Ethnic Market Size and Isolated Labour Pool', *American Sociological Review*, vol.54, pp.950-962.

Evans, A., and Eversley, D. (1980), (ed.), *The Inner City : Employment and Industry*, Heinemann, London.

Fairchild, H.P. (1924), *Immigration*, Macmillan, New York.

Field, S. (1984), The Attitudes of Ethnic Minorities, Home Office Research Study No.80, A Home Office Research and Planning Unit Report.

FitzGerald, M. (1988), 'There is no alternative....Black people and the Labour Party', *Social Studies Review*, September 1988.

Foner, N. (1977), 'The Jamaicans: Cultural and Social Change among Migrants in Britain', in Watson, James L. (ed.), *Between Two Cultures: Migrants and Minorities in Britain*, Basil Blackwell, Oxford.

Fox, R. (1973), 'Pariah Capitalism and Traditional Indian Merchants, Past and Present, in Singer, M. (1973), (ed.), *Entrepreneurship and Modernization of Occupational Cultures in South Asia*, Duke University, Monograph and Occasional Papers series, Durham, North Carolina.

Frazier, E.F. (1957), *The Black Bourgeoisie*, Free Press, New York.

Gambetta, D. (1987), *Were They Pushed Or Did They Jump?* Cambridge University Press, Cambridge.

Gardner, K. (1990), '*From Paddy Field to Jumbo Jet:Out Migration and Village Life in Sylhet*', Ph.D. thesis, London School of Economics.

Gerry, C., and Birkbeck, C. (1981), 'The Petty Commodity Producer in Third World Cities:petit Bourgeois or Disguised Proletarian' in Bechhofer, F., and Elliott, B. (ed.), *The Petite Bourgeoisie*, Macmillan, London.

Gerth, H.H. and Mills, C.W. (1948), *From Max Weber: Essays in Sociology*, Kegan Paul, Trench, Trubner and Co. Ltd., London.

Glass, R. (1960), *Newcomers*, Allen and Unwin, London.

Glazer, N. and Moynihan, D. (1975), (eds.), *Ethnicity:Theory and Experience*, Harvard University Press, Cambridge, Mass.

-------. (1963), *Beyond the Melting Pot*, Harvard University Press, Cambridge, Mass.

Goffee, R., and Scase, R. (1987), (eds.), *Entrepreneurship in Europe*, Croom Helm, London.

Goldthorpe, J., and Lockwood, D. (1963), '*Affluence and the British Class Structure*', Sociological Review, Vol. 11, No.2.

Goldthorpe, J., Lockwood, D., Bechhofer, F., and Platt, J. (1968), *The affluent worker: industrial attitudes and behaviour*, Cambridge University Press, Cambridge.

------. (1968b), *The affluent worker: political attitudes and behaviour*, Cambridge University Press, Cambridge.

------. (1969), *The affluent worker in the class structure*, Cambridge University Press, Cambridge.

Goldthorpe, J. H. (1987), *Social Mobility and Class Structure in Modern Britain*, Clarendon Press, Oxford.

-------.. Revised Class Schema 1983: Based on OPCS Classfication of Occupations 1983. Provided by John Goldthorpe.

Gordon, M. (1964), *Assimilation in American Life: The Role of Race, Religion and National Origin*, Oxford University Press, New York.

Granovetter, M. (1978), 'The strength of weak ties', *American Journal of Sociology*, vol.78(6), pp.1360-380.

Griffith, J.A.G., Henderson, J., Usborne, M., Wood, D. (1960), *Coloured Immigrants in Britain*, Oxford University Press, London.

Hakim, C. (1989), 'New recruits to self-employment in the 1980s', *Employment Gazette*, June, pp.286-297.

Hannerz, U. (1974), 'Ethnicity and Opportunity in Urban America', in Cohen (ed.), *Urban Ethnicity*, Tavistock, London.

Heath, A. (1981), *Social Mobility*, Fontana

------. (1991), *Understanding Political Change: the British Voter 1964-87*, Pergamon, Oxford.

Heath, A., and Ridge, J. (1983), 'Social Mobility of Ethnic Minorities', *Journal of Biosocial Science*, Suppl. 8, pp. 169-184.

Heath, A., Jowell, R., Curtice, J. (1985), *How Britain Votes*, Pergamon Press: Oxford.

Hechter,M. (1974), 'The Political Economy of Ethnic Change', *American Journal of Sociology*, vol.79, pp.1151-1178.

-------. (1978), 'Group formation and the cultural division of labour', *American Journal of Sociology*, 84, pp.298-318.

Hertz, L. (1986), *The Business Amazons*, Andre Deutsch, London.

Himmelfarb,H.S. (1979), Patterns of assimilation: Identification among American Jews, *Ethnicity*, 6, 249-267.

Hiro, D. (1971), *Black British, White British*, Eyre and Spottiswood, Bristol.

Holmes, C. (1988), *John Bull's Island, Immigration and British Society, 1871-1971*, Macmillan, London.

Hope, E., Kennedy, M., and De Winter, A. (1976), 'Homeworkers in North London', in Leonard, D. *et al.* (eds.), *Dependence and Exploitation in Work and Marriage*, Longman, London.

Hoselitz, B.F. (1961), 'Social Stratification and Economic Growth', *International Social Science Journal*, vol.15, pp.237-51.

Hutnik, N. (1985), *Ethnic Minority Identity: the case of second generation South Asians in Britain*, D.Phil thesis, University of Oxford.

------. (1991), *Ethnic Minority Identity: A social psychological perspective*, Oxford University Press, Oxford.

Islam, M.M. (1976), *Bengali Migrant Workers in Britain: A Study of their Position in the Class Structure*, Ph.D. thesis, University of Leeds.

Javillonar, G.V., and Peters, G.R. (1973), 'Sociological and Social Psychological aspects of Indian Entrepreneurship', *British Journal of Sociology*, Vol.24, pp.314-328.

Jeffery, P. (1976), *Migrants and Refugees*, Cambridge University Press, Cambridge.

Jenkins, R. (1984), 'Ethnic minorities in business: a research agenda', in Ward, R., and Jenkins, R., (eds.), *Ethnic Communities in Business*, Cambridge University Press, Cambridge.

Jones, P.N. (1976), 'Coloured Minorities in Birmingham, England', *Annals, Association of American Geographers*, vol.66, pp.89-103.

Jones, T. (1989), Industrial Restructuring and Social Change: The Dawning of a New Era of Flexible accumulation? Conference Paper, Collingwood College, University of Durham, 26-28th September.

------. (1982), 'Small Business Development and the Asian Community in Britain', *New Community*, Vol.9, pp.269-284.

Kasdan, L. (1965), Family Structure, Migration and the Entrepreneur', *Comparative Studies in Society and History*, Vol.7, pp.345-357.

Khan, V.S. (1979), 'Work and Network:South Asian women in South London', in Wallman, S., (ed.), *Ethnicity at work*, Macmillan, London.

Kirby, D.A. (1980), 'The Future of Small Unit Retaining in the UK: the Implications for Planning', in *Local Shopping Centres and Convenience Stores: Report of an URPI workshop*, URPI, Reading.

------. (1976), 'The Convenience Store Phenomenon', *Retail and Distribution Management*, 4(3), pp.31-3.

Kish, L. (1965), *Survey Sampling*, J.Wiley, New York.

Kitay, J. and Lever-Tracy, C. (1990), 'From Survival to Success: Working in Chinese Restaurants in Australia', Paper presented at the International Working Party on Labour Market Segmentation Conference, Trento, Italy

Klandt, H. (1987), 'Trends in Small Business Start-up in West Germany', in Goffee, R., and Scase, R. (eds.), *Entrepreneurship in Europe*, Croom Helm, London.

Klingender, F.D. (1951), The Little Shop, *Current Affairs*, No.127, 3rd March.

Kosmin, B. (1979), 'Exclusion and Opportunity: traditions of work among British Jews', in Wallman, S., (ed.), *Ethnicity at work*, Macmillan, London.

Krausz, E. (1972), 'Factors of Social Mobility in British Minority Groups', *British Journal of Sociology*, vol.xxiii, No.3, pp. 275-285.

Krcmar, K.M. (1984), 'Immigrant Retail in Glasgow', M.B.A. Dissertation, University of Strathclyde.

Ladbury, S. (1984), 'Choice, chance or no alternative? Turkish Cypriots in business in London', in Ward, R., and Jenkins, R., (eds.), *Ethnic Communities in Business*, Cambridge University Press, Cambridge.

Lamb, H.B. (1965), 'The Rise of Indian Business Communities', *Pacific Affairs*, vol.23 (June), pp.98-126.

Lambeth, London Borough of (1982), *Black Business in Lambeth*, Report of Survey, RM20, March.

Laumann, E.O. (1966), *Prestige and Association in an Urban Community*, Bobbs-Merrill, Indianapolis, New York.

Lawrence, D. (1974), *Black Migrants, White Natives: A study of Race Relations in Nottingham*, Cambridge University Press, Cambridge.

Leach, B., Nicholson, D., and Basu, D. (1990), *Ethnic Minority Businesses and Employment in Greater Manchester*, Report Commissioned by Greater Manchester Economic Development Officers Association.

Leo, J.F. (1981), *Ethnic Minorities and Small Firms*, Dissertation for Planning Diploma, Polytechnic of Central London, May 1981.

Lever-Tracy, C., Ip, D., Kitay, J., Phillips, I., and Tracy, N. (1991), *Asian Entrepreneurs in Australia: Ethnic small business in the Chinese and Indian communities of Brisbane and Sydney*, Report to the Office of Multicultural Affairs, Australian Government Publishing Service, Canberra.

Levine, N., and Nayar, T. (1975), 'Modes of Adaptation by Asian Immigrants in Slough', *New Community*, vol.iv, No.3. pp.356-363.

Lewis, R., and Maude, A. (1949), *The English Middle Classes*, Phoenix House, London.

Lieberson, S. (1980), *A Piece of the Pie: Black and White Immigrants Since 1880*, University of California Press, Berkeley.

------. (1961), 'A societal Theory of Race and Ethnic Relations', *American Sociological Review*, Vol.26, pp.902-910.

Lieberson, S., and Waters, M. (1988), *From Many Strands: Ethnic and Racial Groups in Contemporary America*, Russel Sage Foundation, New York.

Light, I. (1972), *Ethnic Enterprise in America: Business and Welfare among Chinese, Japanese and Blacks*, University of California Press, Berkeley.

------. (1980), 'Asian Enterprise in America', in Cummings, S. (ed.), *Self-Help in Urban America*, Kennikat Press, Port Washington.

------. (1984), 'Immigrant and Ethnic Enterprise in North America', in *Ethnic and Racial Studies*, vol.17, pp.195-216.

Light, I., and Bonacich, E. (1988), *Immigrant Entrepreneurs*, University of California Press, Berkeley.

Lipset, S., and Bendix, R. (1959), *Social Mobility in Industrial Society*, Heinemann, London.

------. (1951), 'Social Mobility and Occupational Career Patterns', in American Journal of Sociology, lvii.

Lipset, S.M., Trow, M., Coleman, J. (1977), *Union Democracy*, The Free Press, New York.

Lockwood, D. (1958), *The Blackcoated Worker*, George, Allen and Unwin, London.

London, H. (1967), 'Liberalising the White Australia policy: Integration, assimilation or cultural pluralism', *Australian Outlook*, 21, 338-46.

Lowenthal, D. (1972), *West Indian Societies*, Oxford University Press, London.

Marcson, S. (1950-1), 'A theory of intermarriage and assimilation', *Social Forces*, vol.29, pp.75-8.

Marris, P., and Somerset, A. (1971), *African Businessmen: A study of Entrepreneurship and Development in Kenya*, Routlegde and Kegan Paul, London.

Mars, G., and Ward, R. (1984), 'Ethnic business development in Britain: opportunities and resources', in Ward, R., and Jenkins, R., (eds.), *Ethnic Communities in Business*, Cambridge University Press, Cambridge.

Marx, K. and Engels, F. (1968), *The Manifesto of the Communist Party (1848)*, in Marx, K. and Engels, F., *Selected Works*, London.

Mason, P. (1967), (ed.), *India and Ceylon: Unity and Diversity*, Oxford University Press:London.

Mayer, A. (1975), 'The Lower Middle Class as Historical Problem', *Journal of Modern History*, 47, pp.409-436.

Mayer, K. (1947), 'Small business as a social institution', *Social Research*, Vol.14(3), pp.332-349.

------. (1953), Business Enterprise: Traditional symbol of Opportunity', *British Journal of Sociology*, Vol.iv, pp.160-180.

Mayer, N. (1987), 'Small Business and Social Mobility in France', in Goffee, R., and Scase, R. (eds.), *Entrepreneurship in Europe*, Croom Helm, London.

McEvoy, D., Aldrich H.E., Cater, J.C., and Jones, T.P., (1979), *Retail and Service Business and the Immigrant Community, Final Report*, Project HR5520, Social Sciences Research Council, London.

McHugh, J. (1979), 'The self-employed and the small independent entrepreneur', in King, R., and Nugent, N. (ed.), *Respectable Rebels*, Hodder asnd Stoughton, London.

McClelland, D.C. (1963), *The Achieving Society*, Van Nostrand, Princeton.

Mills, C.W. (1951), *White Collar*, Oxford University Press, Oxford.

Mines, M. (1973), 'Tamil Muslim Merchants in India's Industrial Development', in Singer, M. (ed.), *Entrepreneurship and Modernization of Occupational Cultures in South Asia*, Duke University, Monograph and Occasional Papers series, Durham, North Carolina.

Morris, J. (1965), *Oxford*, Oxford University Press, Oxford.

Moser, C.A. and Scott, W. (1961), *British Towns: a Statistical Study of their Social and Economic Differences*, Oliver and Boyd, London.

Moser, C.A. and Kalton, G. (1971), *Survey Methods in Social Investigation*, Gower, England.

Mullins, D. (1979), 'Asian Retailing in Croydon', *New Community*, Vol.vii, No.3, pp.403-405.

Nandy, A.(1973), quoted by Singer, M. in Singer, M. (ed.), *Entrepreneurship and Modernization of Occupational Cultures in South Asia*, Duke University, Monograph and Occasional Papers series, Durham, North Carolina.

Nowikowski, S. (1984), 'Snakes and ladders: Asian business in Britain', in Ward, R., and Jenkins, R., (eds.), *Ethnic Communities in Business*, Cambridge University Press, Cambridge.

Nowikowski, S. and Ward, R. (1978-79), 'Middle class and British? An analysis of South Asians in suburbia', *New Community*, Vol.vii, No.1, pp.1-10.

OECD, (1980), *Labour Force Statistics 1967-1978*, Organisation for Economic Cooperation and Development, Paris.

Office of Population Census and Survey, (1979).

------. (1980), *Classification of Occupations*.

------. (1992), County Monitor, *1991 Census Oxfordshire*, June.

Owen, D., and Green, A. (1992), Labour market experience and change among ethnic groups in Great Britain, *New Community*, Vol.19, No.1, pp.7-29.

Pacione, M. (1983), (ed.), *Progress in Urban Geography*, Croom Helm, London.

Papanek, H. (1973), 'Pakistan's New Industrialists and Businessmen: Focus on the Memons', in Singer, M. (ed.), *Entrepreneurship and Modernization of Occupational Cultures in South Asia*, Duke University, Monograph and Occasional Papers series, Durham, North Carolina.

Park, R., and Burgess, E. (1921), *Introduction to the Science of Sociology*, University Press, Chicago.

Park, R (1926), 'The Urban Community as a Spatial Pattern and a Moral Order', reprinted in Peach, C. (ed.), (1975), *Urban Social Segregation*, Longman, London.

Parkin, F. (1974), (ed.), *The Social Analysis of Class Structure*, Tavistock, London.

Parsons, T. (1975), 'Some Theoretical Considerations on the Nature and Trends of Change of Ethnicity', in Glazer, N., and Moynihan, P. (eds.), *Ethnicity: Theory and Experience*, Harvard University Press, Cambridge, Mass.

Patel, S (1987), *The Nature and Dynamics of Asian Retailing in Britain*, Ph.D thesis, Open University.

Patel, S. (1991), 'Patterns of Growth: Asian Retailing in Inner and Outer Areas of Birmingham', in Vertovec, S. (ed.), *Aspects of the South Asian Diaspora*, Oxford University Press, Delhi.

Patterson, O. (1983), 'The nature, causes and implications of ethnic identification', in Fried, C. (ed.), *Minorities: Community and Identity*, Springer, New York.

Patterson, S. (1965), *Dark Strangers*, Tavistock, London.

------. (1968), *Immigrants in Industry*, Oxford University Press, London.

Payne, S.L. (1951), *The Art of Asking Questions*, Princeton University Press.

Peach, G.C.K. (1991), 'The Caribeans in Europe: Contrasting Patterns of Migration and Settlement in Britain, France and Netherland', ESRC Research Paper, No. 15.

------... (1968), *West Indian Migration to Britain: A Social Geography*, Oxford University Press, London.

------. (1983), 'Ethnicity', in Pacione, M. (ed.), *Progress in Urban Geography*, Croom Helm, London.

------. (1983), 'Factors Affecting the Distribution of West Indians in Great Britain', *Journal of Biosocial Science Supplement*, 8, pp.151-163.

Peach, C., Robinson, V., Maxted, J., and Chance, J. (1988), 'Immigration and Ethnicity', in Halsey, A.H. (ed.), *British Social Trend Since 1900: A Guide to the Changing Social Structure of Britain*, Macmillan, London.

Penn, R., and Scattergood, H. (1992), 'Ethnicity and career aspirations in contemporary Britain', *New Community*, Vol.19, No.1, pp.75-98.

Pettigrew, T.F. (1978), 'Three Issues in Ethnicity: Boundaries, Deprivations, and Perceptions', in Yinger, J.M., and Cutler, S.J., (eds.), *Major Social Issues*, The Free Press, New York.

Portes, A., and Stepick, A. (1985), 'Unwelcome Immigrants: The labour market experiences of 1980 Cuban and Haitian refugees in South Florida', *American Sociological Review*, Vol.50, pp.493-514.

Poulantzas, N. (1975), *Classes in Contemporary Capitalism*, NLB, London.

Prasad, K.K. (1978), '*The Gujeratis of Fiji, 1900-1945: A Study of an Immigrant Trade Community*', Ph.D. thesis, University of British Columbia.

Price, C. (1969), 'The Study of Assimilation', in Jackson, J.A. (ed.), *Migration*, Cambridge University Press, Cambridge.

Rafiq, M. (1992), 'A comparison of Muslim and non-Muslim owned Asian businesses in Britain', *New Community*, Vol.19, No.1, pp.43-60.

Rafiq, M. (1988), *Asian Businesses in Bradford, West Yorkshire*, Ph.D. thesis, University of Bradford.

Reeves, F., and Ward, R. (1984), West Indian business in Britain, in Ward, R., and Jenkins, R., (eds.), *Ethnic Communities in Business*, Cambridge University Press, Cambridge.

Rex, J.A. (1970), *Race Relations in Sociological Theory*, Weidenfeld and Nicholson, London.

------. (1973), *Race, Colonialism and the City*, Routledge and Kegan Paul, London.

------. (1986), *Race and Ethnicity*, Open University Press, Milton Keynes.

Rex, J., and Mason (1986), *Theories of Race and Ethnic Relations*, Cambridge University Press, Cambridge.

Rex, J., and Tomlinson, S. (1979), *Colonial Immigrants in a British City*, Routledge and Kegan Paul, London.

Rex, J., and Moore, R. (1967), *Race, Community and Conflict*, Oxford University Press, London.

Richardson, A. (1967), 'A theory and method for the psychological study of assimilation', *International Migration Review*, 2, pp.3-30.

Richmond, A. (1990), 'Race Relations and Immigration: A Comparative Perspective', *International Journal of Comparative Sociology*, XXXI, pp.156-176.

------. (1972), *Readings in Race and Ethnic Relations*, Pergamon Press, Oxford.

------. (1988), *Immigration and Ethnic Conflict, Macmillan*, London.
Robinson, V. (1990), 'Boom and Gloom: the Success and Failure of South Asians in Britain', in Clarke, C., Peach, C., and Vertovec, S. (ed.), *South Asians Overseas: Migration and Ethnicity*, Cambridge University Press, Cambridge.

------. (1986), *Transients, Settlers and Refugees*, Clarendon Press, Oxford.

------. (1982), 'The Assimilation of South and East African Asian Immigrants', in Coleman, D.A. (ed.), *Demography of Immigrants and Minority Groups in the United Kingdom*, Academic Press, London.

------. (1980a), 'Correlates of Asian immigration to Britain', *New Community*, Vol.8, pp.115-23.

Rose, A.M. (1969), *Migrants in Europe: Problems of Acceptance and Adjustment*, Minnesota.

Rose, E.J.B. (1969), *Colour and Citizenship*, Oxford University Press, London.

Rosentraub, M., and Taebel, P. (1980), 'Jewish Enterprise in Transition', in Cummings, S. (ed.), *Self-Help in Urban America*, Kennikat Press, Washington.

Rughani, M. (1981), '*A Descriptive Survey Of Management Practices of Asian Businessmen*', MBA Dissertation, University of Aston.

Scarman, Lord (1982), *The Scarman Report: The Brixton Disorders, 10-12 April 1981*, Pelican, Harmondsworth.

Scase, R. (1982), 'The Petty Bourgeoisie and Modern Capitalism: A consideration of recent theories', in Giddens, A., and Mackenzie, G. (eds.), *Social Class and the Division of Labour*, Cambridge University Press, Cambridge.

Scase, R., and Goffee, R. (1982), *The Entrepreneurial Middle Class*, Croom Helm, London.
-------. (1981), 'Traditional' Petty Bourgeois Attitudes: The case of self-employed craftsmen, *Sociological Review*, Vol.29, No.4.

-------. (1980), *The real World of the Small Business Owner*, Croom Helm, London.

Shaw, A. (1988), *A Pakistani Community in Britain*, Basil Blackwell, Oxford.

Singer, M. (1973), (ed.), *Entrepreneurship and Modernization of Occupational Cultures in South Asia*, Duke University, Monograph and Occasional Papers series, Durham, North Carolina.

-------. (1972), *When a Great Tradition Modernizes*, London.

Snow, P. (1991), *Oxford Observed:Town and Gown*, John Murray, London.

Spooner, A.J. (1979), *Migration and the City of Oxford*, Unpublished Dissertation, School of Geography, Oxford University.

Srinivasan, S. (1992), 'The class position of the Asian petty bourgeoisie', *New Community*, Vol.19, No.1, pp.61-74.

------. (1984), *Impact of Emigration on Social Structure*, unpublished M.Phil Dissertation, Delhi University.

Stanworth, J., Blythe, S., Granger, B., and Stanworth, C. (1989), 'Who Becomes an Entrepreneur?', *International Small Business Journal*, vol.8, no.1, pp. 11-22.

Steen A-B.(1992), *Varieties of the Refugee Experience: Sri Lankan Tamils in Denmark and England*, D.Phil thesis, Institute of Anthropology, University of Copenhagen.

Storey, (ed.), (1983), *The Small Firm: an International Survey*, Croom Helm, London.

Strahan, K.W., and Williams, A.J. (1988), *Immigrant Entrepreneurs in Australia*, Report to the Office of Multicultural Affairs, Australian Government Publishing Service, Canberra.

Studlar, D.T. (1986), 'Non-white Policy Preferences, Political Participation, and the Political agenda in Britain', in Layton-Henry, Z., and Rich, P.B. (eds.), *Race, Government and Politics in Britain*, Macmillan, Basingstoke.

Suttles, G.D. (1968), *The social order of the slum: Ethnicity and Territory in the Inner City*, University of Chicago Press, Chicago.

Tajfel, H. (1978), *The social psychology of minorities*, Minority Rights Group, London.

Taeuber, K.E., and Taeuber, A.F. (1964), 'The negro as an American group', *American Journal of Sociology*, 69, pp.374-382.

Taylor, J.H. (1976), *The Half-Way Generation: A study of Asian youths in Newcastle Upon Tyne*, National Foundation for Educational Research, Windsor.

Taylor, L. (1992), *Asian Business*, vol.4, no.12, 31st July - 14th August 1992, p.8.

Tawney, R.H. (1921), *The Acquisitive Society*, Bell, London.

Thakrar, P. (1992), 'Ethnic Foods', in *Asian Business*, vol.4, no.9, 23 May - 19th June 1992, p.29.

Tinker, H. (1977), *The Banyan Tree: Overseas Immigrants from India, Pakistan and Bangladesh*, Oxford University Press, London.

Useem, O. C., and Useem, R.H. (1945), 'Minority Group Pattern in Prairie Society', *American Journal of Sociology*, Vol.50, pp.377-389.

van den Berghe, P.L. (1967), *Race and Racism: A Comparative Perspective*, Wiley: New York.
-------. (1975), *Man in Society: A Biosocial View*, Elsevier, New York.

Vertovec, S. (1991), (ed.), *Aspects of the South Asian Diaspora*, Oxford University Press, Delhi.

Vidich, A.J., and Shapiro, G. (1970), 'A comparison of Participant Observation and Survey data', in Denzin, N.K. (ed.), *Sociological Methods*, Butterworths, London.

Waldinger, R. (1983), *Ethnic Enterprise and Industrial Change: A Case Study of the New York Garment Industry*. Ph.D. Thesis. University of Harvard, 1983.

------. (1984), 'Immigrant Enterprise and the Structure of the labour Market', in Finnegan, R., and Gallie, D. (ed.), *New Approaches to Economic Life*, Manchester University Press, Manchester.

Waldinger, R., Ward, R. and Aldrich, H. (1985), 'Ethnic Business and Occupational Mobility in Advanced Societies, *Sociology*, Vol.19, No.4, pp.586-97.

Wallman, S. (1979), (ed.), *Ethnicity at work*, Macmillan, London.

------. (1979), 'Introduction: The Scope of Ethnicity', in Wallman, S., (ed.), *Ethnicity at work*, Macmillan, London.

------. (1983), 'Identity Options', in Fried, C. (ed.), *Minorities: Community and Identity*, Springer, New York.

Ward, R., and Jenkins, R. (1984), (eds.), *Ethnic Communities in Business*, Cambridge University Press, Cambridge.

Ward, R. (1988), 'Caribbean business enterprise in Britain', in Cross and Entzinger (ed.), *Lost Illusions*, Routledge, London.

------. (1987), 'Ethnic Entrepreneurship in Britain and Europe', in Goffee, R., and Scase, R. (eds.), *Entrepreneurship in Europe*, Croom Helm, London.
------. (1991), 'Economic development and ethnic business', in Curran, J. and Blackburn, R. (eds.), *Paths of Enterprise: The Future of the Small Business*, Routlegde, London and New York.

Watson, James L. (1977), (ed.), *Between Two Cultures: Migrants and Minorities in Britain*, Basil Blackwell, Oxford.

Weinfeld, M. (1977), 'Determinants of Ethnic Identification of Jews, Slavs, and Italians in Toronto: The Assimilationist Model', Unpublished manuscript, Harvard University.

Werbner, P. (1979b), '*Avoiding the Ghetto: Pakistani Migrants and Settlement Shifts in Manchester*', New Community, Vol.7, pp.376-89.

------. (1981), 'Manchester Pakistanis: Life Styles, Ritual and the making of social Distinctions', *New Community*, Vol.9, pp.216-29

------. (1984), 'Business on trust: Pakistani entrepreneurship in the Manchester garment trade', in Ward, R., and Jenkins, R., (eds.),

Ethnic Communities in Business, Cambridge University Press, Cambridge.

-------. (1985a), 'The organisation of giving and ethnic elites: voluntary associations among Manchester Pakistanis', *Ethnic and Racial Studies*, vol.8, no.3, July 1985, pp. 368-388.

-------. (1985b), 'How Immigrants can Make it in Britain', *New Society*, 20th September, pp.411-14.

-------. (1986), 'Evaluation of Shopping Centre Improvements Funded Under the Urban Programme in the West Midlands: the Ethnic Dimension', Working Paper No.8, Birmingham, Aston University Public Sector Management Research Unit.

-------. (1987), 'Barefoot in Britain:anthropological research on Asian immigrants', in *New Community*, Vol.xiv, No.1/2.

-------. (1990), 'Manchester Pakistanis: division and Unity', in Clarke, C., Peach, C., and Vertovec, S. (eds), *South Asians Overseas*, Comparative ethnic and race relations series, Cambridge University Press, Cambridge.

Whiting, R. (1978), *'The Working Class in the "New Industry" Towns between the Wars:the Case of Oxford'*, D.Phil thesis, University of Oxford.

Wilken, P.H. (1979), *Entrepreneurship: a comparative and historical study*, Norwood, N.J.

Williams, V. (1986), *The Needs of Ethnic Minorities in Oxford City*, Oxford County Council Social Service Dept.

Wilson, K. L. and A. Portes (1980), 'Immigrant Enclaves: An Analysis of the Labour Market Experiences of Cubans in Miami', *American Journal of Sociology*, 86, pp.295-319.

Wilson, P. (1983), *Black Business Enterprise in Britain: A Survey of Afro-Caribbean and Asian Small Businesses in Brent*, Runnymede Trust, London.

Wilson, P. and Stanworth, J. (1985), *Black Business in Brent*, Small Business Research Trust, London.

Winchester, S.W.C. (1975), *Spatial Structure and Social Activity: A Social Geography of Coventry*, D.Phil thesis, university of Oxford.

Wright, P.L. (1968), *The Coloured Worker in British Industry*, Oxford University Press, London.

Wright, E.O. (1978), *Class, Crisis and the State*, NLB, London.

Yancey, W.L., Ericksen, E., and Juliani, R.M. (1976), 'Emergent Ethnicity: A Review and Reformulation', *American Sociological Review*, 41, 3, pp.391-403.

Yinger, J.M., and Cutler, S.J., (1978), (eds.), *Major Social Issues*, The Free Press, New York.

Yinger, J.M. (1981), 'Towards a theory of assimilation and dissimilation', *Ethnic and Racial Studies*, 4, pp.249-264.

Young, M. and Wilmott, P. (1957), *Family and Kinship in East London*, Routledge and Kegan Paul, London.

Zarwan, J.I. (1977), *Indian businessmen in Kenya during the 20th Century, A Case Study* , Ph.D Dissertation, Yale University.

Index

Response rate, 12
Retaurants, 4, 12, 19, 20, 21, 24, 33, 34, 35, 38, 39, 40, 44, 56, 57, 60, 61, 62, 76, 95, 100, 127, 130, 131, 134, 136, 137, 146, 187
Retailers, 9, 14, 64
Rotating Credit Associations, 42, 43, 57, 187

-S-

Sample survey, 12
Self-employed, 2, 3, 5, 6, 12, 13, 42, 52, 74, 78, 89, 90, 98, 100, 107, 109, 114, 115, 116, 118, 119, 124, 130, 131, 134, 139, 140, 146, 148, 172, 173, 174, 175, 180, 181, 182
Self-employment, 2, 5, 6, 9, 11, 13, 16, 36, 38, 47, 51, 52, 53, 56, 65, 66, 67, 68, 69, 72, 78, 81, 82, 84, 85, 87, 889, 90, 92, 97, 98, 100, 105, 106, 108, 109, 122, 124, 130, 137, 138, 139, 140, 141, 159, 186, 187, 188, 190
Self-employment, attitudes to, 8, 12, 73, 122
Small business owners, 1, 7, 8, 9, 13, 14, 35, 36, 38, 51, 54, 55, 56, 71, 79, 90, 91, 92, 93, 94, 95, 99, 100, 105, 106, 109, 112, 114, 115, 119, 121, 122, 123, 124, 125, 126, 127, 128, 129, 131, 132, 135, 137, 138,

139, 140, 141, 143, 144, 145, 147, 148, 168, 172, 182, 187, 188, 189, 191, 192
Small-business owners, class position of, 13
Small-business owners, economic situation of, 69
Small business owners, home country, 55, 73, 75, 76, 157, 160, 161, 162
Small business owners, hours worked, 8, 50, 55, 72, 87, 104, 111, 122, 187, 188
Small business owners, market situation of, 91, 99
Small business owners, political participation, 158, 163, 181
Small business owners, prestige of, 107
Social mobility, 1, 6, 7, 113, 86, 90, 109, 186, 190
Sojourner mentality, 45
Small business owners, aspriations, 12, 75, 78, 82, 85, 86, 87, 114, 115, 139, 140, 141, 142, 143, 144, 145, 147, 188, 190
Small-business owners, ethnically distinctive features of, 119
Small business owners, status, 6, 11, 13, 14, 24, 31, 36, 46, 52, 72, 75, 76, 79, 81, 82, 83, 84, 85, 86, 87, 91, 97, 107, 108, 109, 111, 112, 115, 116, 129, 132, 139, 145, 146, 148, 171, 172, 177, 188, 190